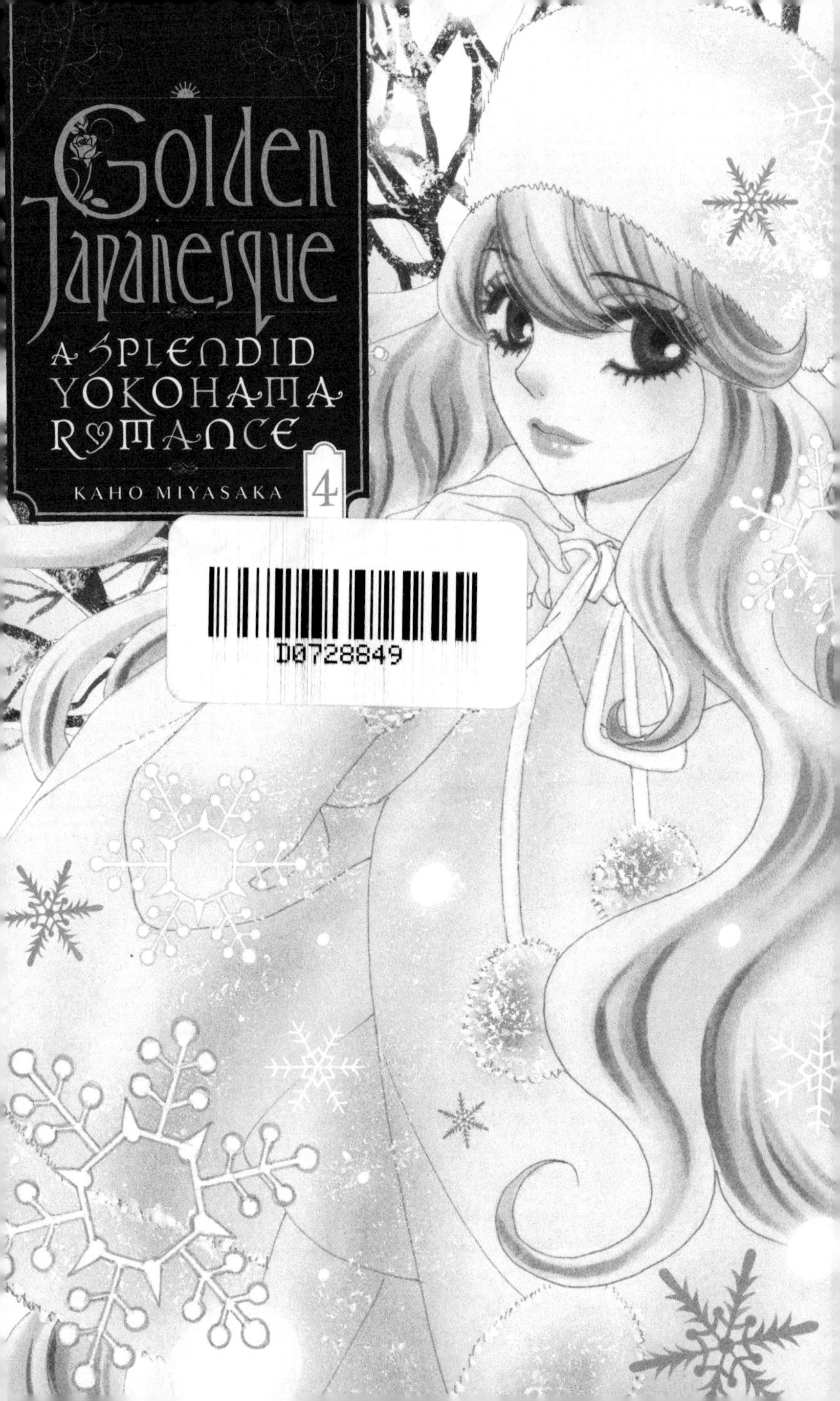
Golden Japanesque
A Splendid Yokohama Romance
4
KAHO MIYASAKA

Golden Japanesque
A Splendid Yokohama Romance

4

Story

◆ The port town of Yokohama, during the Meiji era— Maria inherited blond hair and blue eyes from her father, and her mother strictly trained her to hide them so she wouldn't be the target of discrimination.

◆ One day, she met Rintarou, the son of the distinguished family that employed her mother. Although Maria hated him at first, every time they met, she found herself more and more drawn to him. Although their families objected, eventually they became engaged, with certain conditions attached.

◆ While Rintarou studied overseas, Maria spent her days learning the skills she'd need as his wife. One day, she met Chiaki, a womanizing older relative of Rintarou. Just then, a letter from Rintarou arrived, with the news that he'd be returning earlier than anticipated—!!

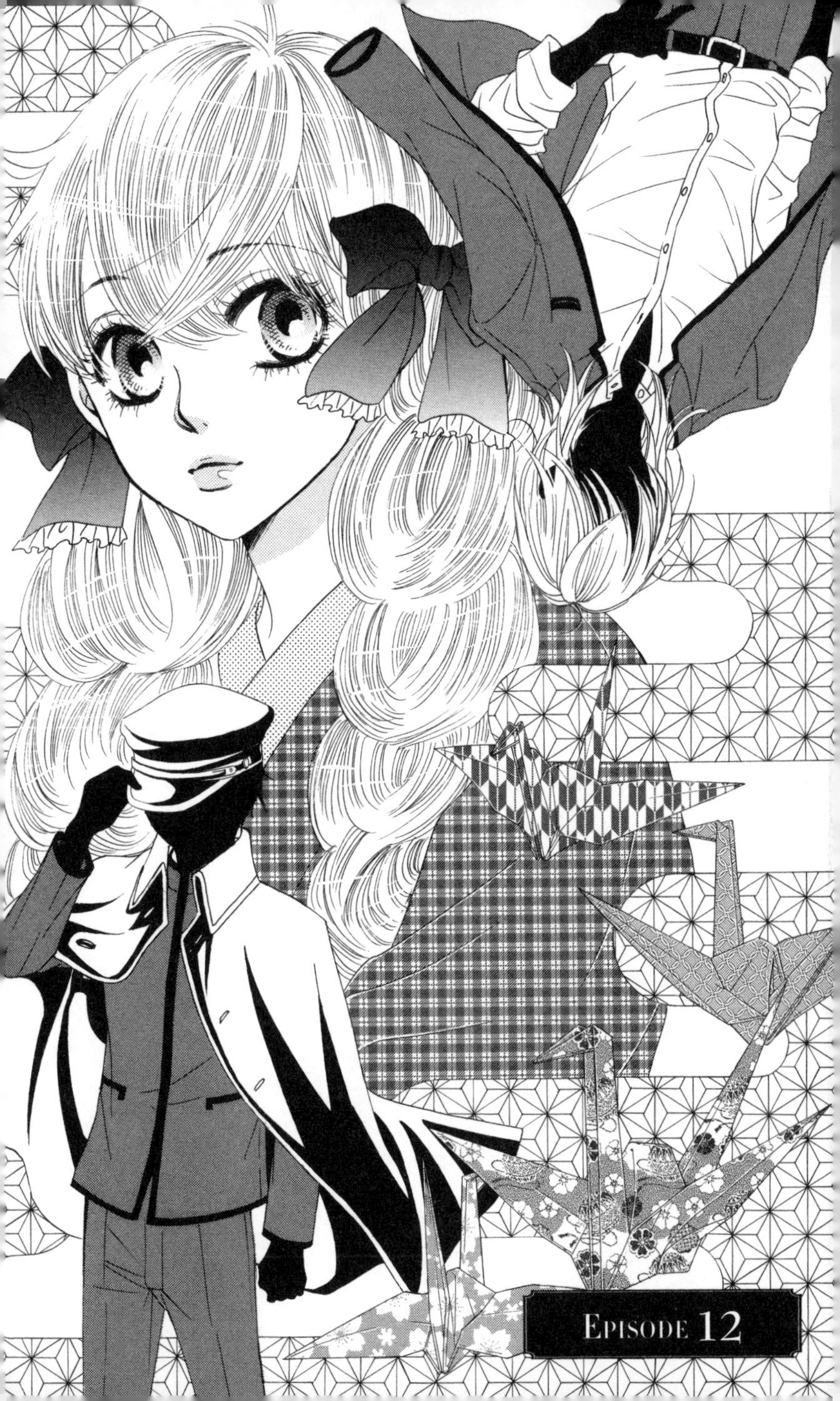
EPISODE 12

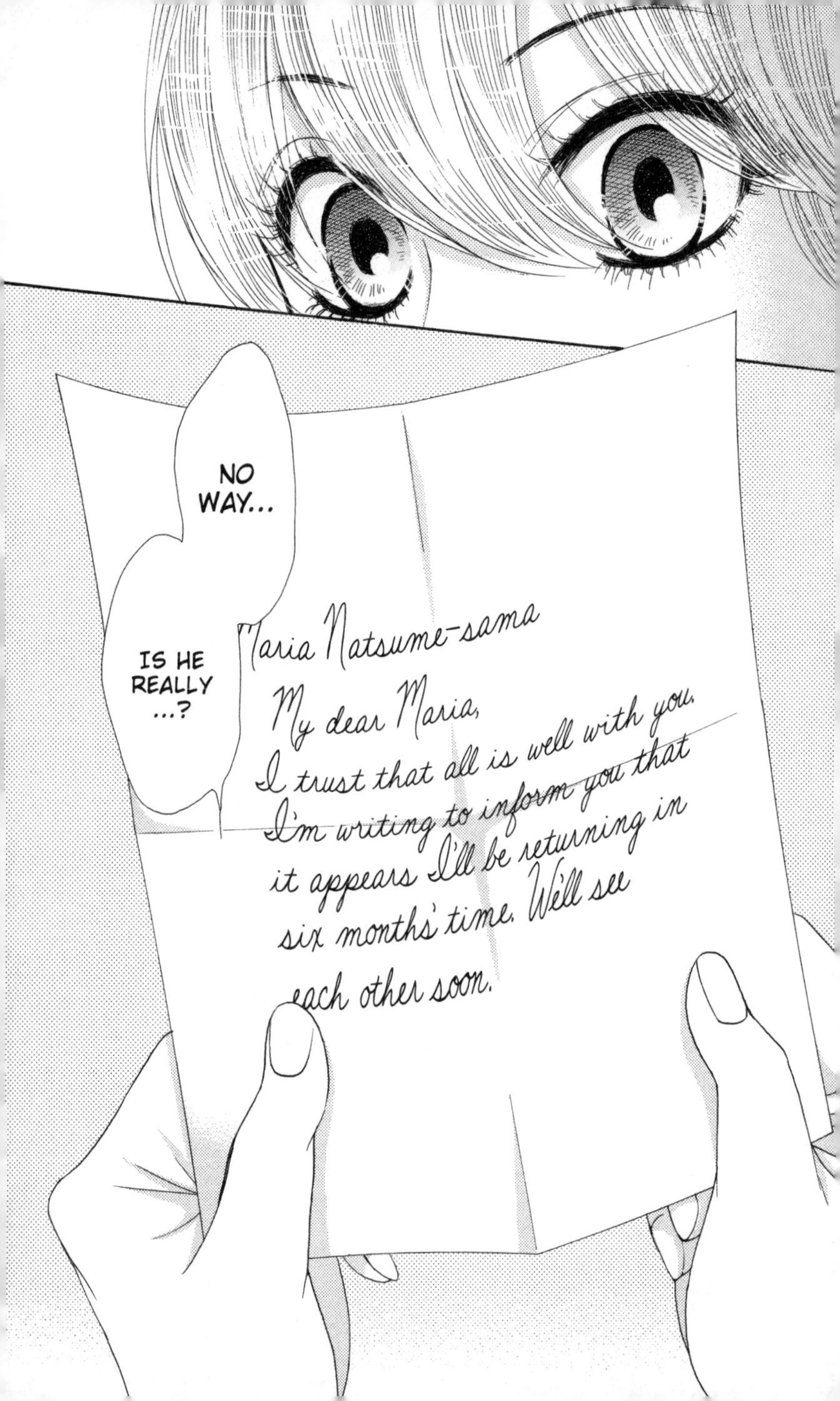
NO WAY...
IS HE REALLY ...?
Maria Natsume-sama
My dear Maria,
I trust that all is well with you.
I'm writing to inform you that
it appears I'll be returning in
six months' time. We'll see
each other soon.

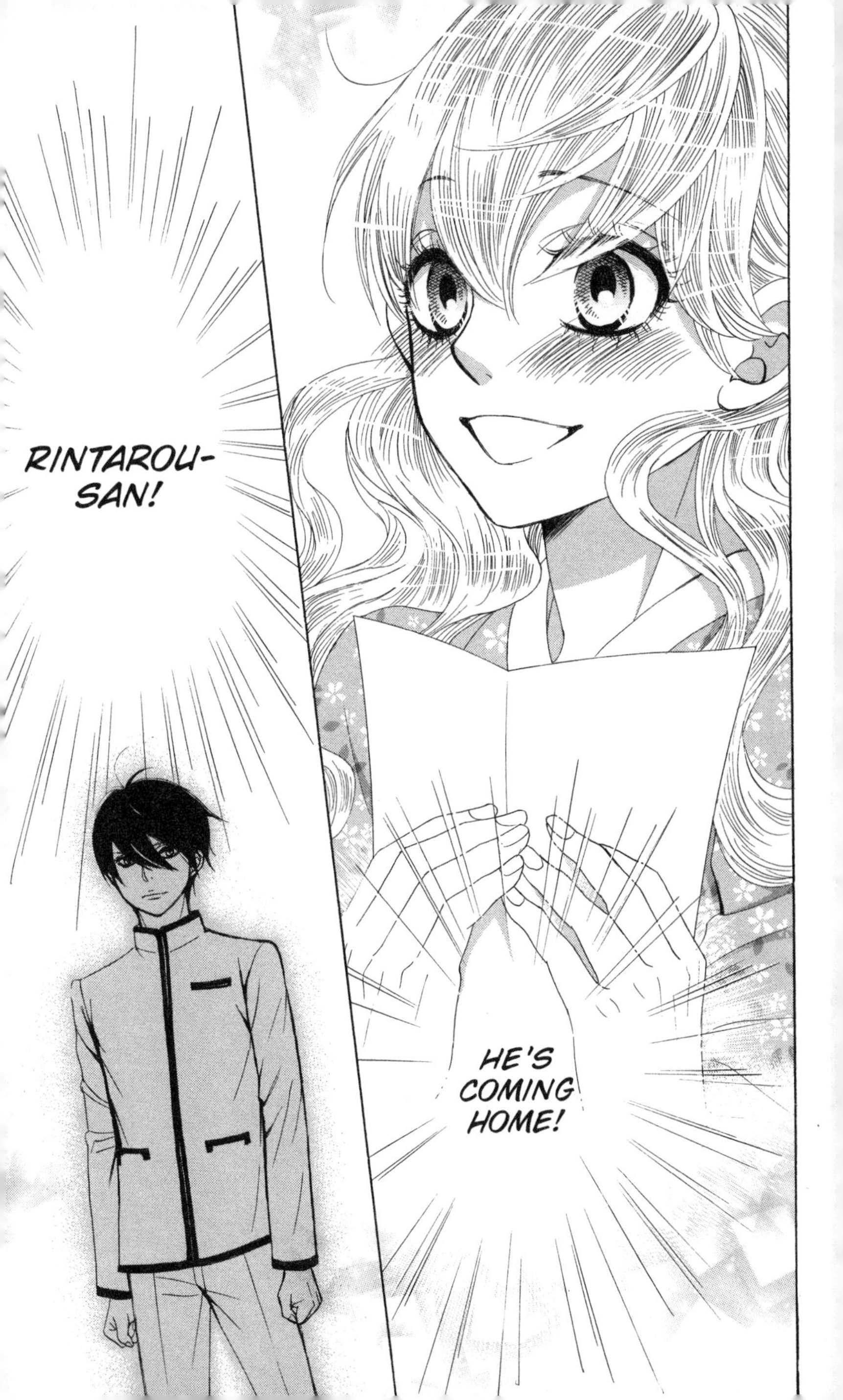
HE'S COMING HOME!
RINTAROU-SAN!

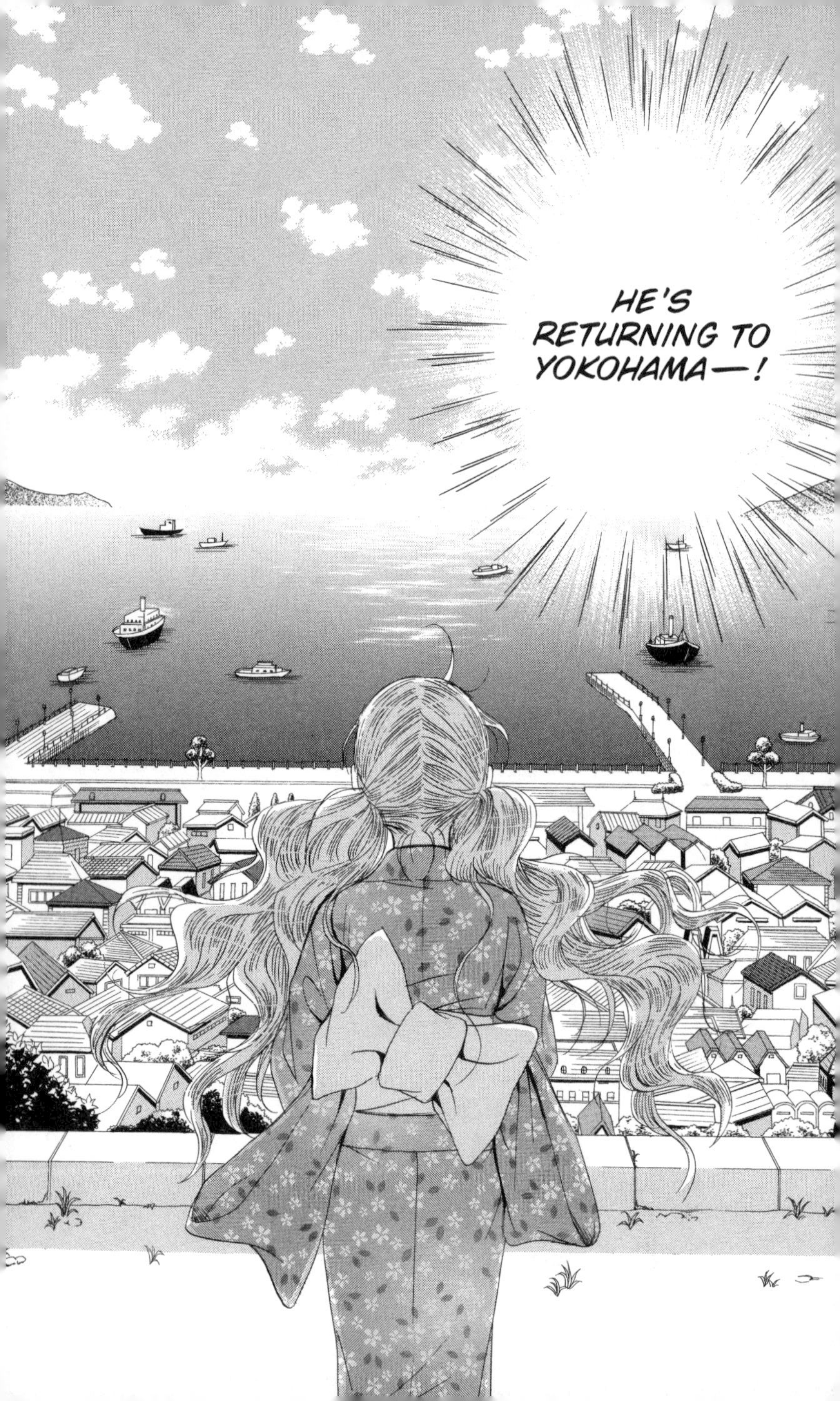
HE'S RETURNING TO YOKOHAMA—!

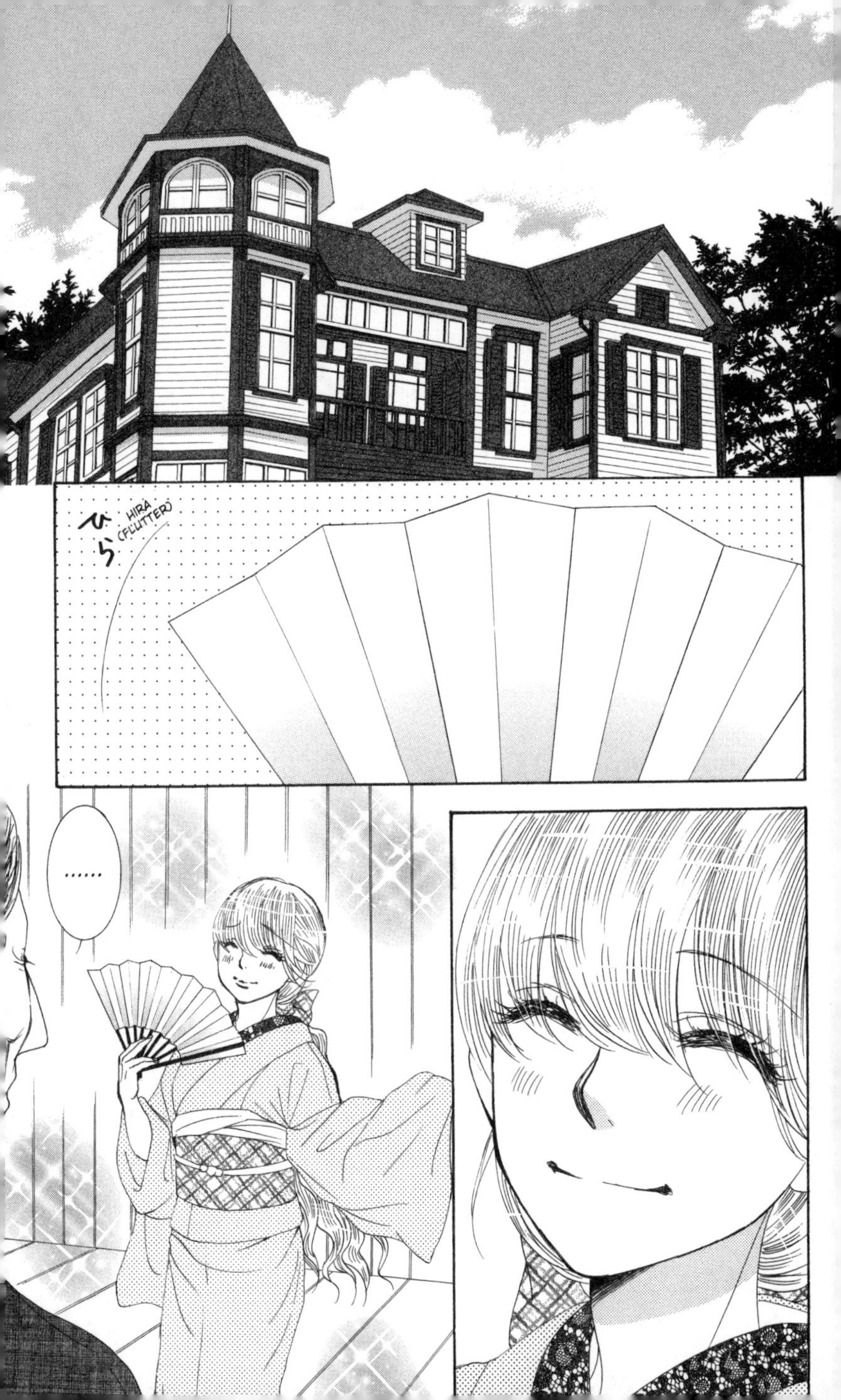
ひら HIRA (FLUTTER)
......

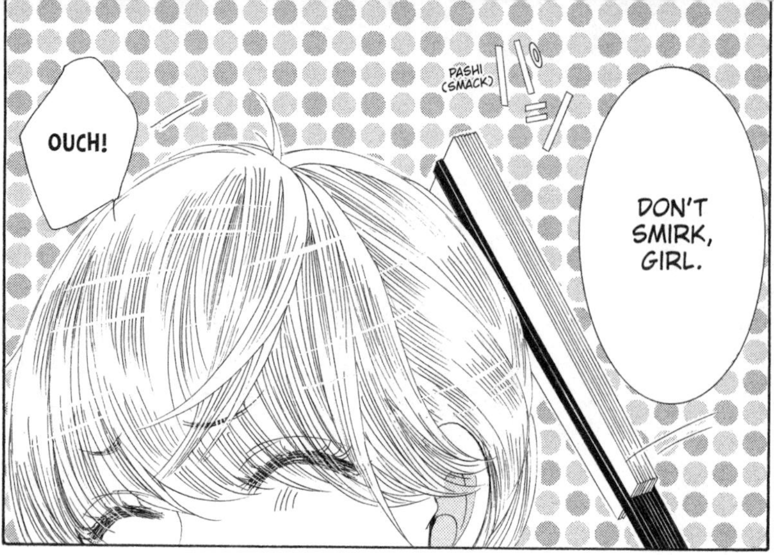
DON'T SMIRK, GIRL.
PASHI (SMACK)
OUCH!

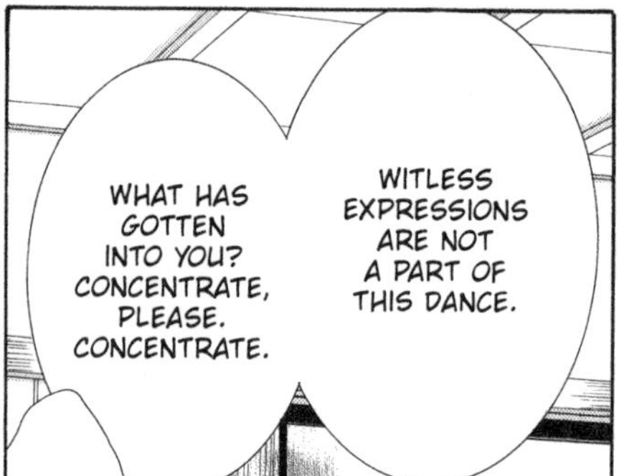
WITLESS EXPRESSIONS ARE NOT A PART OF THIS DANCE.
WHAT HAS GOTTEN INTO YOU? CONCENTRATE, PLEASE. CONCENTRATE.
I...I'M SORRY...

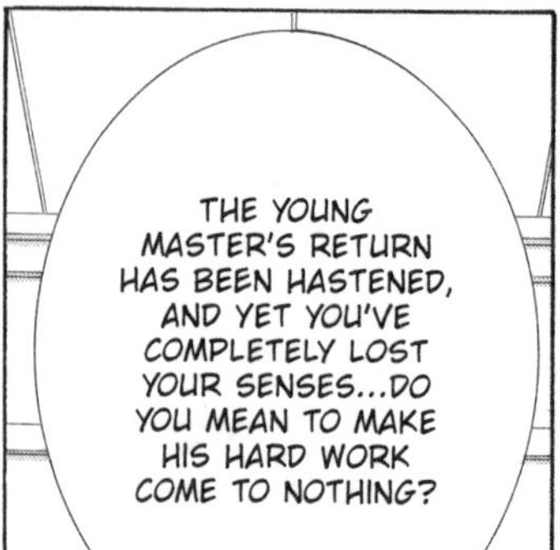
THE YOUNG MASTER'S RETURN HAS BEEN HASTENED, AND YET YOU'VE COMPLETELY LOST YOUR SENSES...DO YOU MEAN TO MAKE HIS HARD WORK COME TO NOTHING?
HONESTLY!

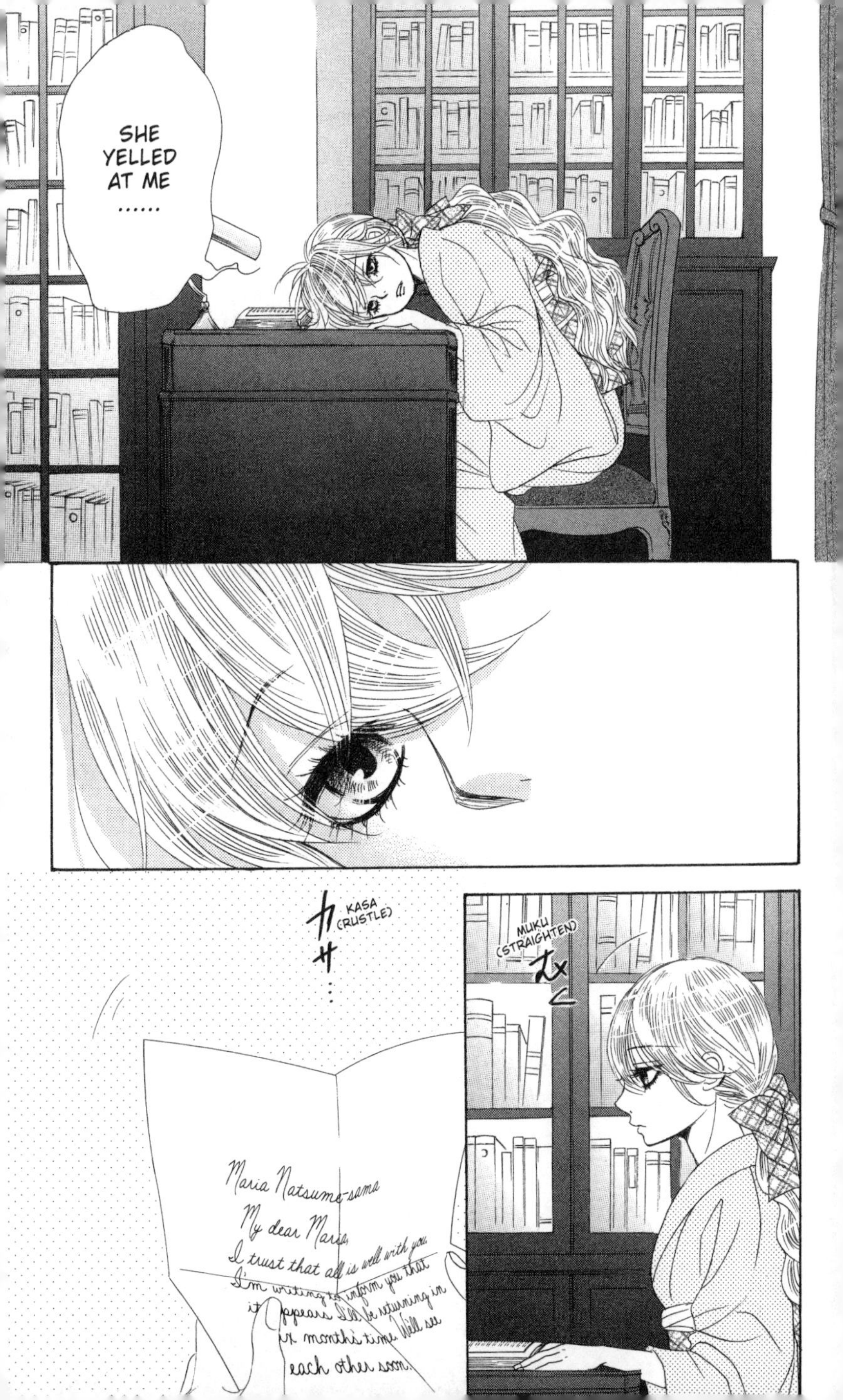
SHE YELLED AT ME ......
KASA (RUSTLE)
MUKU (STRAIGHTEN)
Maria Natsume-sama
My dear Maria,
I trust that all is well with you.
I'm writing to inform you that it appears I'll be returning in six month's time. We'll see each other soon.

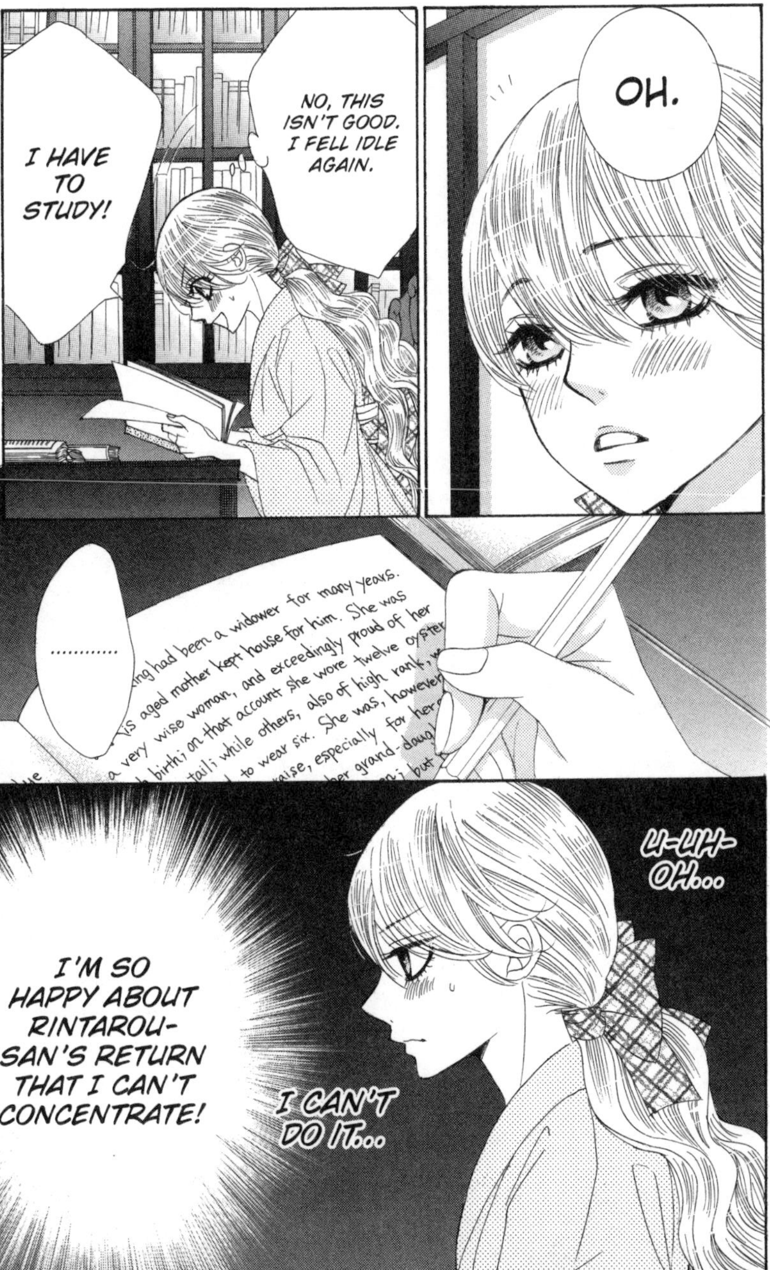
OH.
NO, THIS ISN'T GOOD. I FELL IDLE AGAIN.
I HAVE TO STUDY!
....
U-UH-OH...
I'M SO HAPPY ABOUT RINTAROU-SAN'S RETURN THAT I CAN'T CONCENTRATE!
I CAN'T DO IT...

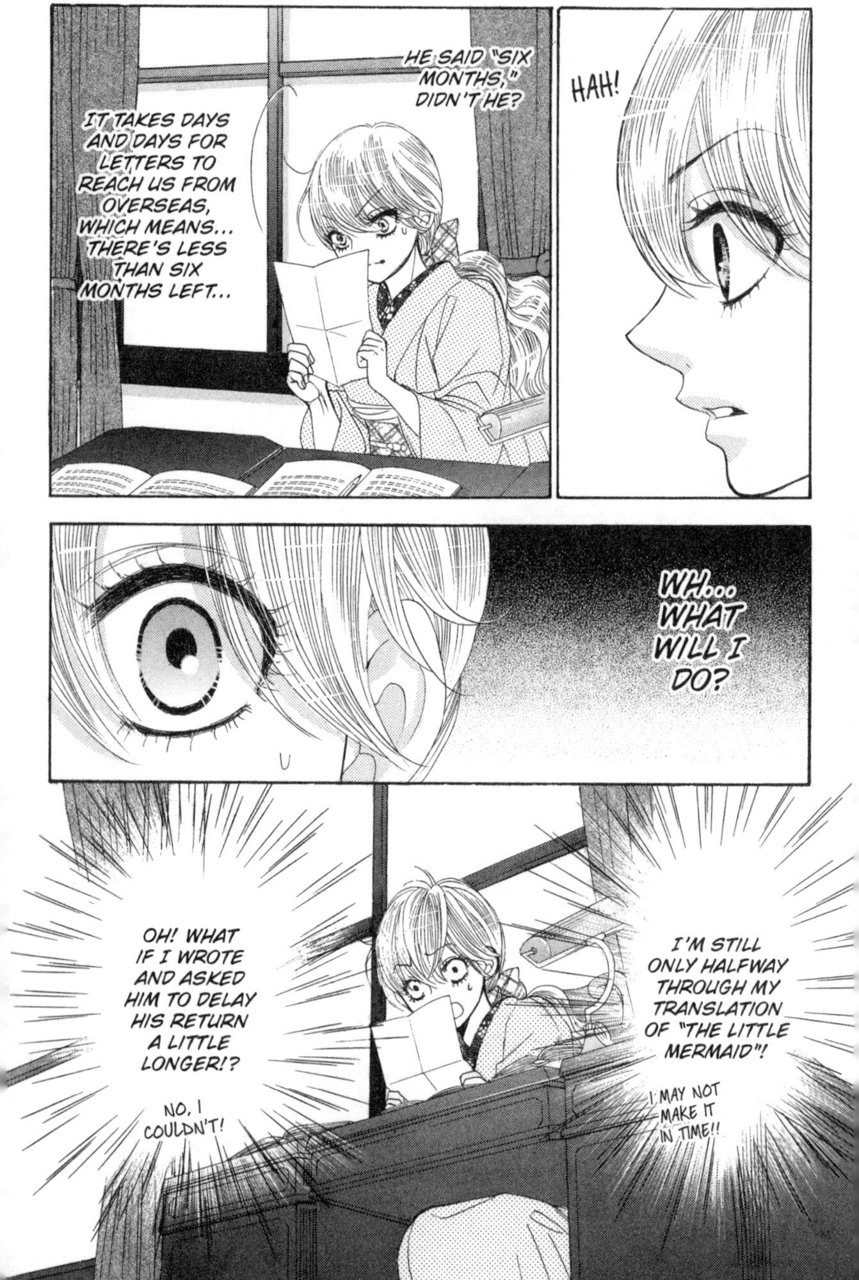
HAH!
HE SAID "SIX MONTHS," DIDN'T HE?
IT TAKES DAYS AND DAYS FOR LETTERS TO REACH US FROM OVERSEAS, WHICH MEANS... THERE'S LESS THAN SIX MONTHS LEFT...
WH... WHAT WILL I DO?
I'M STILL ONLY HALFWAY THROUGH MY TRANSLATION OF "THE LITTLE MERMAID"!
I MAY NOT MAKE IT IN TIME!!
OH! WHAT IF I WROTE AND ASKED HIM TO DELAY HIS RETURN A LITTLE LONGER!?
NO, I COULDN'T!

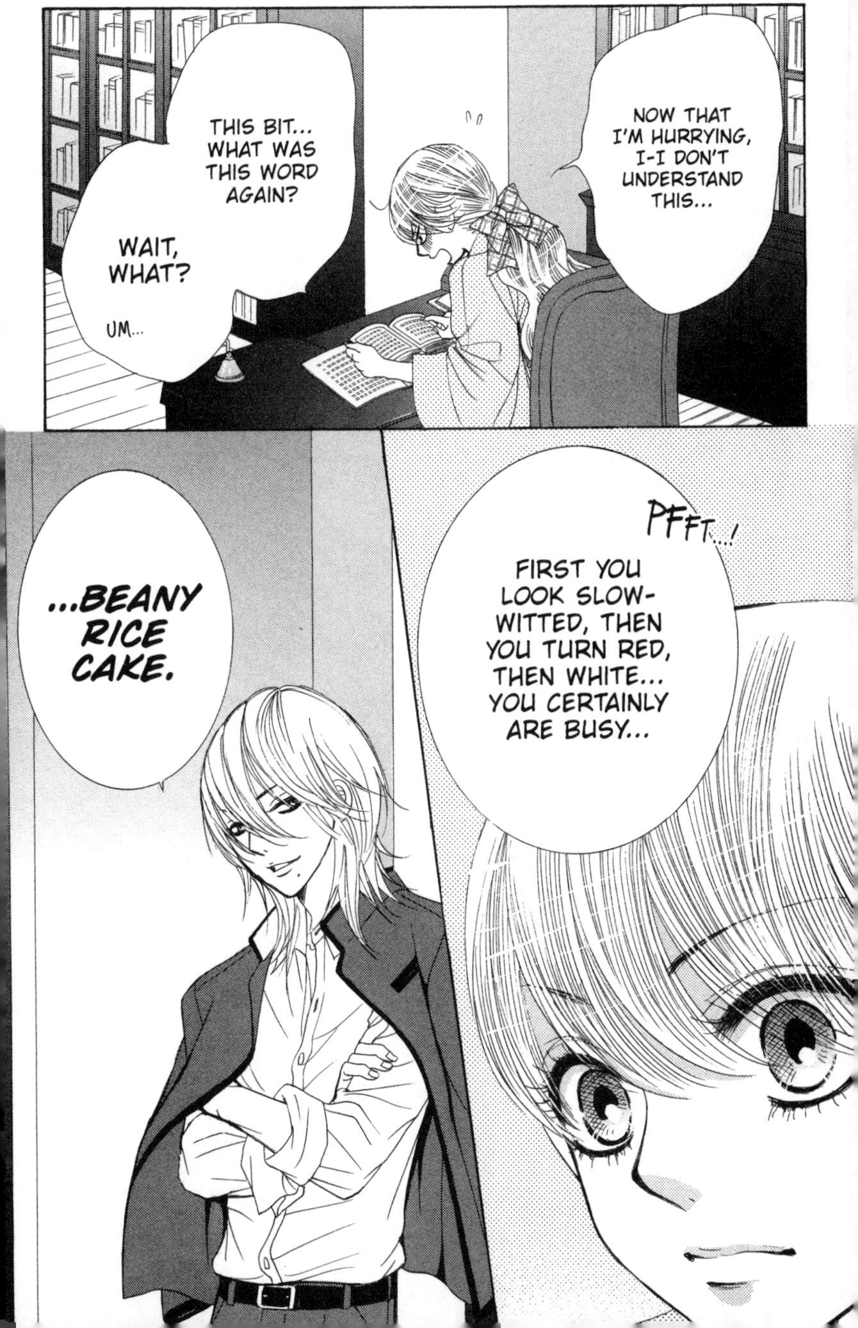
NOW THAT I'M HURRYING, I-I DON'T UNDERSTAND THIS...
THIS BIT... WHAT WAS THIS WORD AGAIN?
WAIT, WHAT?
UM...
PFFT...!
FIRST YOU LOOK SLOW-WITTED, THEN YOU TURN RED, THEN WHITE... YOU CERTAINLY ARE BUSY...
...BEANY RICE CAKE.

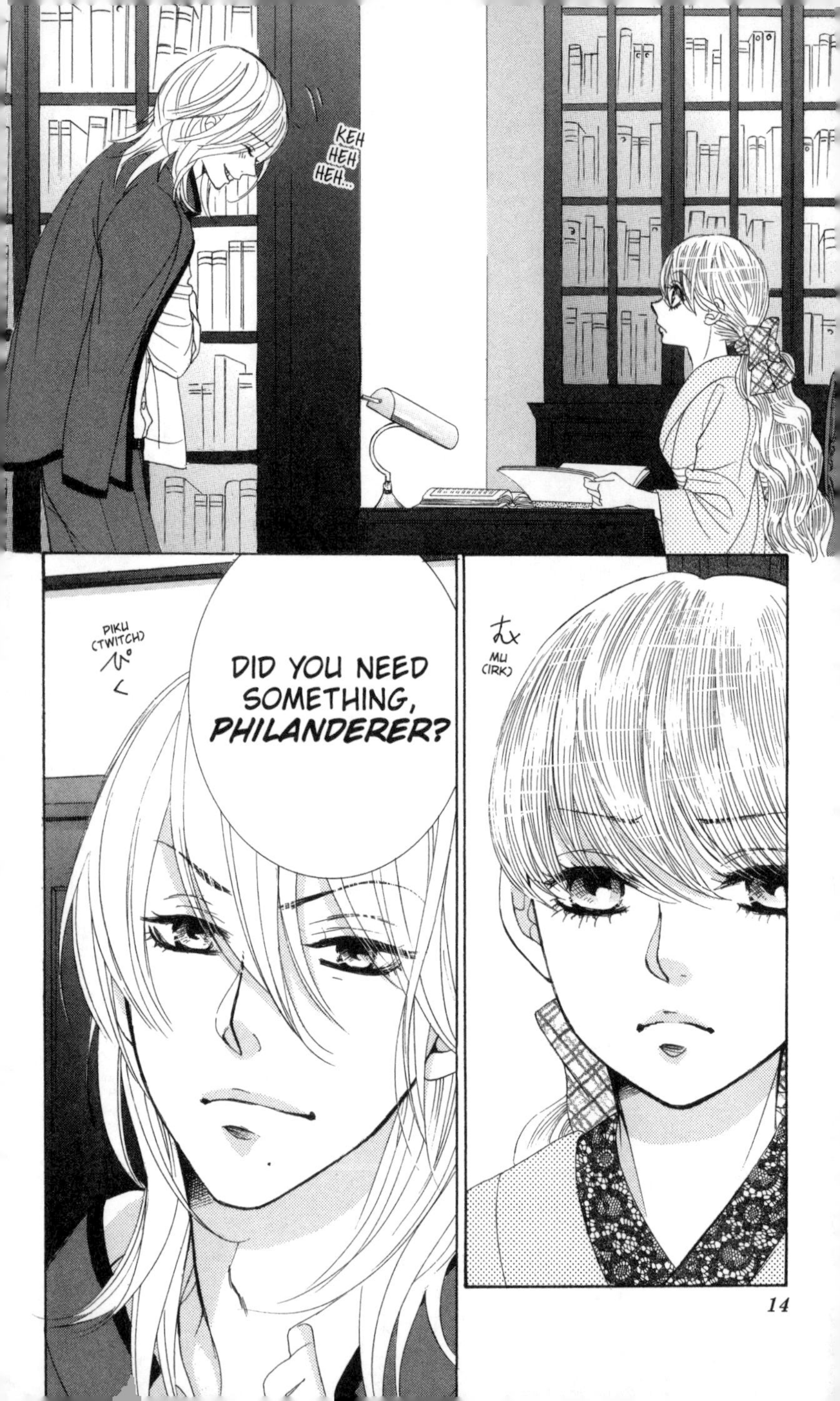
KEH HEH HEH...
む
MU (IRK)
DID YOU NEED SOMETHING, **PHILANDERER?**
ぴく
PIKU (TWITCH)

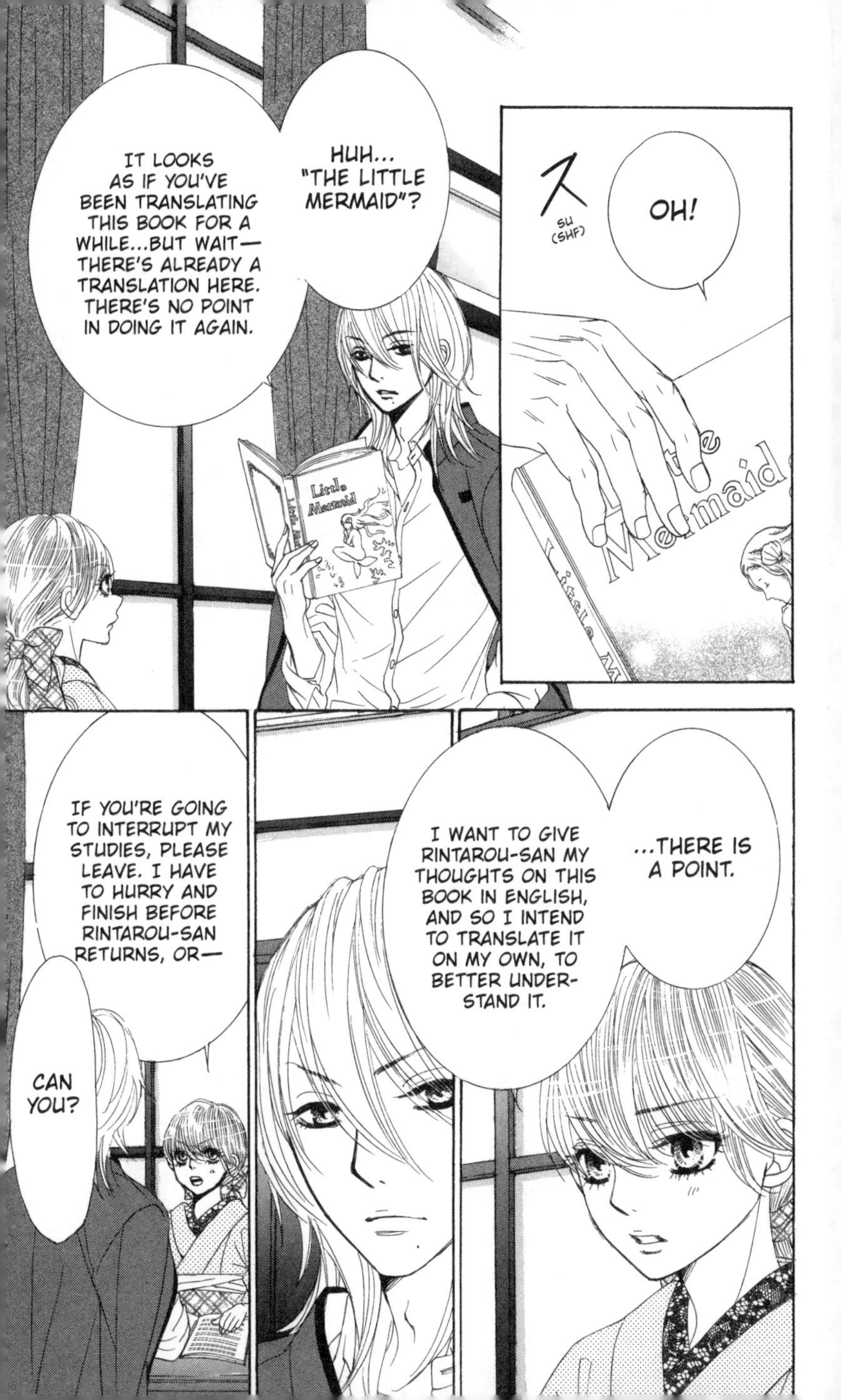
ス
SU (SHF)
OH!
HUH... "THE LITTLE MERMAID"?
IT LOOKS AS IF YOU'VE BEEN TRANSLATING THIS BOOK FOR A WHILE...BUT WAIT—THERE'S ALREADY A TRANSLATION HERE. THERE'S NO POINT IN DOING IT AGAIN.
...THERE IS A POINT.
I WANT TO GIVE RINTAROU-SAN MY THOUGHTS ON THIS BOOK IN ENGLISH, AND SO I INTEND TO TRANSLATE IT ON MY OWN, TO BETTER UNDER-STAND IT.
IF YOU'RE GOING TO INTERRUPT MY STUDIES, PLEASE LEAVE. I HAVE TO HURRY AND FINISH BEFORE RINTAROU-SAN RETURNS, OR—
CAN YOU?

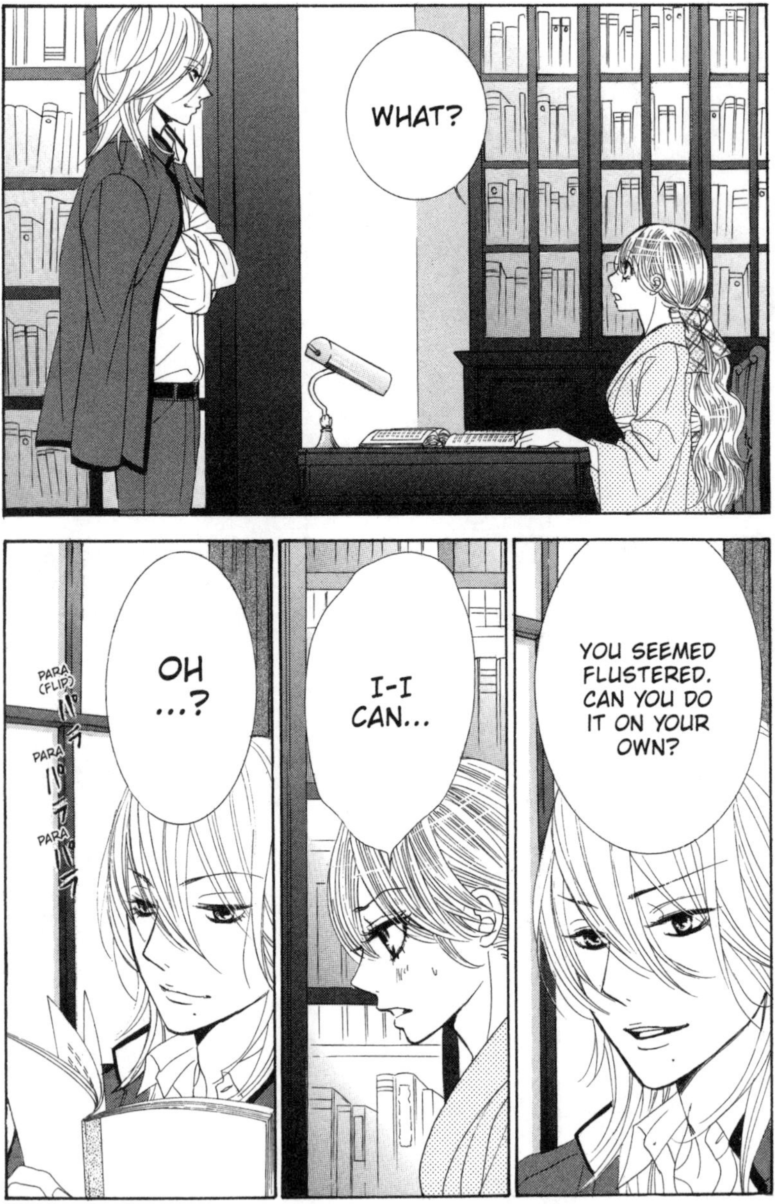
WHAT?
YOU SEEMED FLUSTERED. CAN YOU DO IT ON YOUR OWN?
I-I CAN...
OH ...?
PARA (FLIP)
PARA
PARA

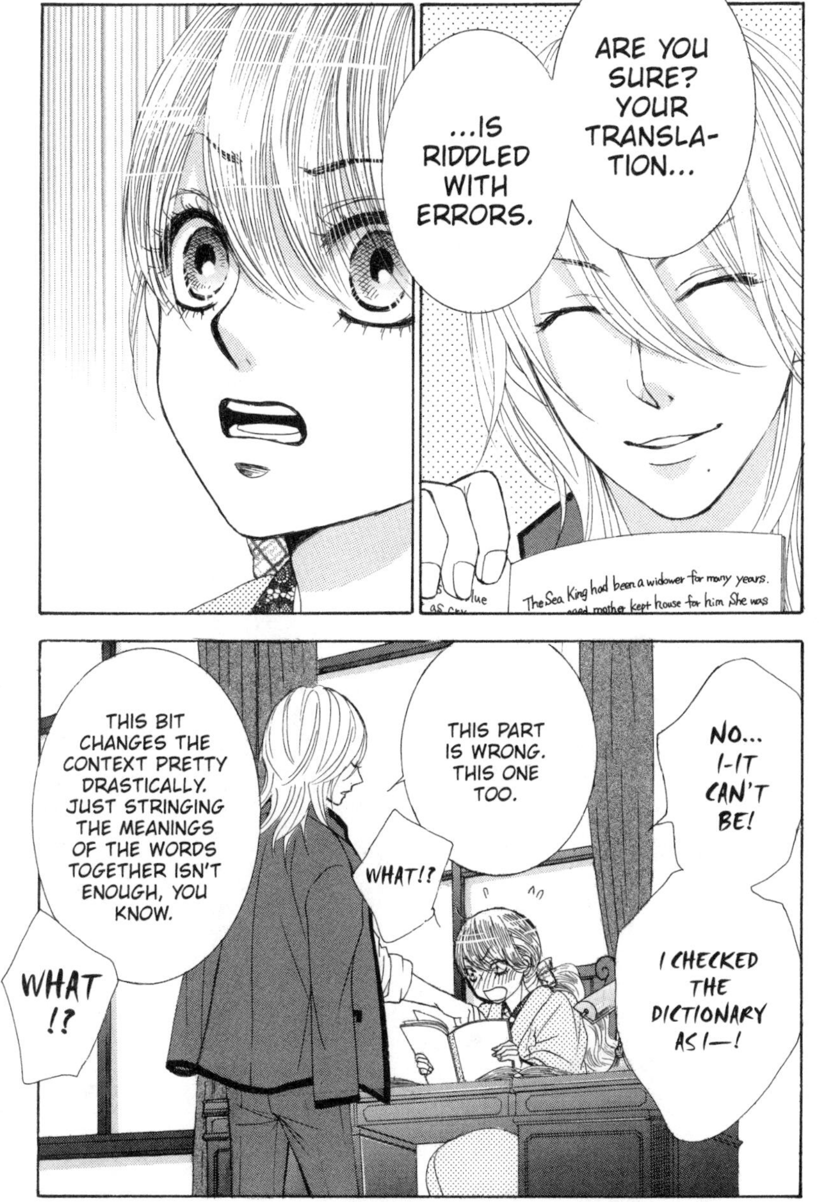
ARE YOU SURE? YOUR TRANSLA-TION...
...IS RIDDLED WITH ERRORS.
The Sea King had been a widower for many years.
NO... I-IT CAN'T BE!
I CHECKED THE DICTIONARY AS I—!
THIS PART IS WRONG. THIS ONE TOO.
WHAT!?
THIS BIT CHANGES THE CONTEXT PRETTY DRASTICALLY. JUST STRINGING THE MEANINGS OF THE WORDS TOGETHER ISN'T ENOUGH, YOU KNOW.
WHAT !?

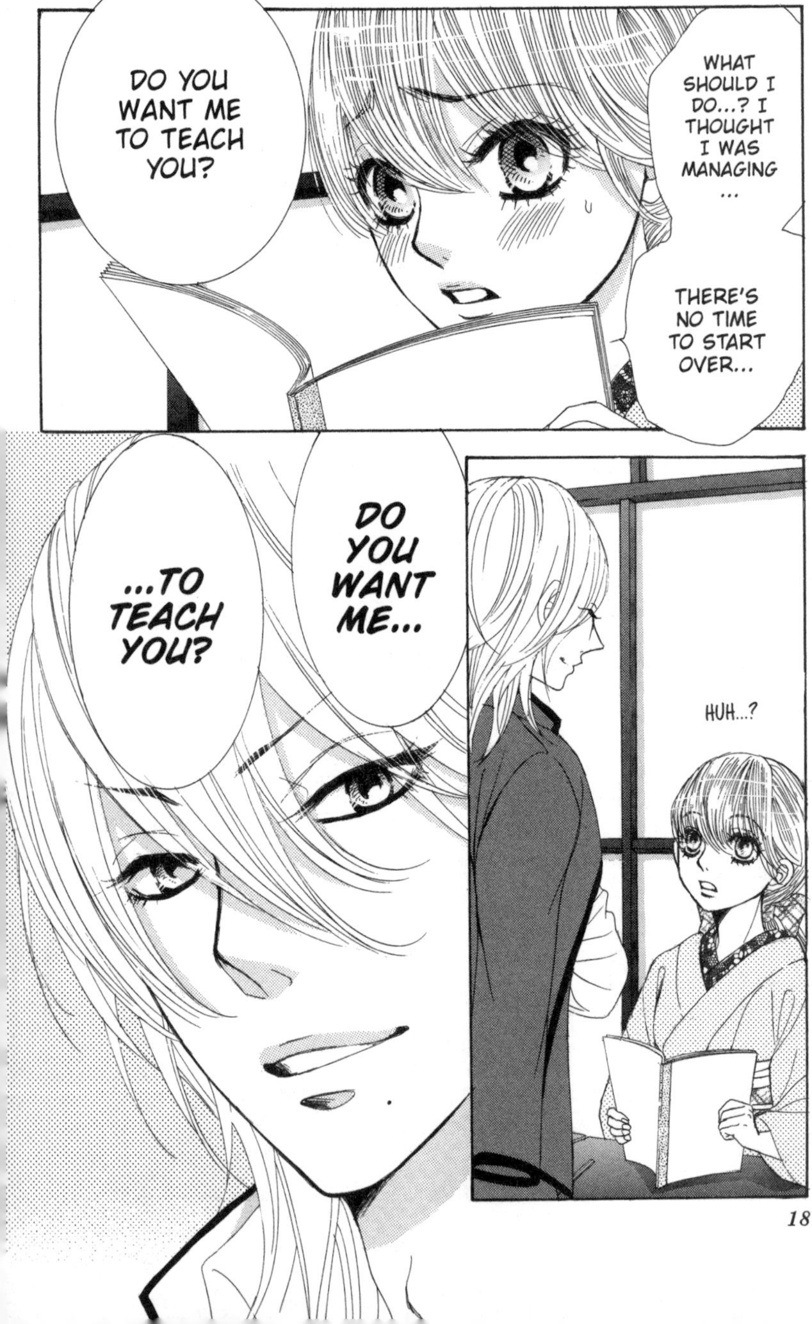
WHAT SHOULD I DO...? I THOUGHT I WAS MANAGING...
THERE'S NO TIME TO START OVER...
DO YOU WANT ME TO TEACH YOU?
HUH...?
DO YOU WANT ME...
...TO TEACH YOU?

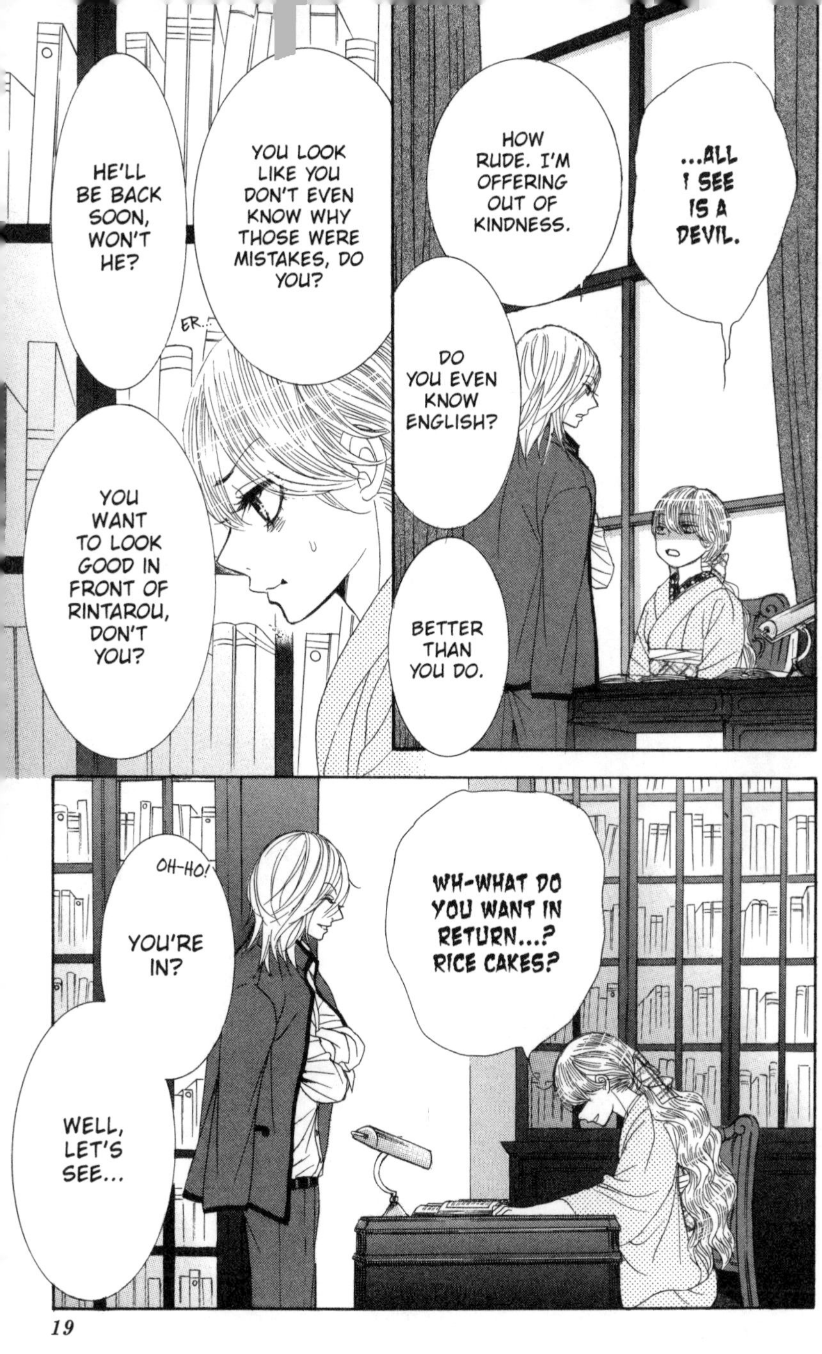
...ALL I SEE IS A DEVIL.
HOW RUDE. I'M OFFERING OUT OF KINDNESS.
DO YOU EVEN KNOW ENGLISH?
BETTER THAN YOU DO.
YOU LOOK LIKE YOU DON'T EVEN KNOW WHY THOSE WERE MISTAKES, DO YOU?
HE'LL BE BACK SOON, WON'T HE?
ER...
YOU WANT TO LOOK GOOD IN FRONT OF RINTAROU, DON'T YOU?
WH-WHAT DO YOU WANT IN RETURN...? RICE CAKES?
OH-HO!
YOU'RE IN?
WELL, LET'S SEE...

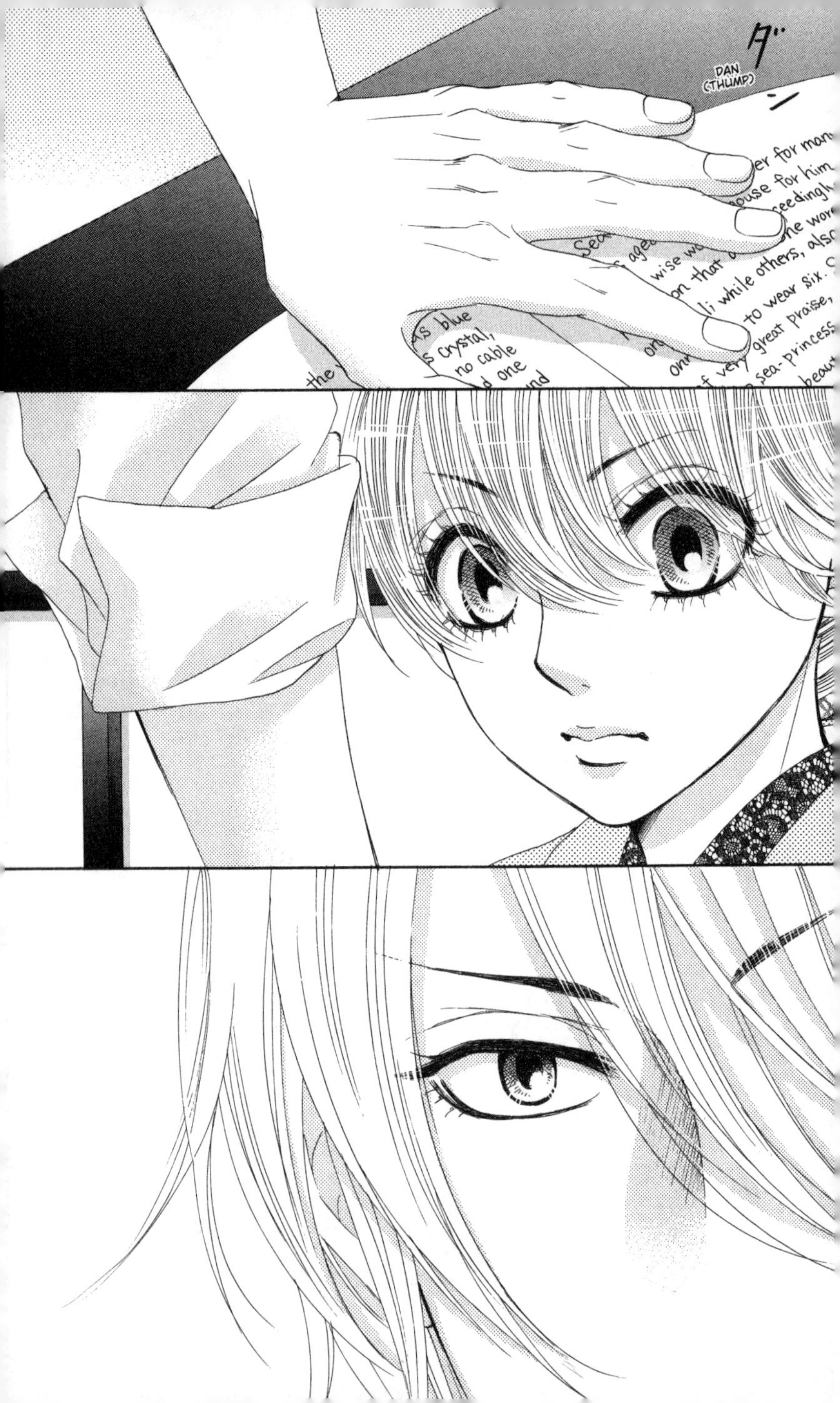

ダ
DAN (THUMP)

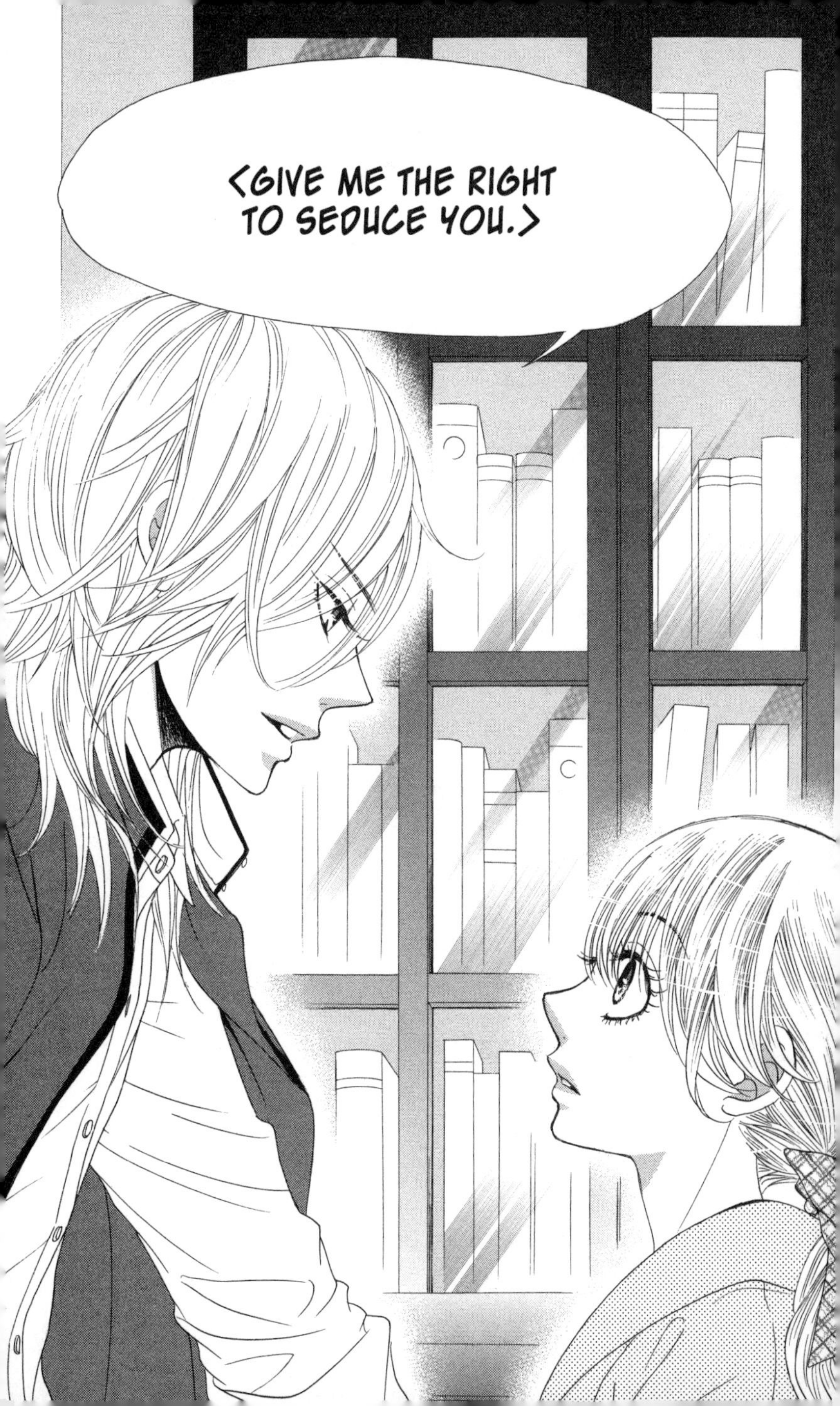
<GIVE ME THE RIGHT TO SEDUCE YOU.>

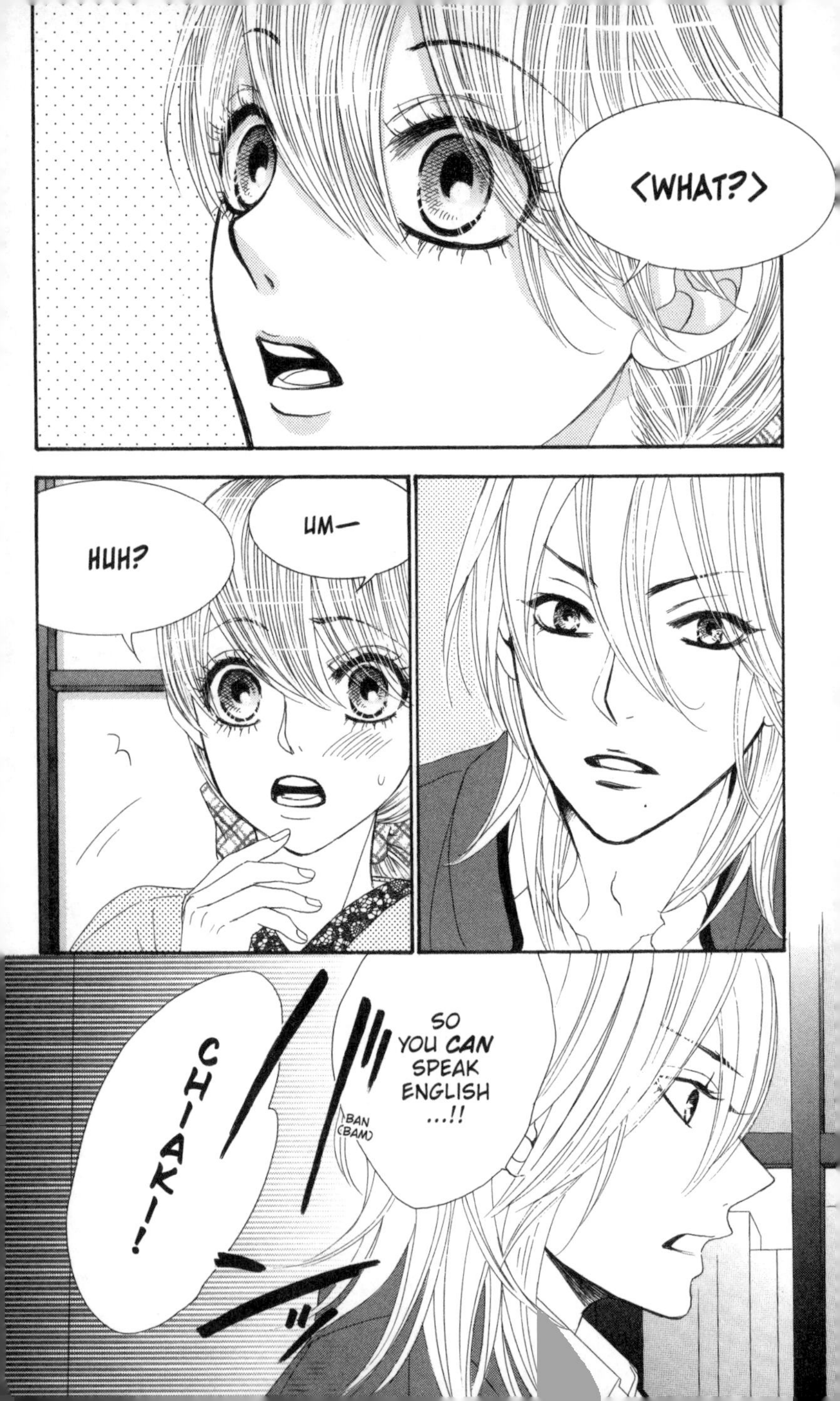
<WHAT?>
UM—
HUH?
SO YOU CAN SPEAK ENGLISH ...!!
BAN (BAM)
CHIAKI—!

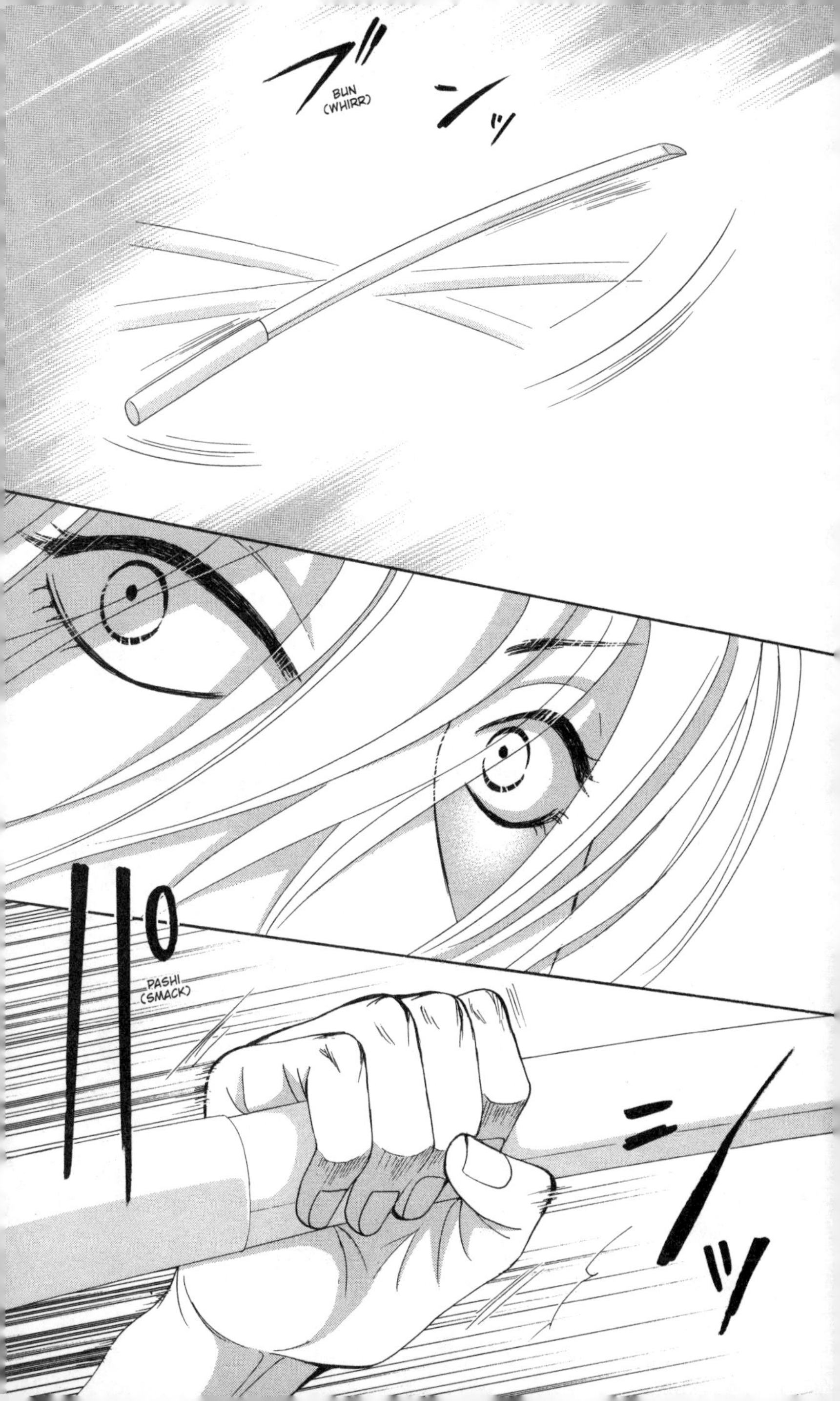
ブンッ
BUN (WHIRR)
パシ
PASHI (SMACK)
ニイッ

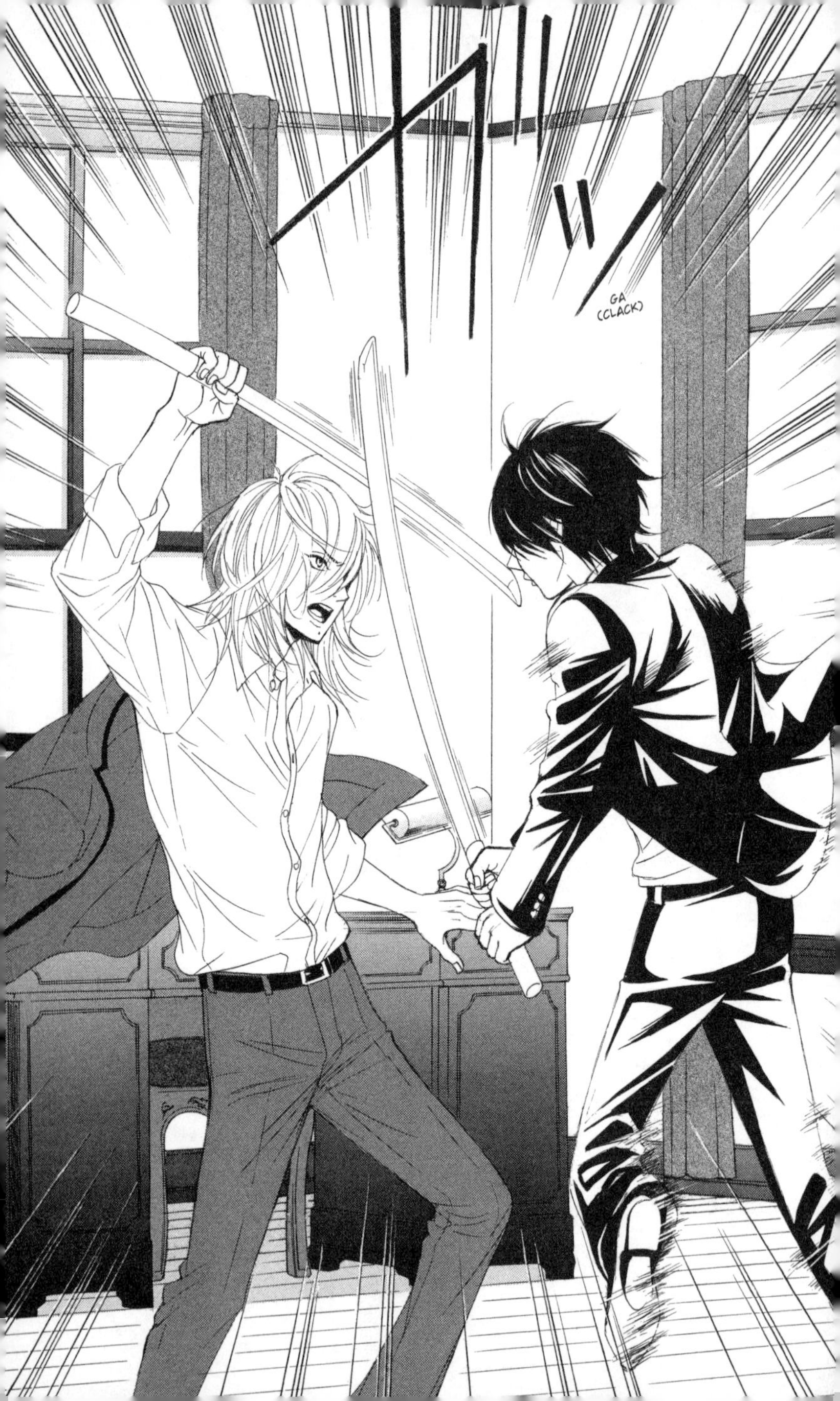
GA
(CLACK)

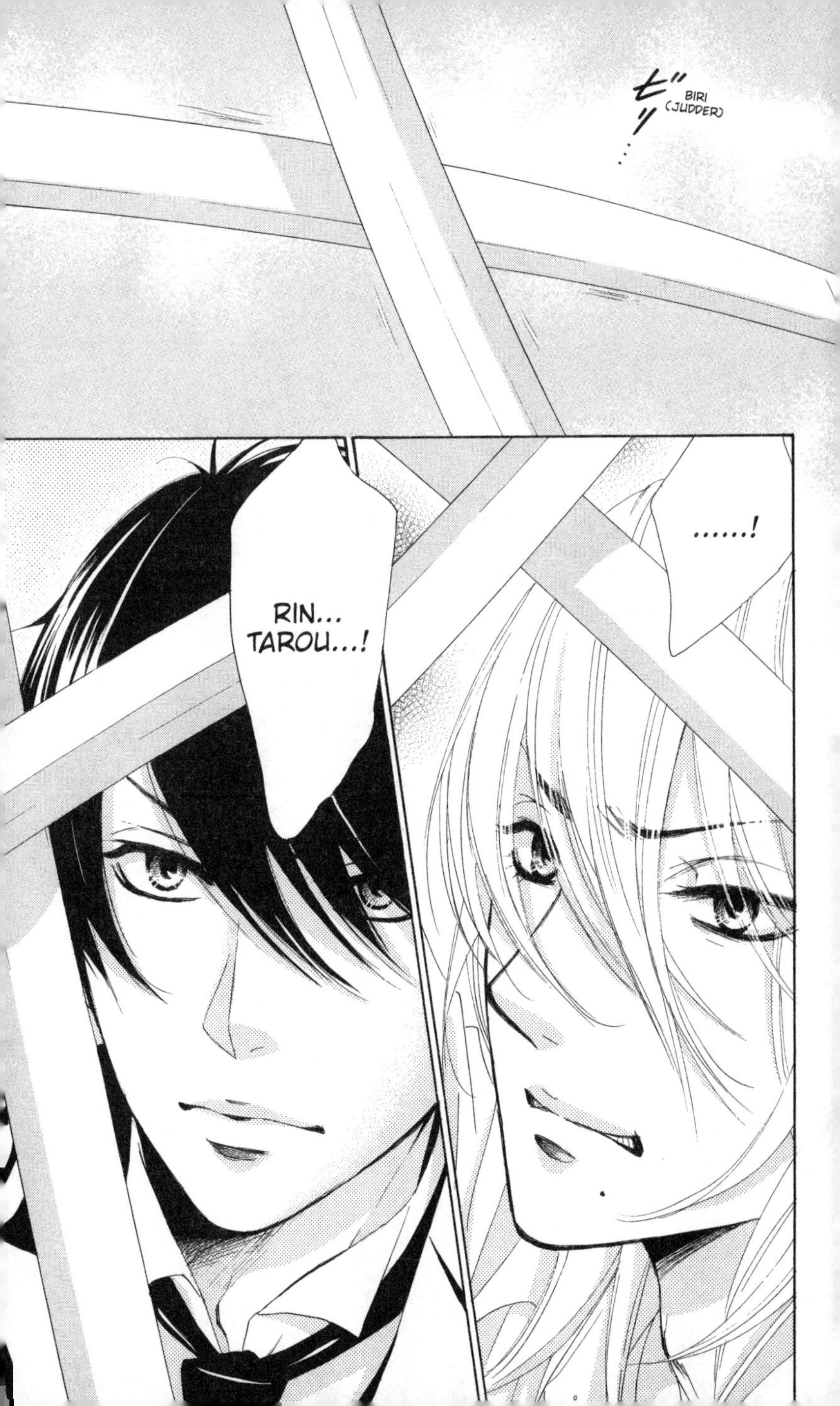
ビリ BIRI (JUDDER)
......!
RIN... TAROU...!

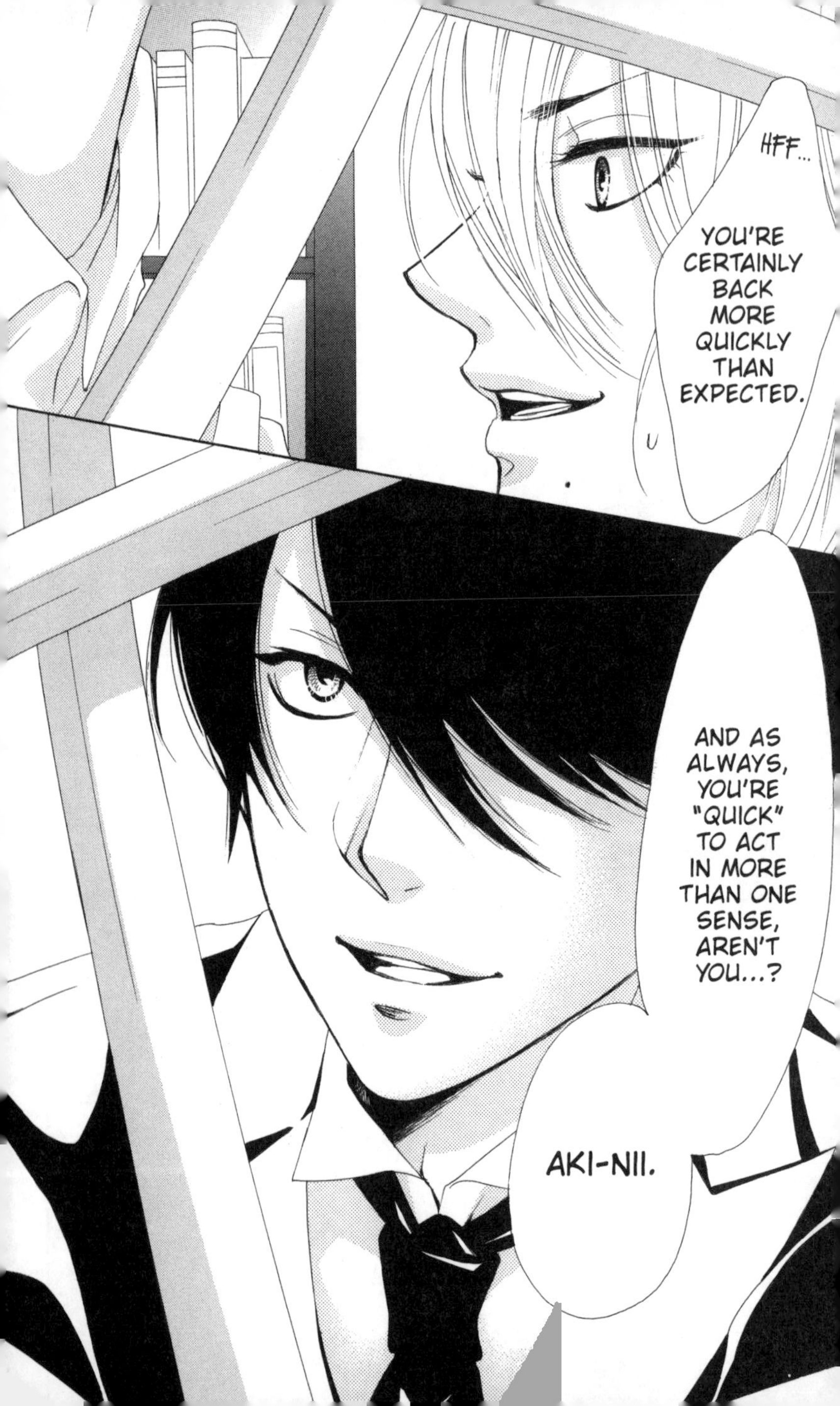
HFF...
YOU'RE CERTAINLY BACK MORE QUICKLY THAN EXPECTED.
AND AS ALWAYS, YOU'RE "QUICK" TO ACT IN MORE THAN ONE SENSE, AREN'T YOU...?
AKI-NII.

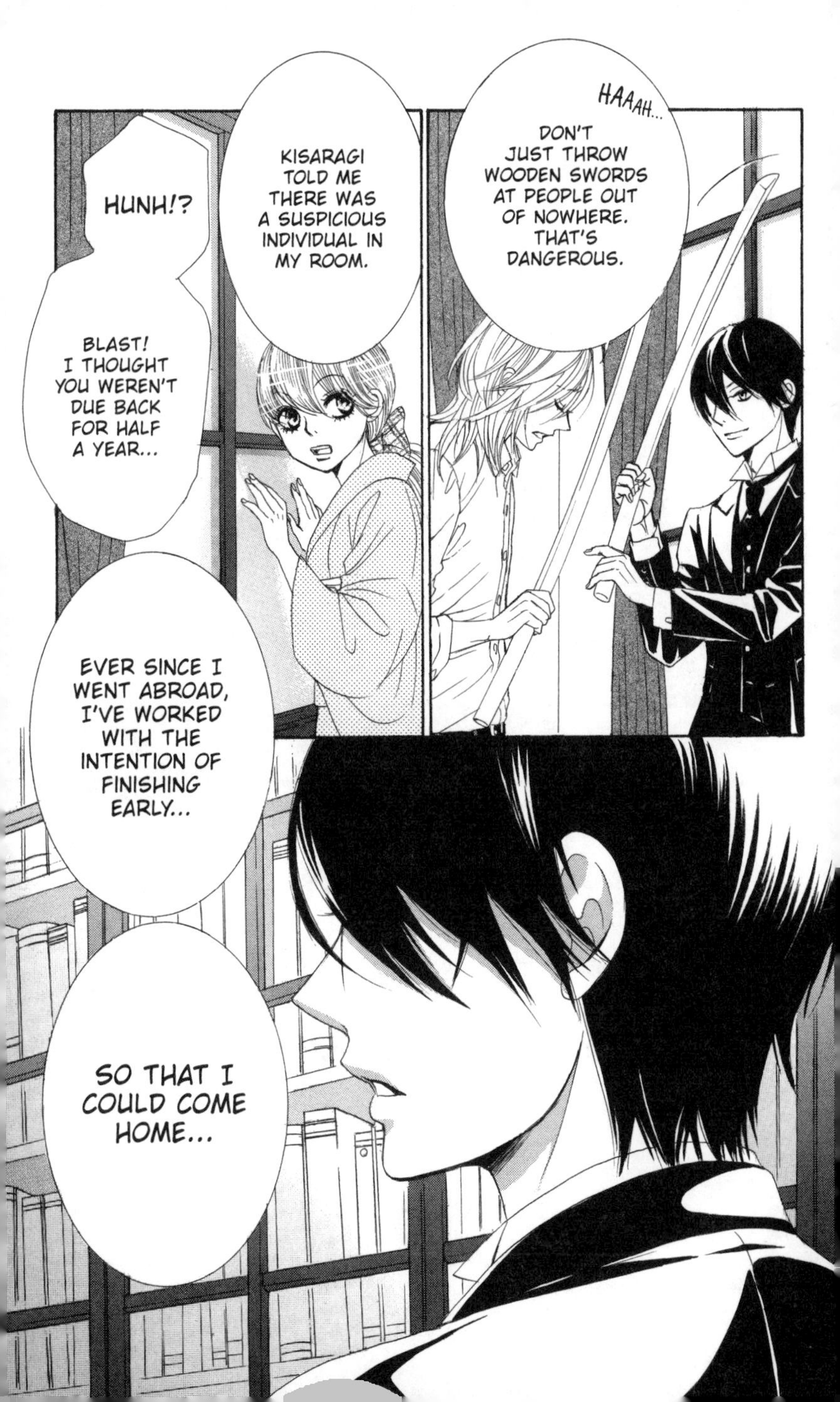
HAAAH...
DON'T JUST THROW WOODEN SWORDS AT PEOPLE OUT OF NOWHERE. THAT'S DANGEROUS.
KISARAGI TOLD ME THERE WAS A SUSPICIOUS INDIVIDUAL IN MY ROOM.
HUNH!?
BLAST! I THOUGHT YOU WEREN'T DUE BACK FOR HALF A YEAR...
EVER SINCE I WENT ABROAD, I'VE WORKED WITH THE INTENTION OF FINISHING EARLY...
SO THAT I COULD COME HOME...

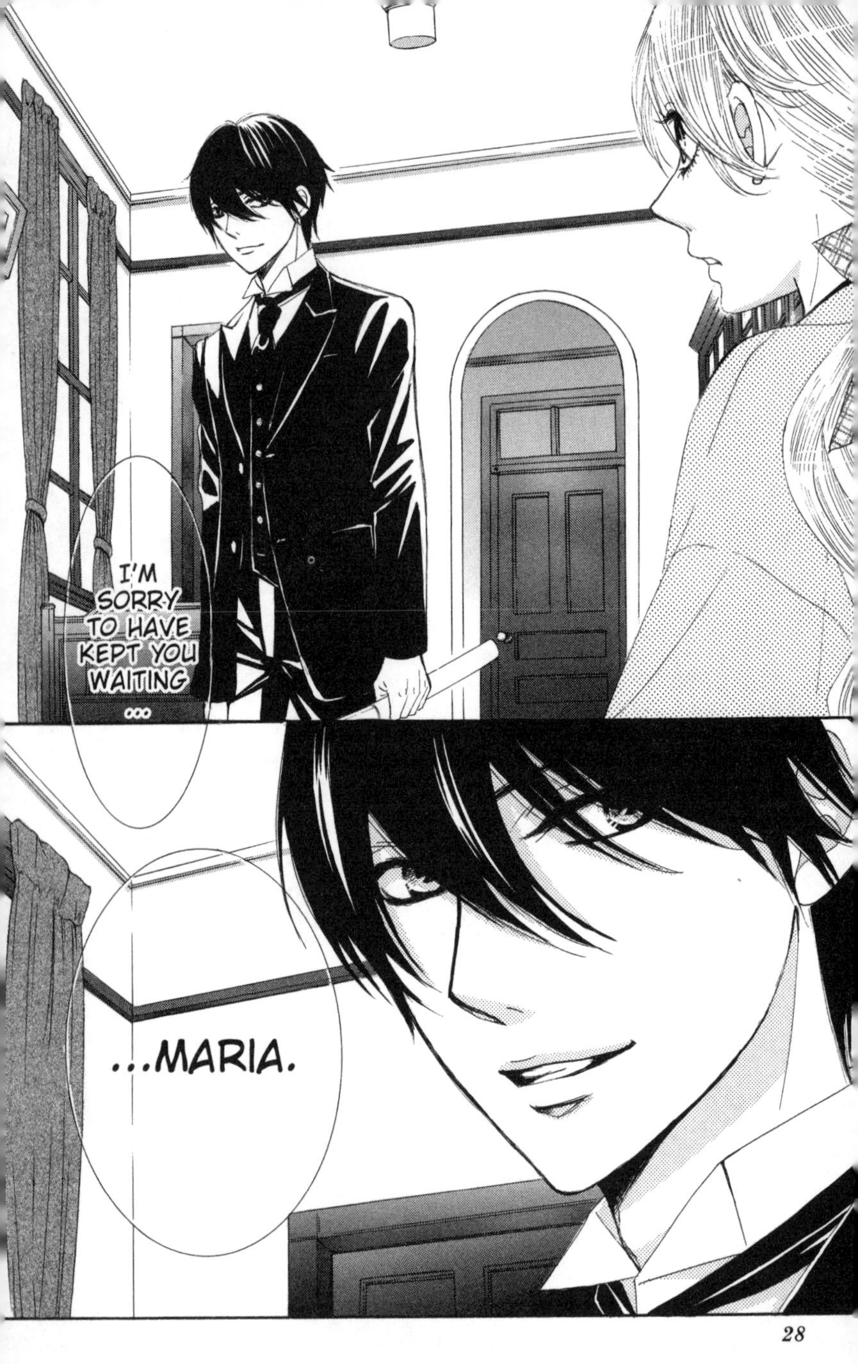
I'M SORRY TO HAVE KEPT YOU WAITING...
...MARIA.

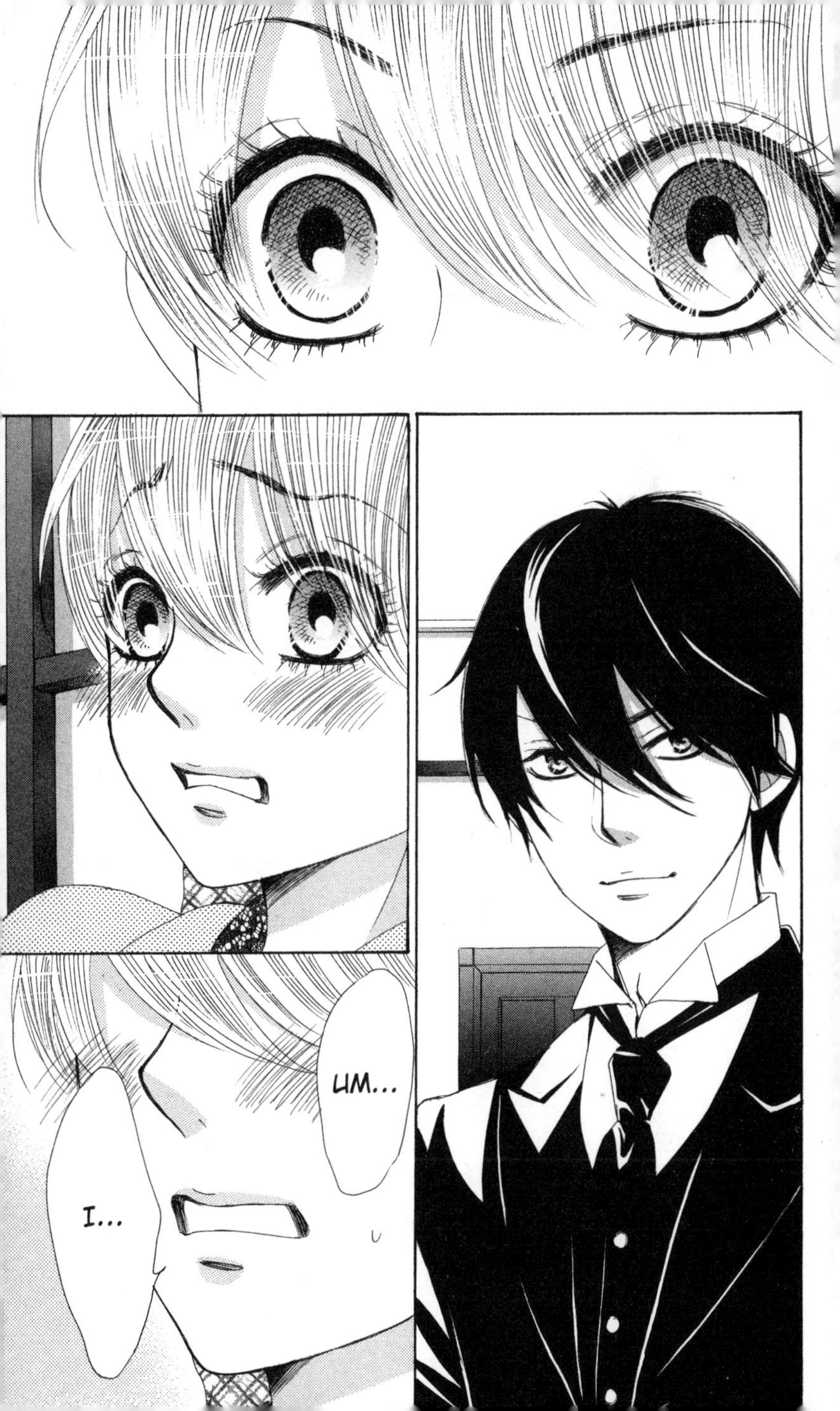
UM...
I...

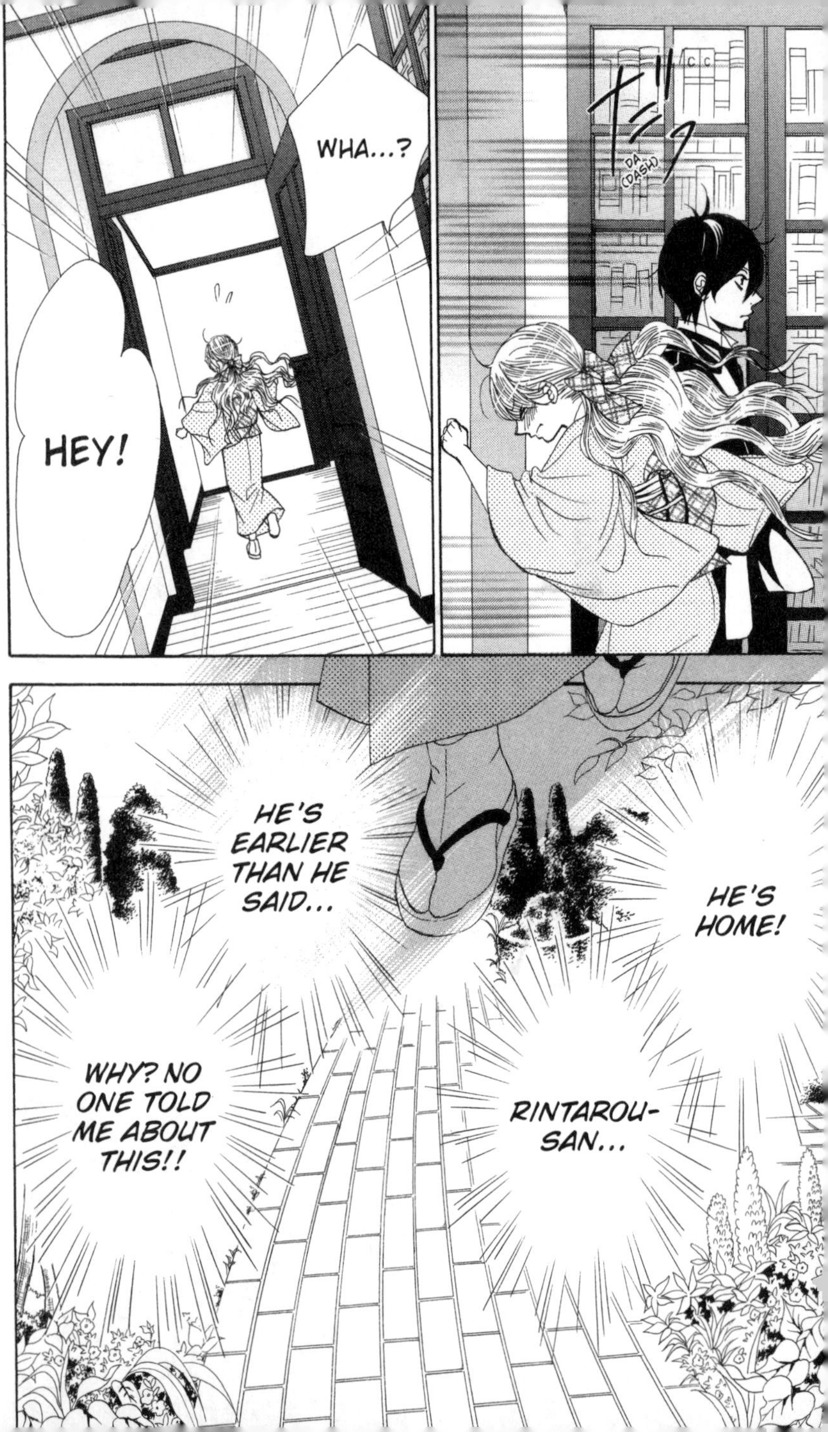
DA (DASH)
WHA...?
HEY!
HE'S HOME!
HE'S EARLIER THAN HE SAID...
RINTAROU-SAN...
WHY? NO ONE TOLD ME ABOUT THIS!!

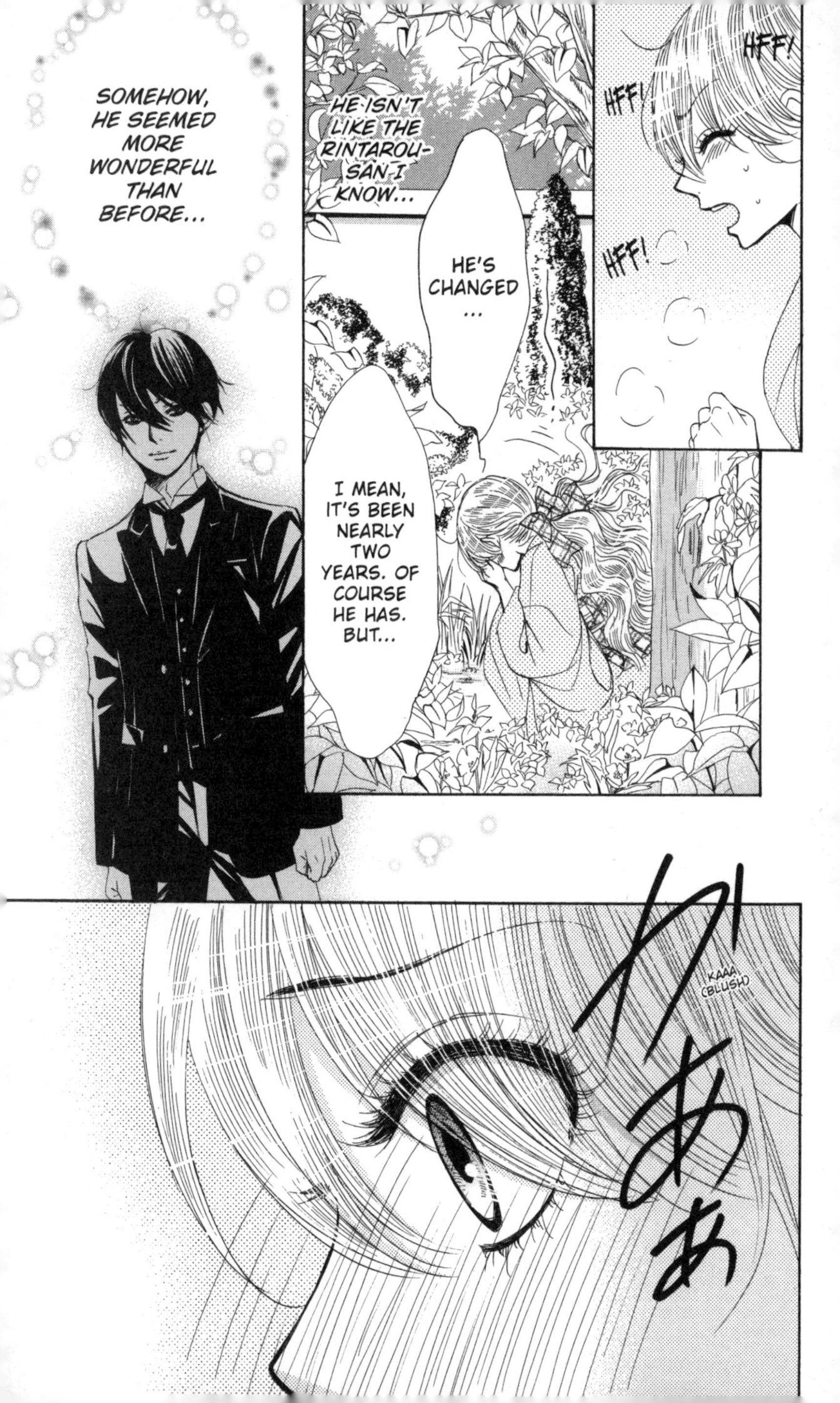
HFF!
HFF!
HFF!
HE ISN'T LIKE THE RINTAROU-SAN I KNOW...
HE'S CHANGED...
I MEAN, IT'S BEEN NEARLY TWO YEARS. OF COURSE HE HAS. BUT...
SOMEHOW, HE SEEMED MORE WONDERFUL THAN BEFORE...
かぁぁ
KAAA (BLUSH)

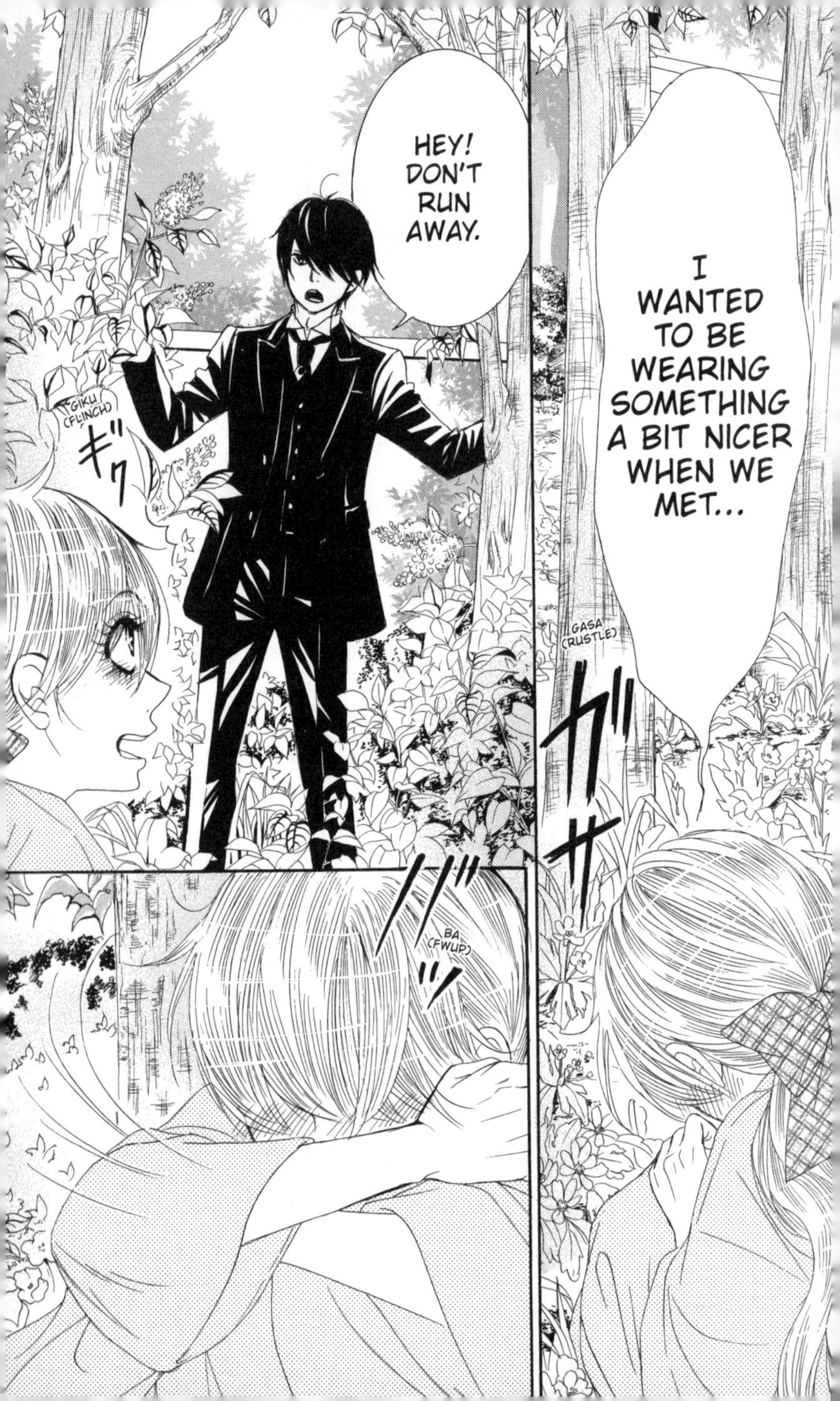
I WANTED TO BE WEARING SOMETHING A BIT NICER WHEN WE MET...
GASA (RUSTLE)
HEY! DON'T RUN AWAY.
GIKU (FLINCH)
BA (FWUP)

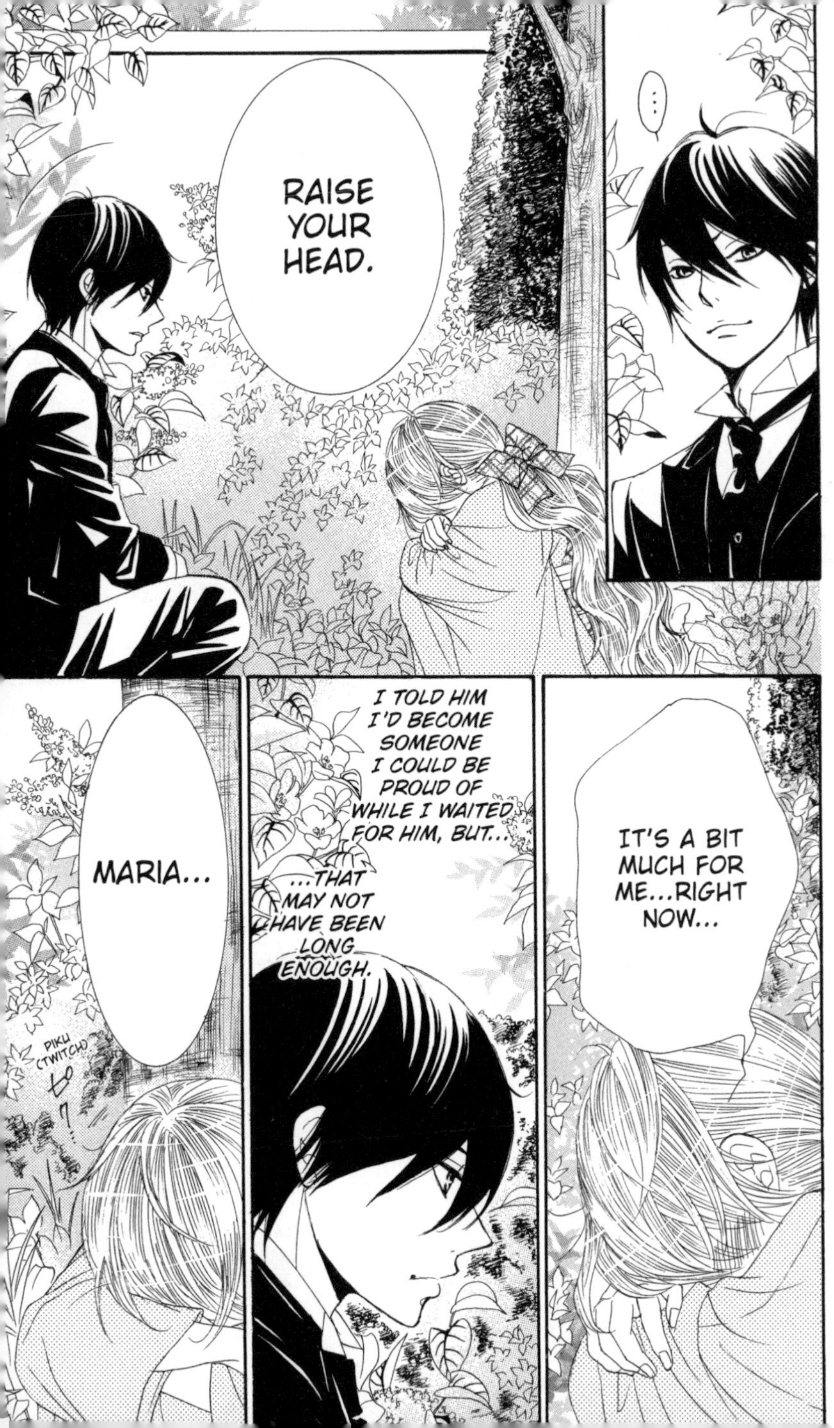
…
RAISE YOUR HEAD.
IT'S A BIT MUCH FOR ME…RIGHT NOW…
I TOLD HIM I'D BECOME SOMEONE I COULD BE PROUD OF WHILE I WAITED FOR HIM, BUT…
…THAT MAY NOT HAVE BEEN LONG ENOUGH.
MARIA…
PIKU (TWITCH)

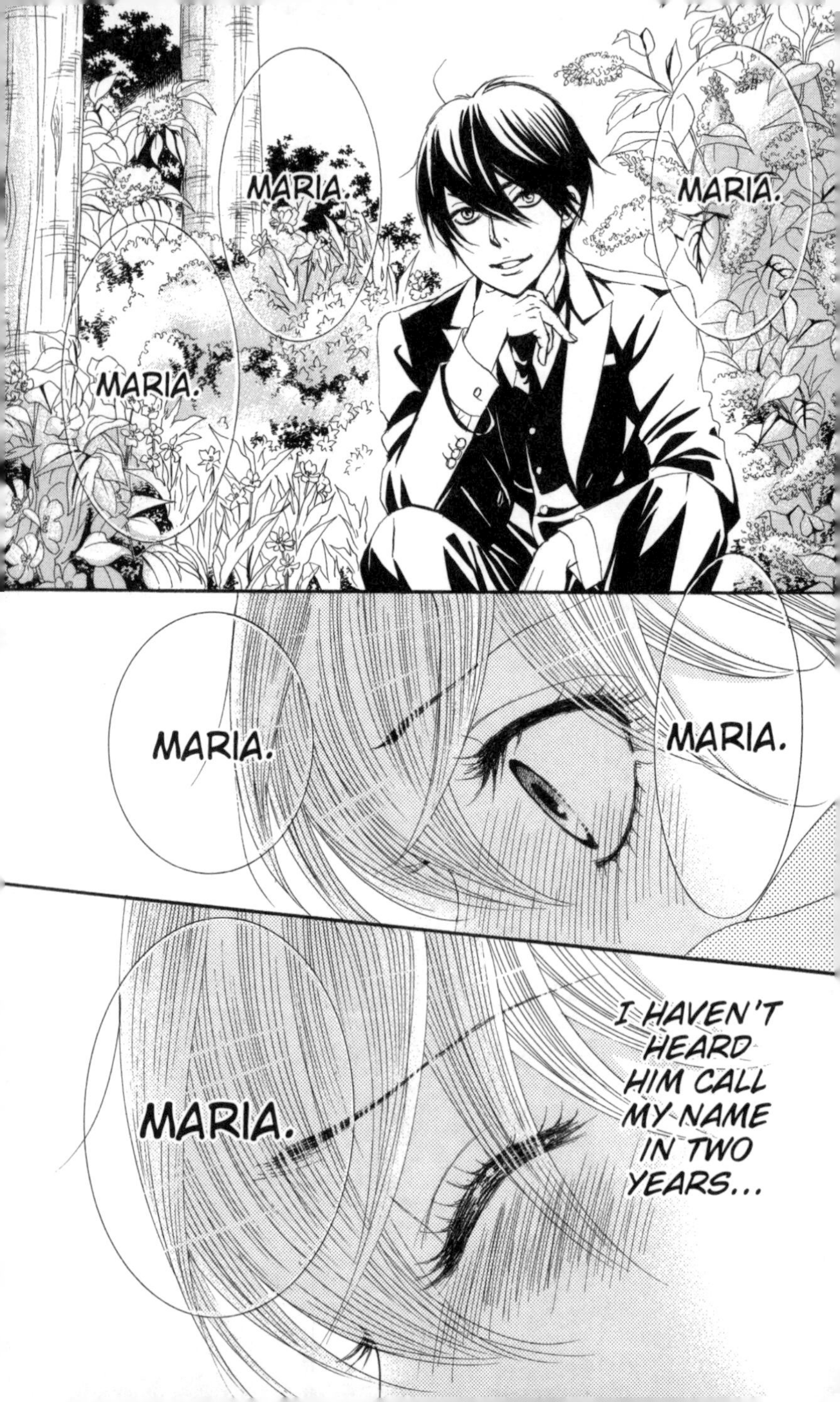
MARIA.
MARIA.
MARIA.
MARIA.
MARIA.
I HAVEN'T HEARD HIM CALL MY NAME IN TWO YEARS...
MARIA.

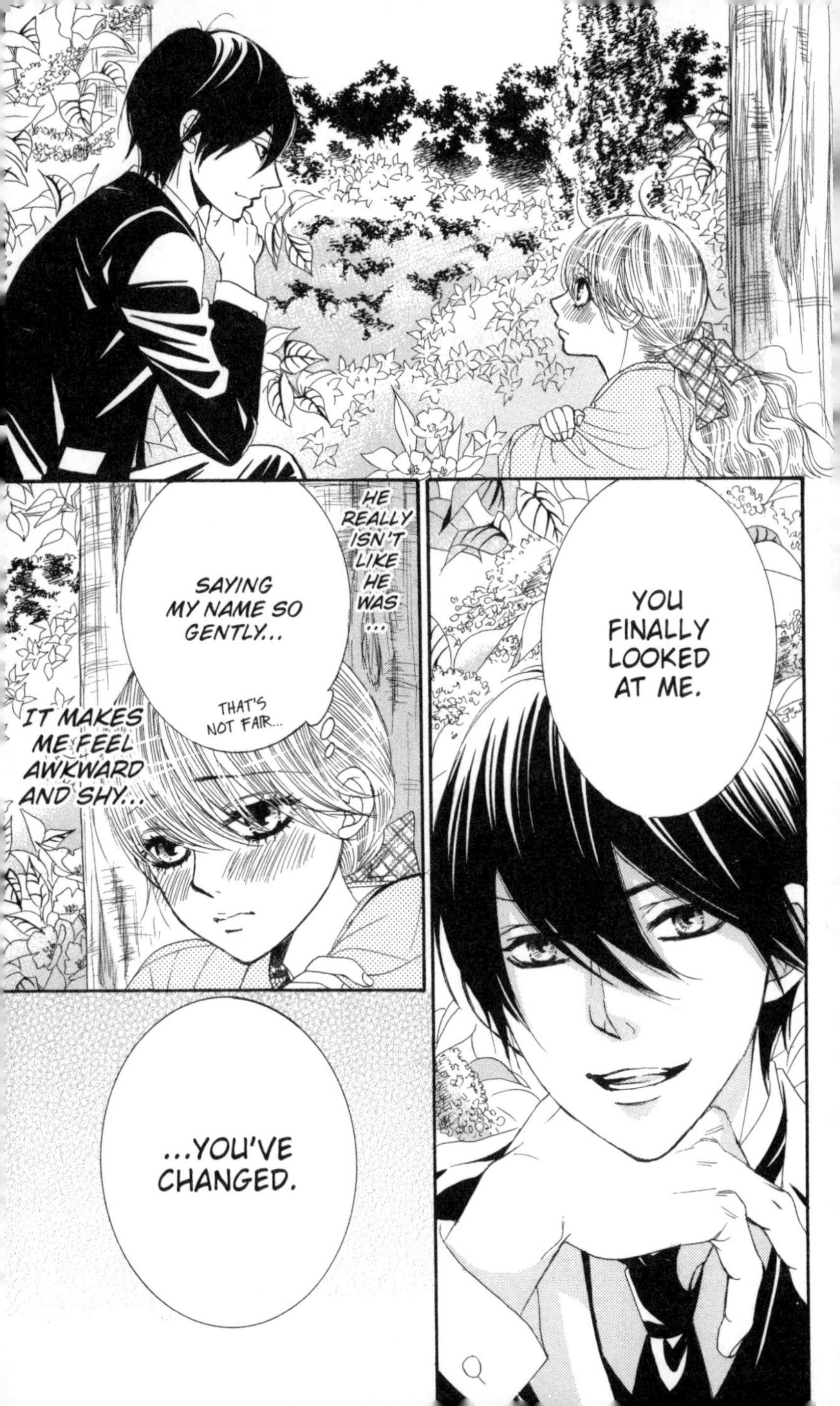
YOU FINALLY LOOKED AT ME.
HE REALLY ISN'T LIKE HE WAS...
SAYING MY NAME SO GENTLY...
THAT'S NOT FAIR...
IT MAKES ME FEEL AWKWARD AND SHY...
...YOU'VE CHANGED.

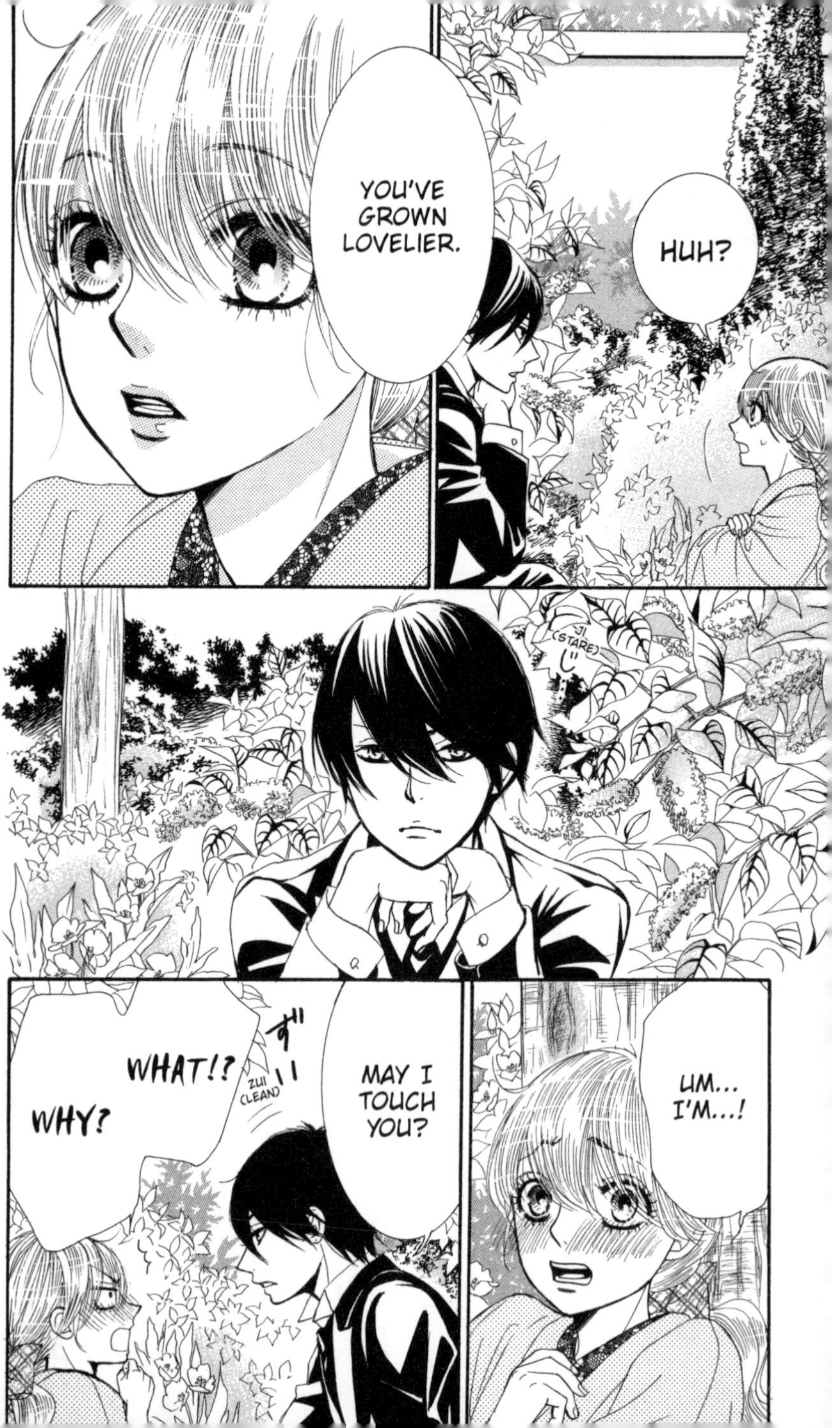
HUH?
YOU'VE GROWN LOVELIER.
じ
JI (STARE)
UM... I'M...!
MAY I TOUCH YOU?
ずい
ZUI (LEAN)
WHAT!?
WHY?

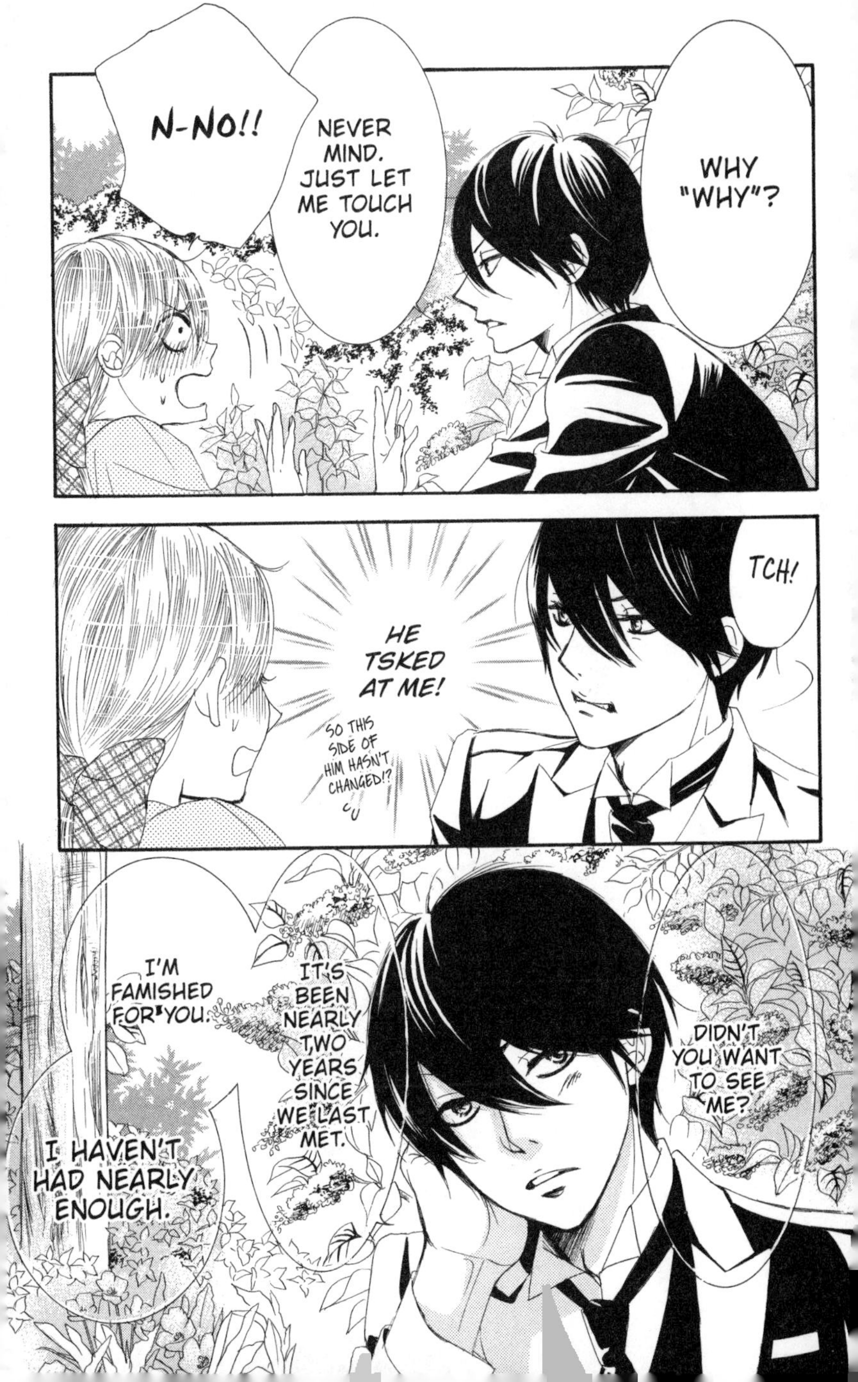
WHY "WHY"?
NEVER MIND. JUST LET ME TOUCH YOU.
N-NO!!
TCH!
HE TSKED AT ME!
SO THIS SIDE OF HIM HASN'T CHANGED!?
DIDN'T YOU WANT TO SEE ME?
IT'S BEEN NEARLY TWO YEARS SINCE WE LAST MET.
I'M FAMISHED FOR YOU.
I HAVEN'T HAD NEARLY ENOUGH.

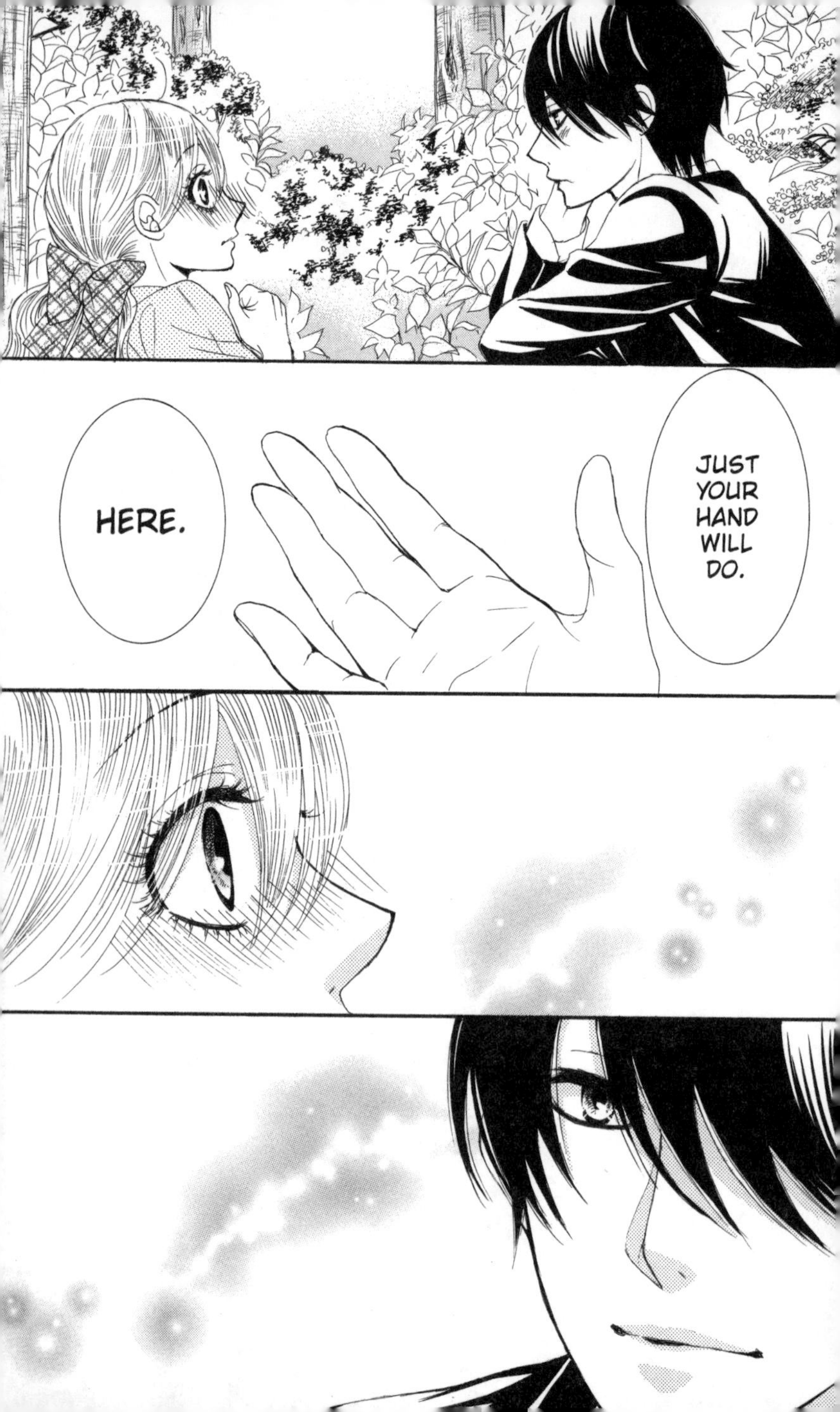
JUST YOUR HAND WILL DO.
HERE.

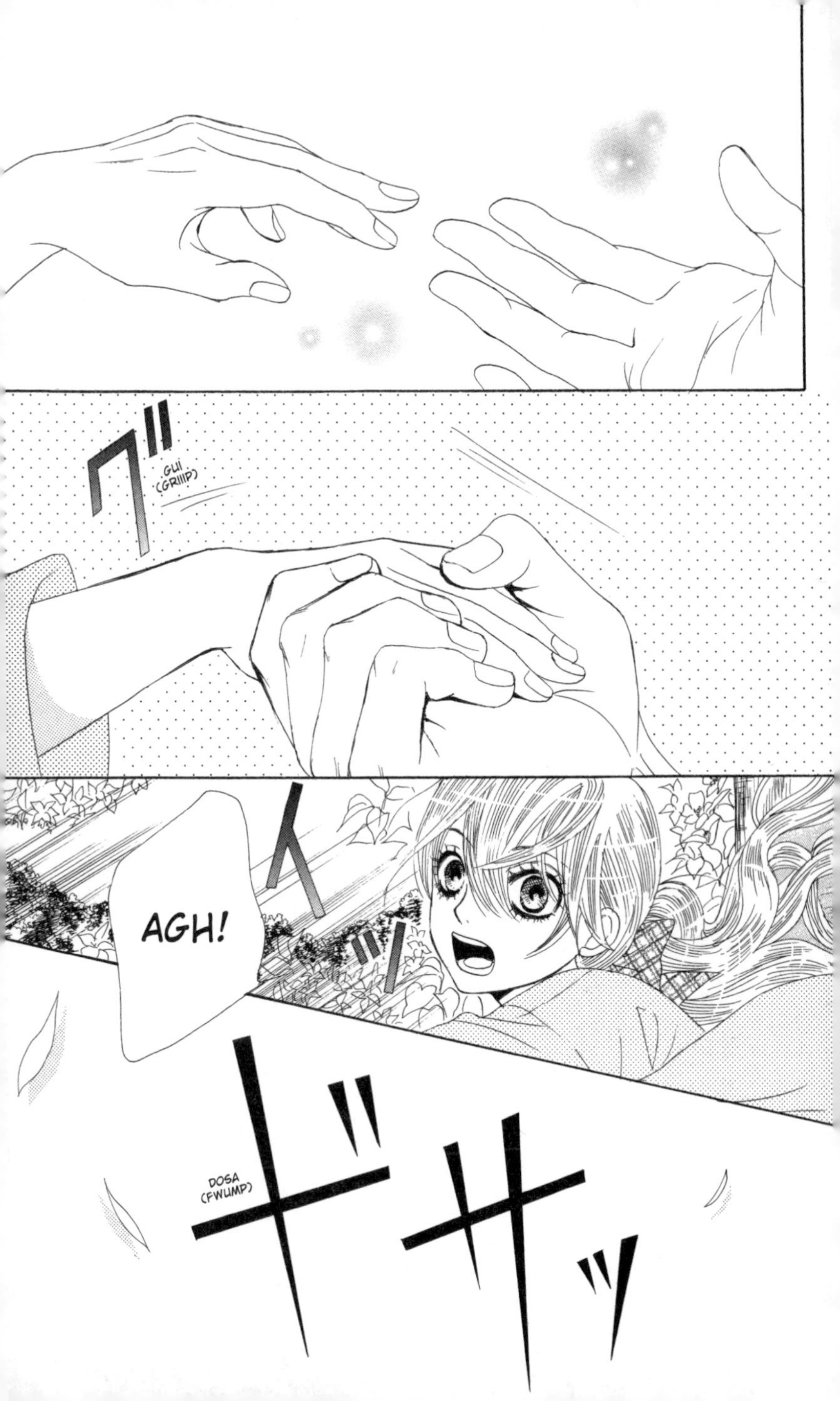
GUI (GRIIIP)
AGH!
DOSA (FWUMP)

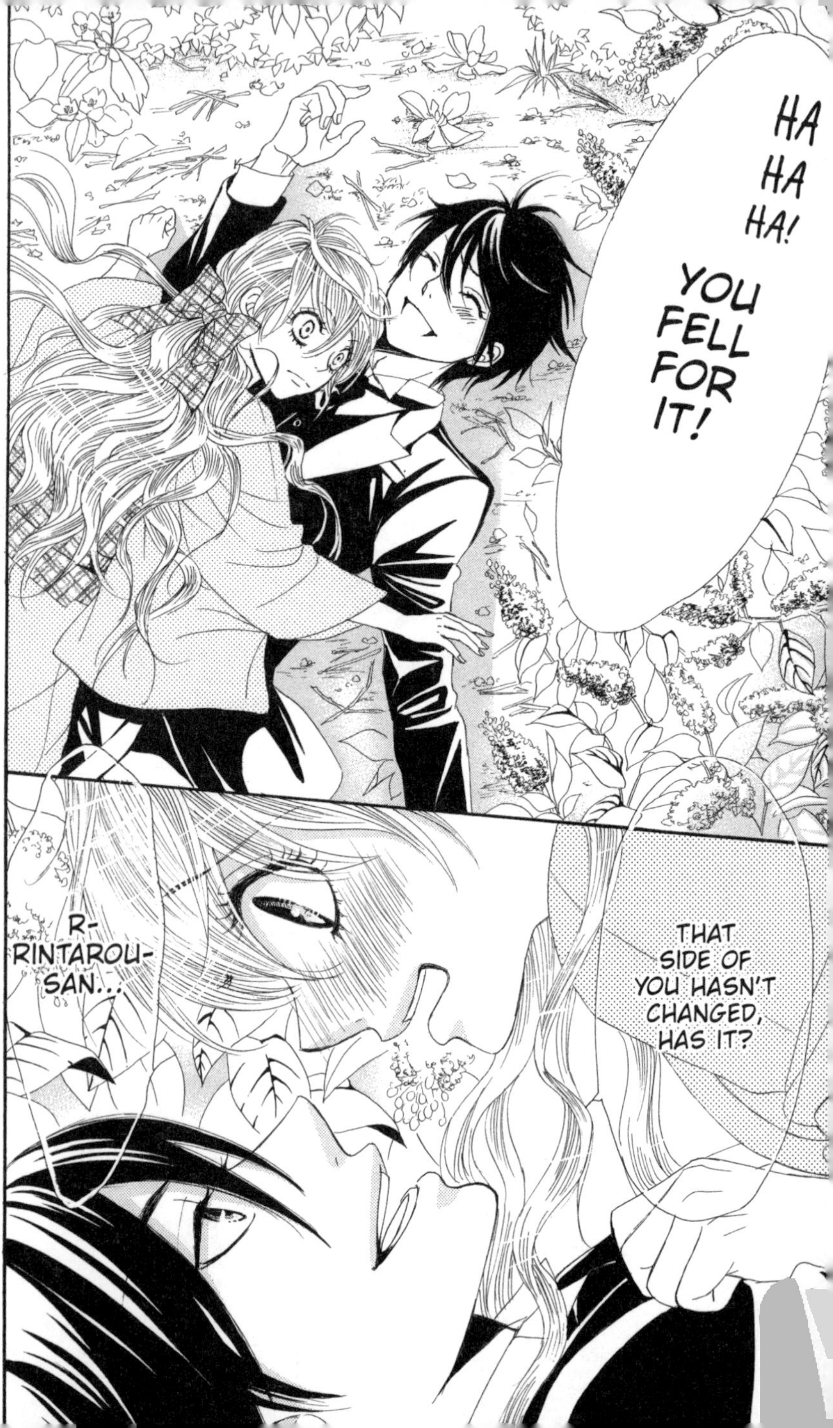
HA HA HA! YOU FELL FOR IT!
THAT SIDE OF YOU HASN'T CHANGED, HAS IT?
R-RINTAROU-SAN...

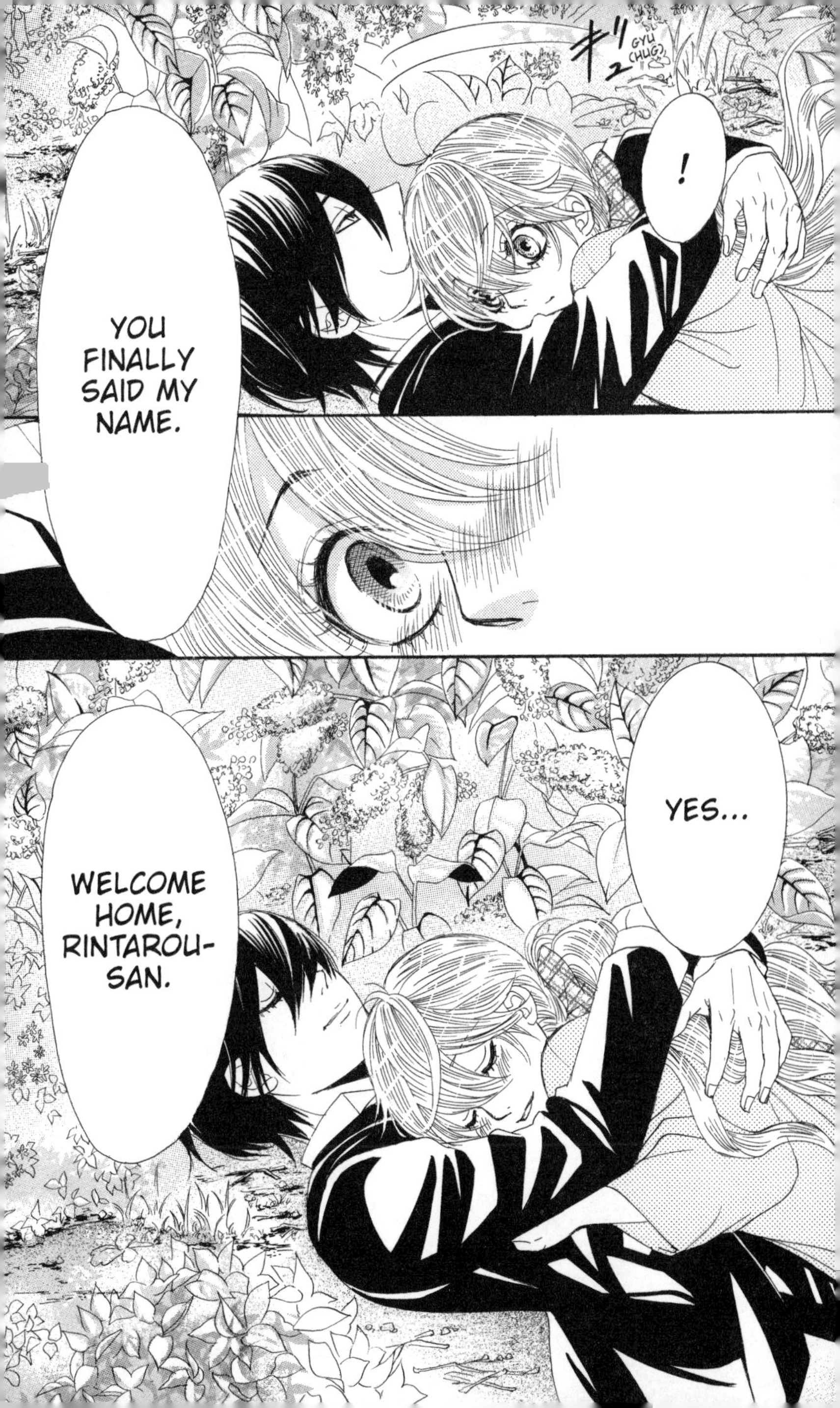
ギュ
GYU (HUG)
!
YOU FINALLY SAID MY NAME.
YES...
WELCOME HOME, RINTAROU-SAN.

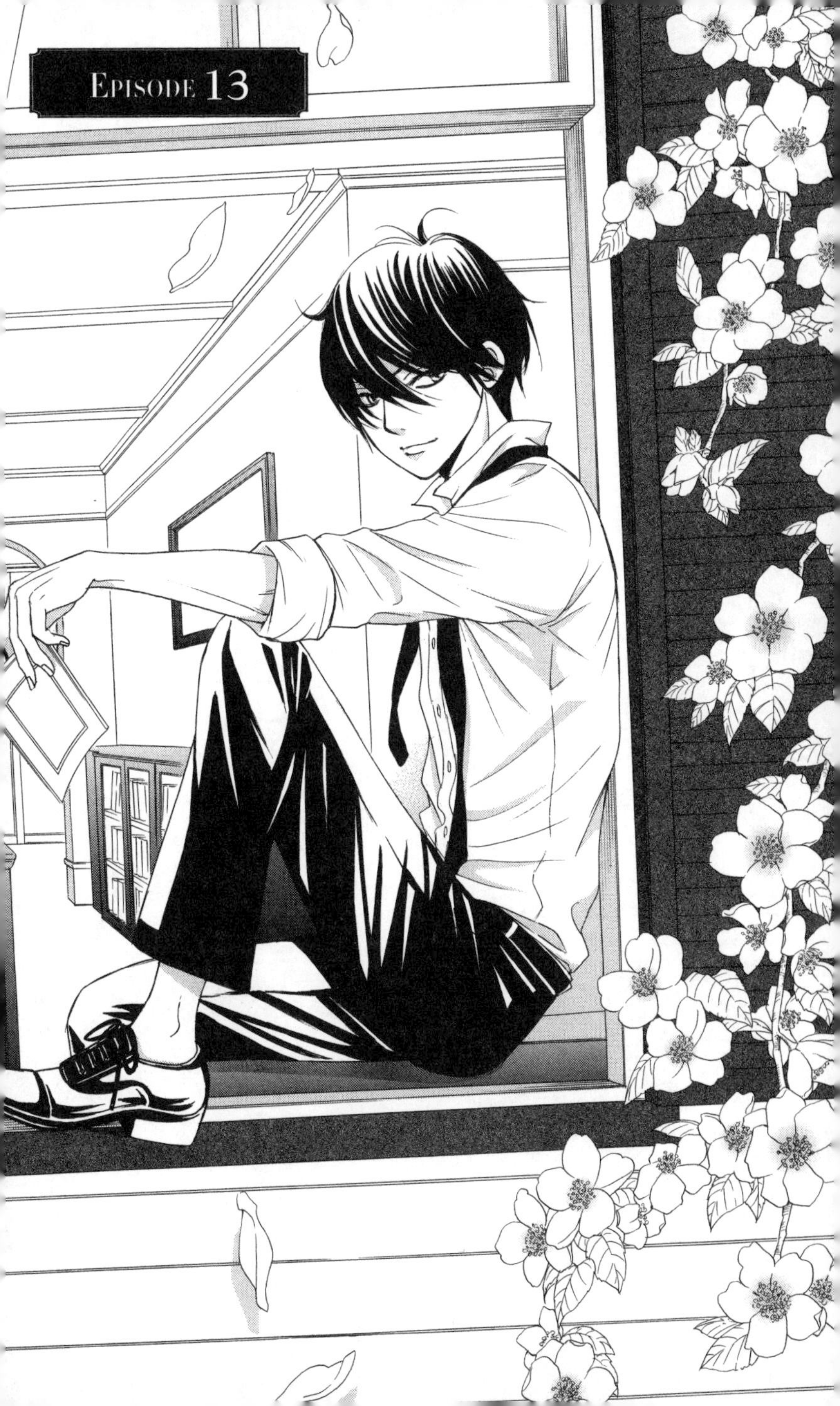
EPISODE 13

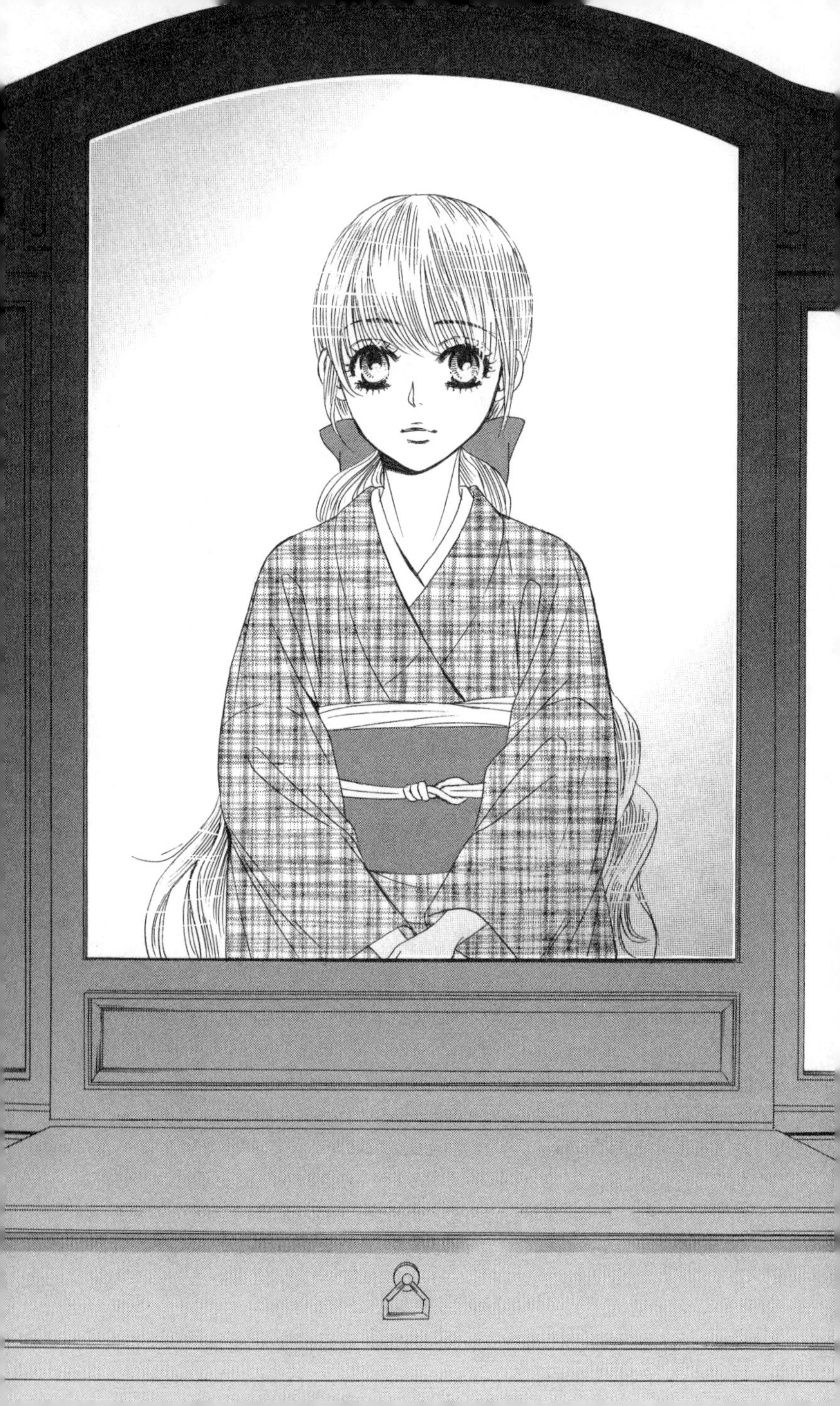

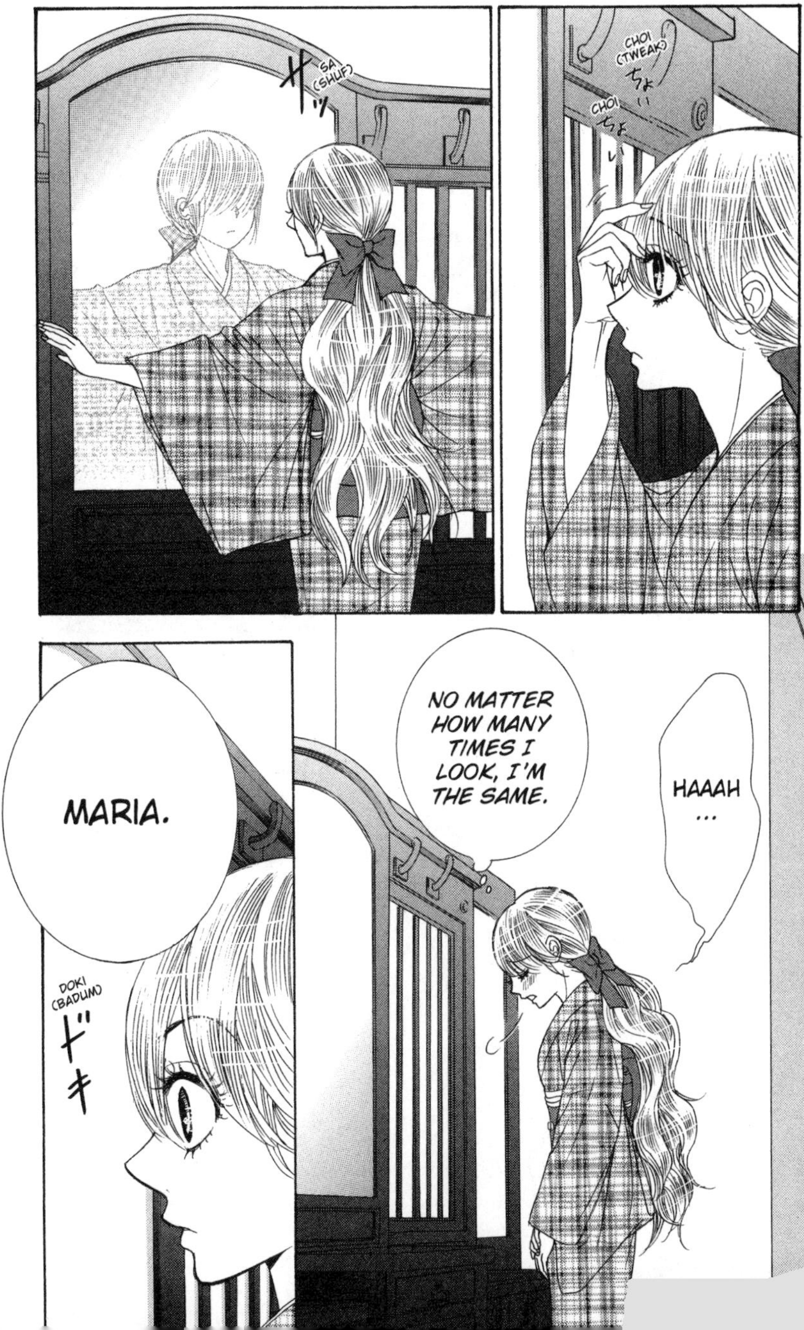
CHOI (TWEAK)
ちょい
CHOI
ちょい
SA (SHUF)
サッ
HAAAH ...
NO MATTER HOW MANY TIMES I LOOK, I'M THE SAME.
MARIA.
DOKI (BADUM)
ドキ

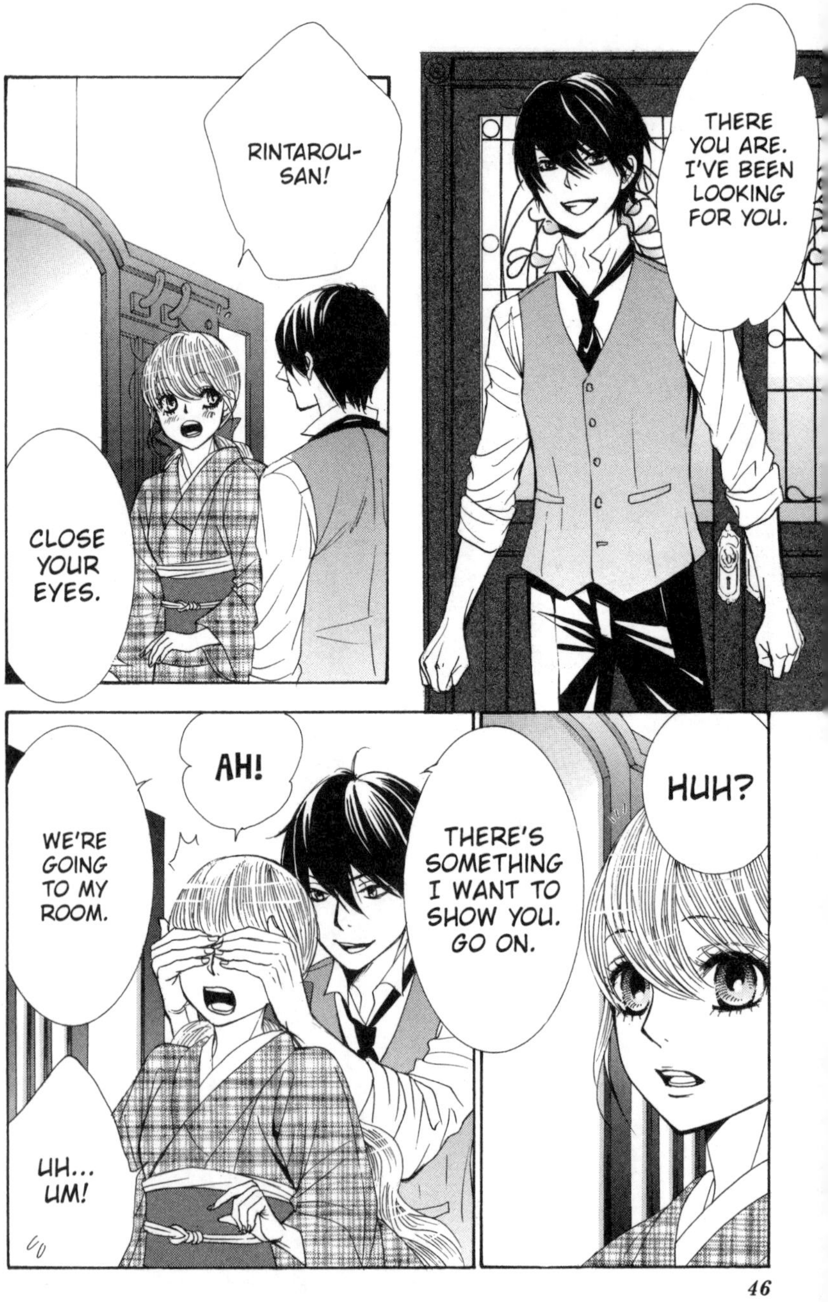
THERE YOU ARE. I'VE BEEN LOOKING FOR YOU.
RINTAROU-SAN!
CLOSE YOUR EYES.
HUH?
THERE'S SOMETHING I WANT TO SHOW YOU. GO ON.
AH!
WE'RE GOING TO MY ROOM.
UH... UM!

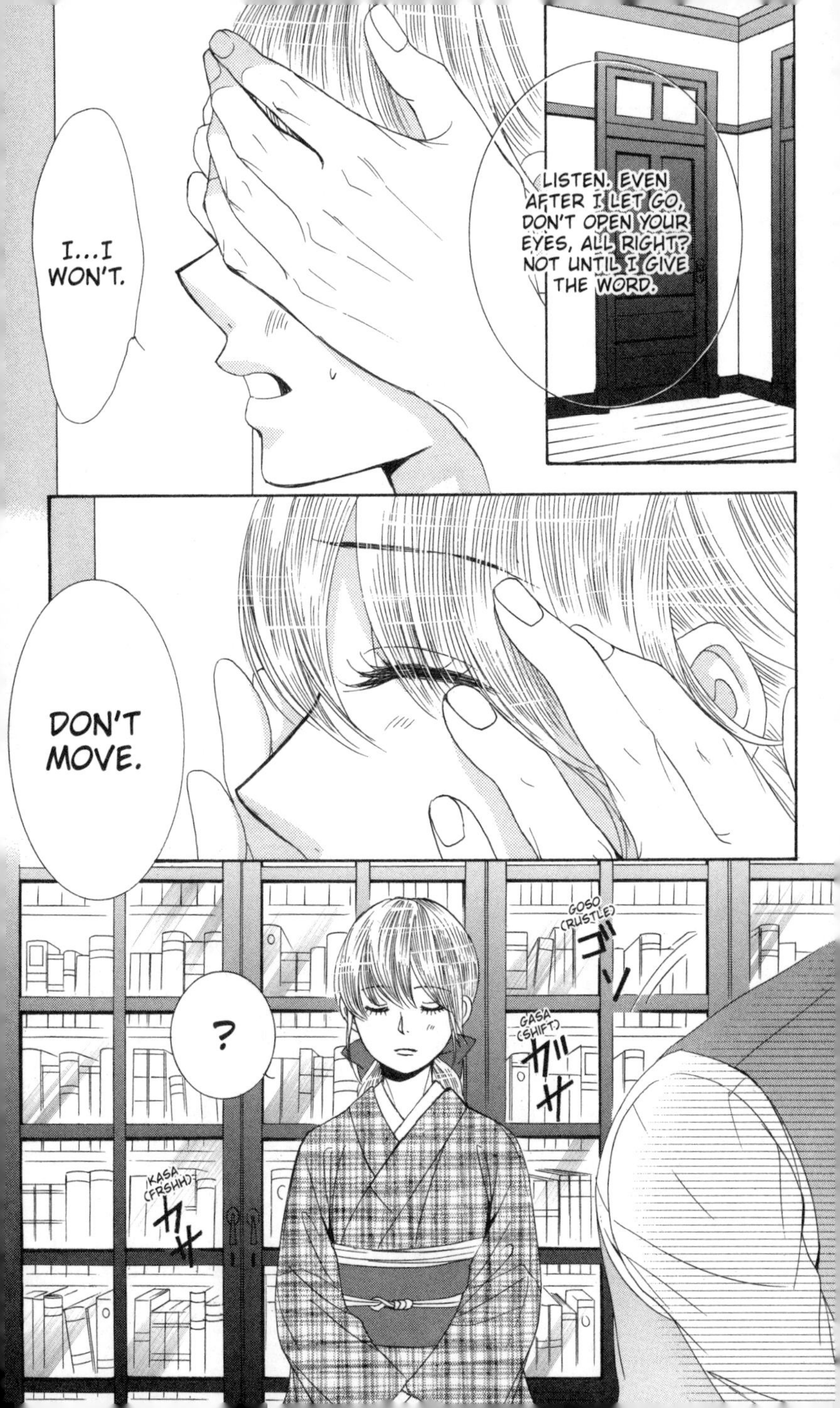
LISTEN. EVEN AFTER I LET GO, DON'T OPEN YOUR EYES, ALL RIGHT? NOT UNTIL I GIVE THE WORD.
I...I WON'T.
DON'T MOVE.
GOSO (RUSTLE)
GASA (SHIFT)
?
KASA (FRSHH)

WHAT IS THIS, ALL OF A SUDDEN?
I CAN HEAR HIM RUMMAGING AROUND, BUT...
....
...YOU REALLY ARE OBEDIENT AT TIMES LIKE THIS.
IT ACTUALLY WORRIES ME.
WHY?
NO, NEVER MIND.

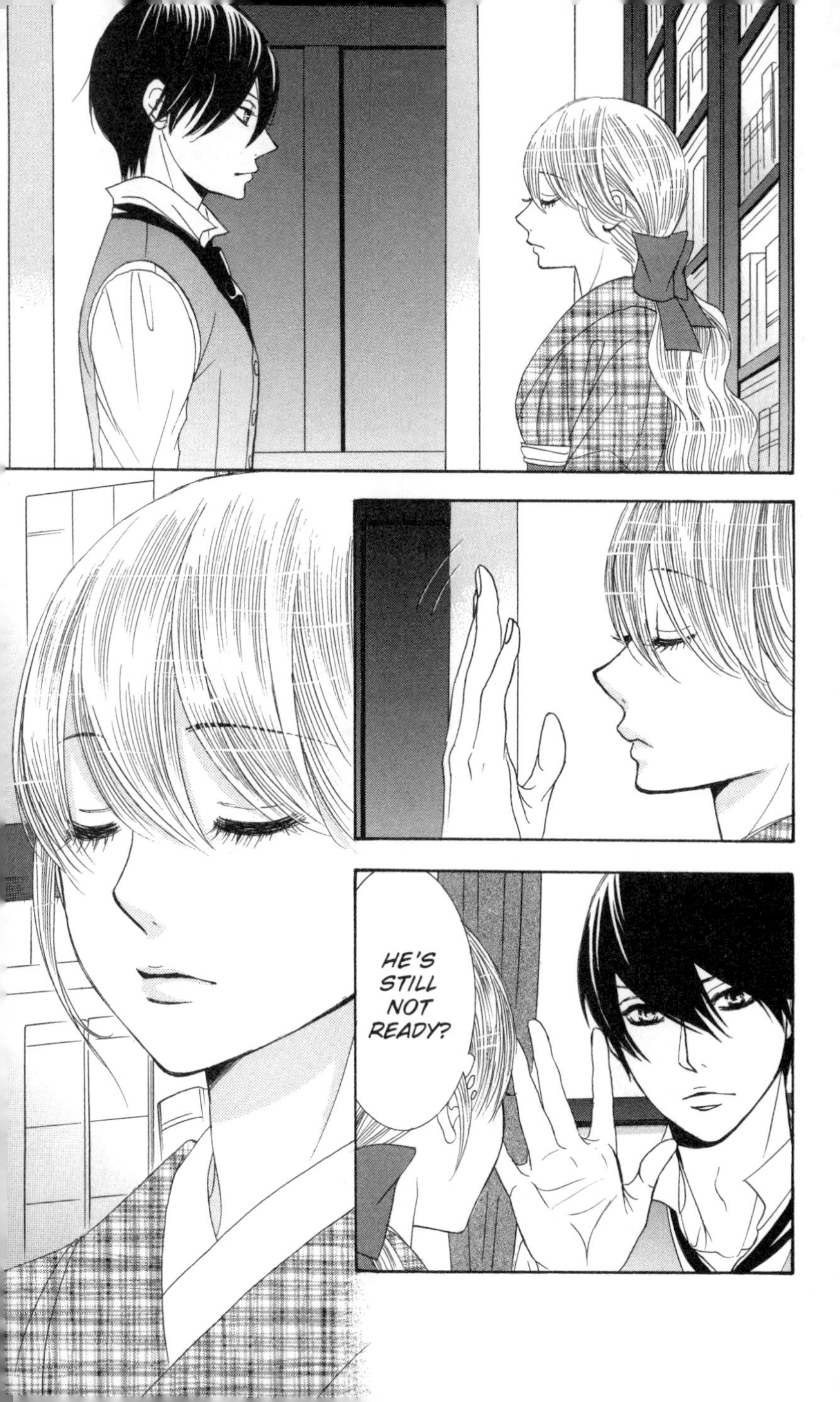
HE'S STILL NOT READY?

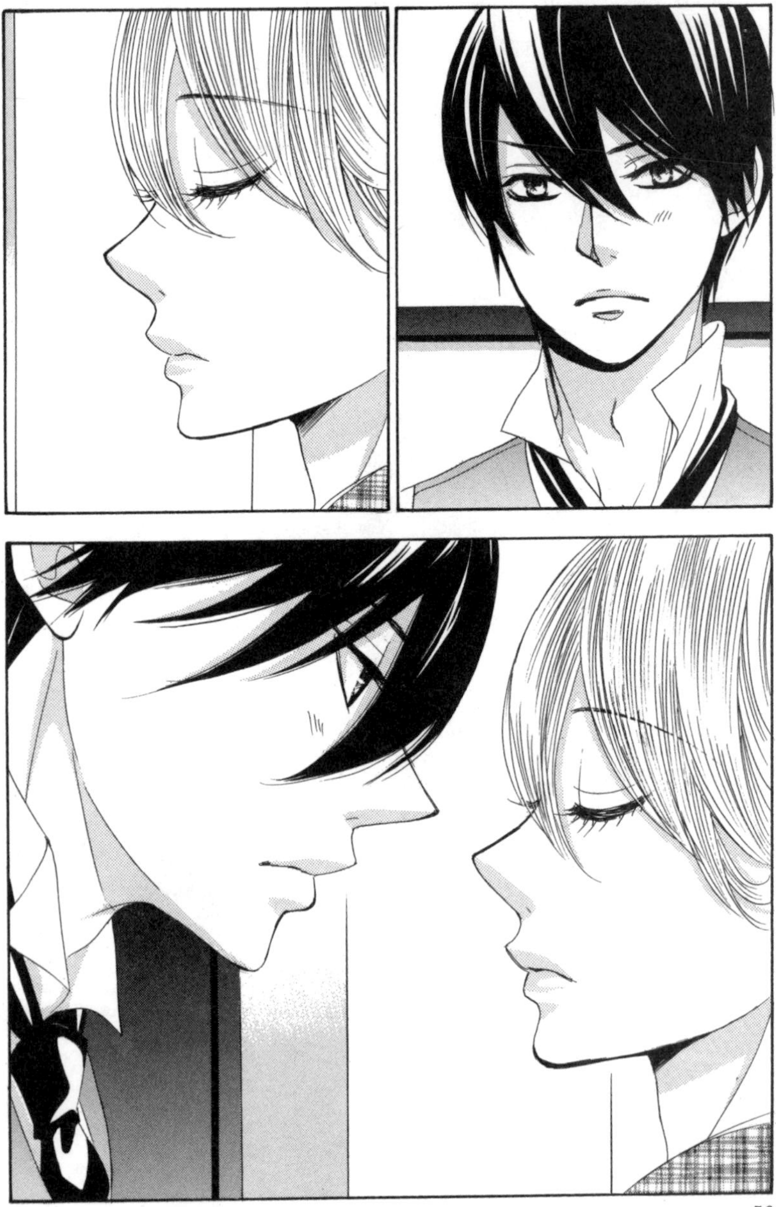

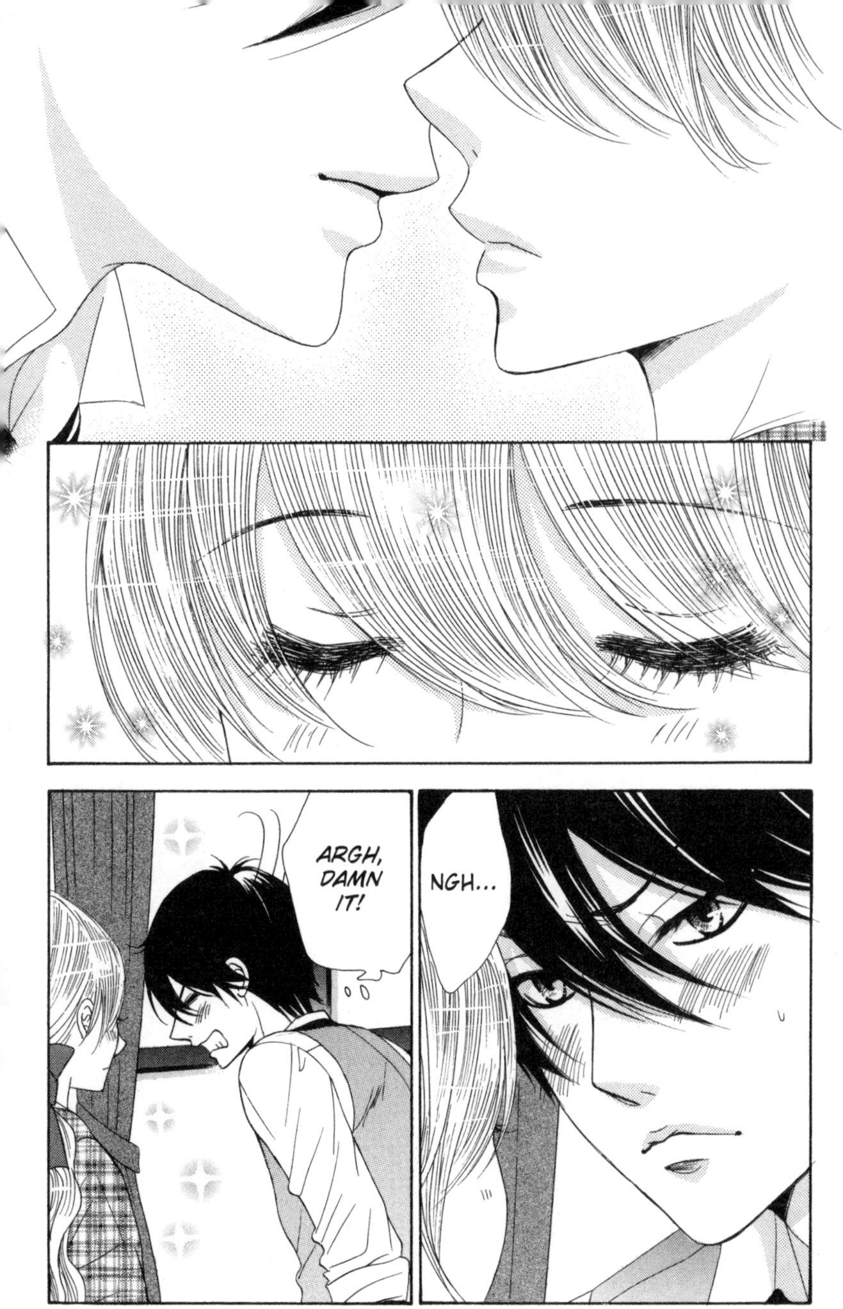
NGH...
ARGH, DAMN IT!

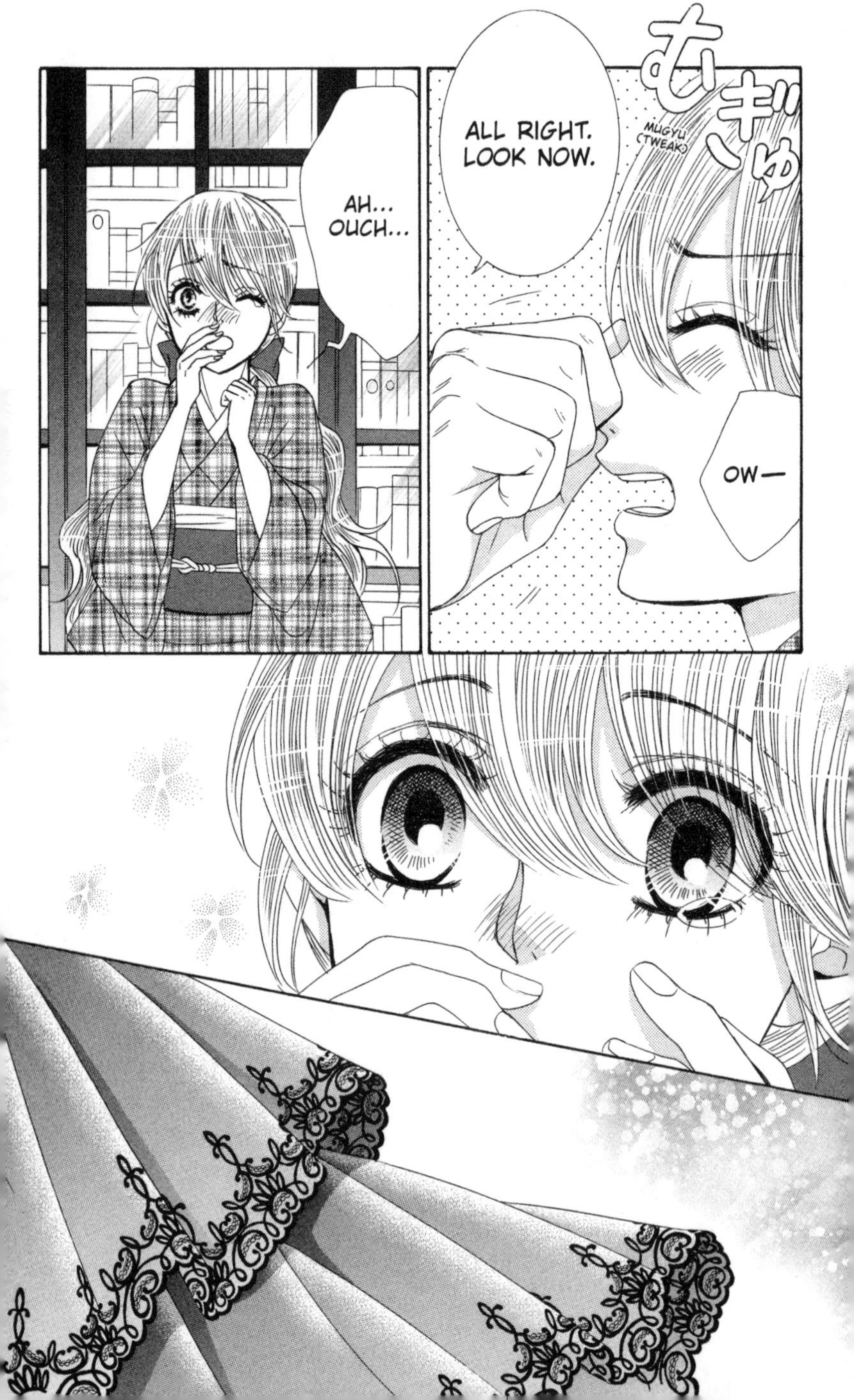
むぎゅ
MUGYU (TWEAK)
ALL RIGHT. LOOK NOW.
OW—
AH... OUCH...

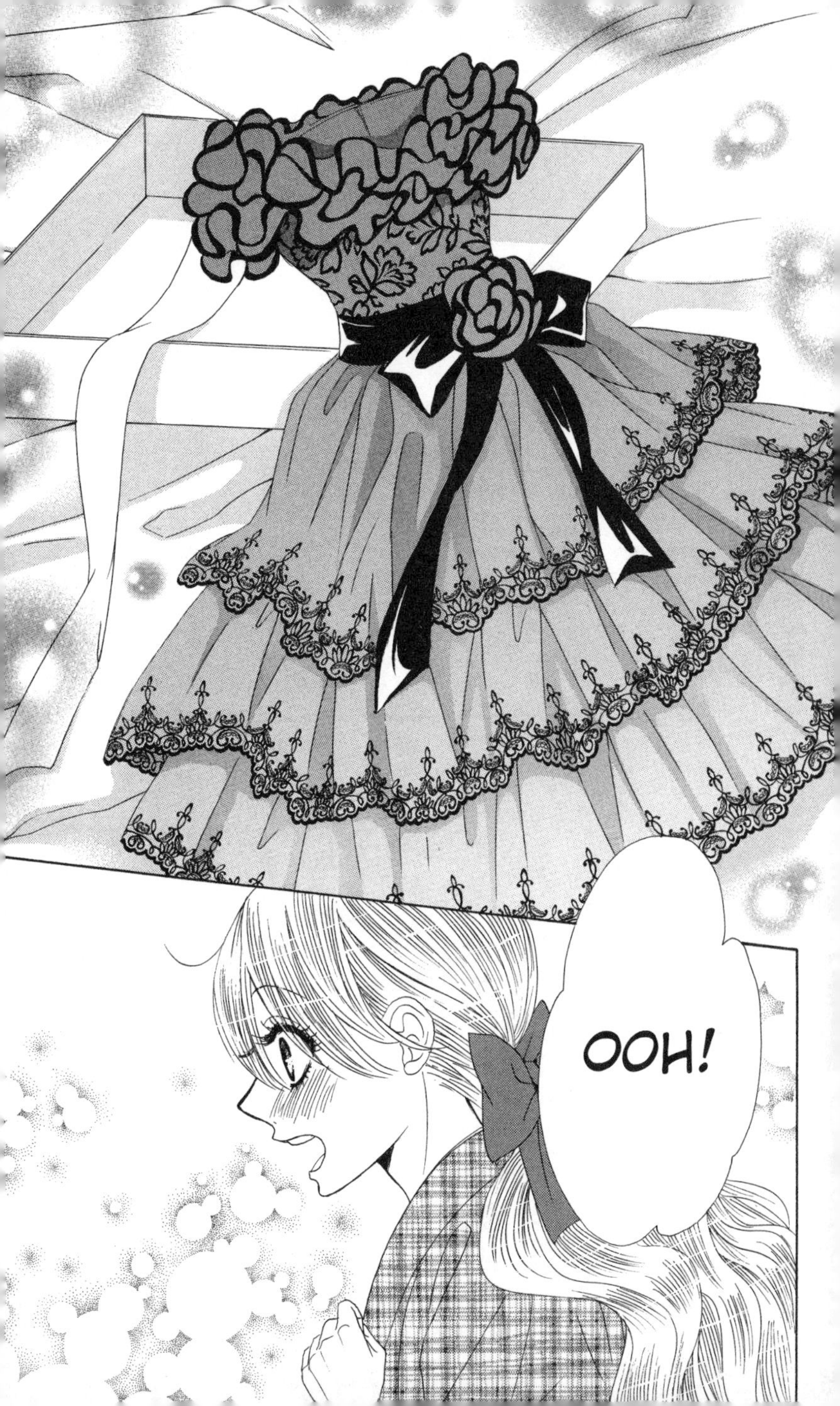
OOH!

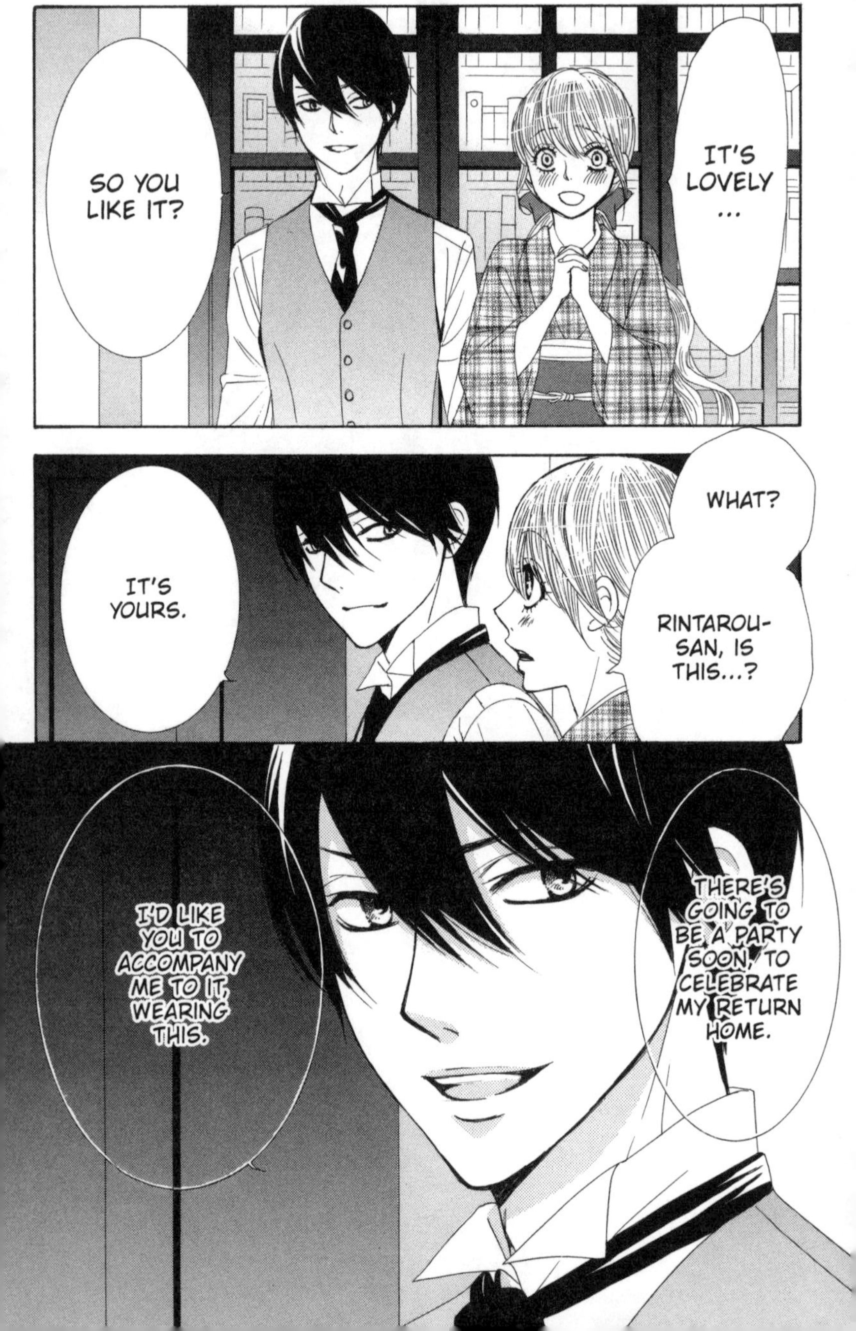
IT'S LOVELY ...
SO YOU LIKE IT?
WHAT?
RINTAROU-SAN, IS THIS...?
IT'S YOURS.
THERE'S GOING TO BE A PARTY SOON, TO CELEBRATE MY RETURN HOME.
I'D LIKE YOU TO ACCOMPANY ME TO IT, WEARING THIS.

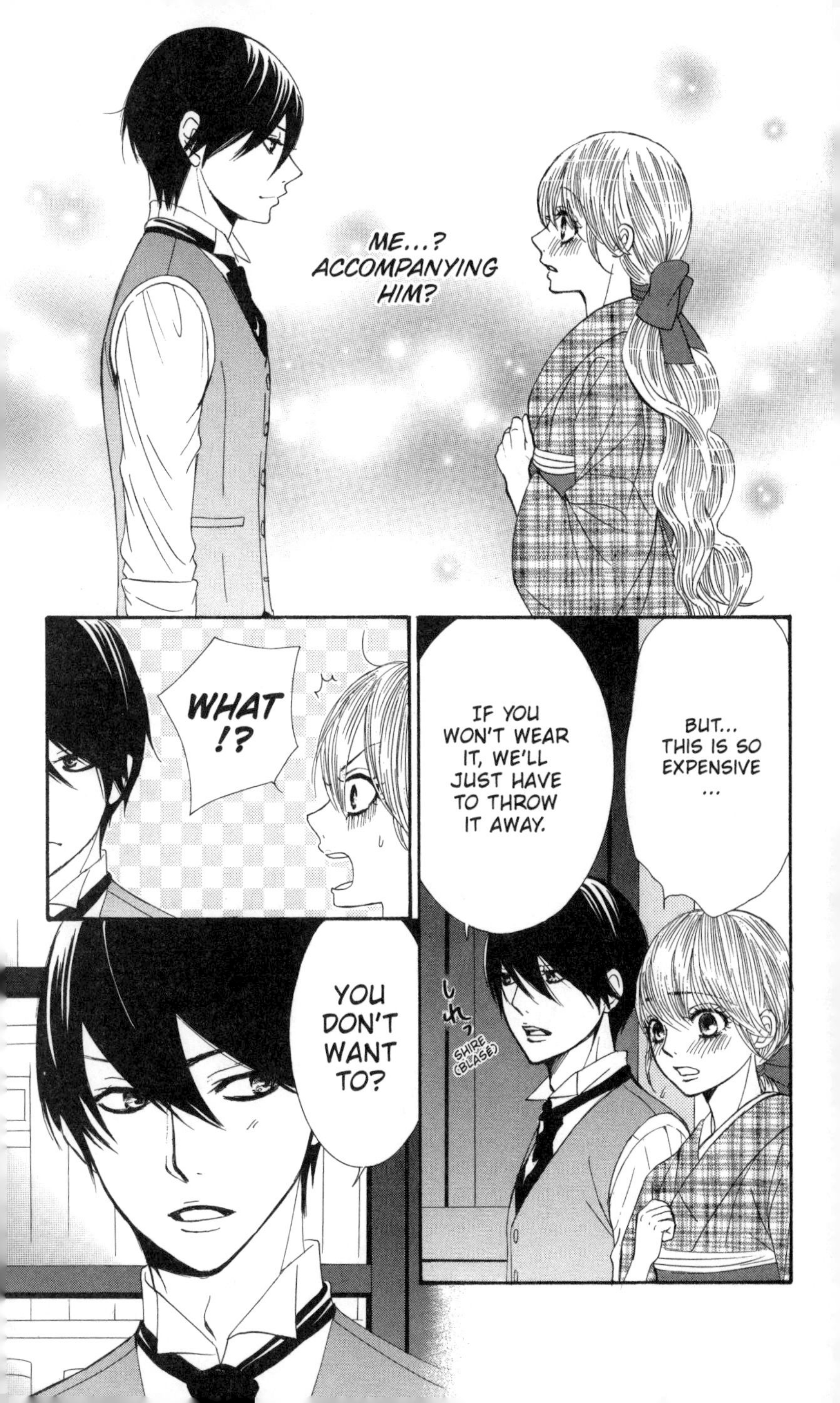
ME...? ACCOMPANYING HIM?
BUT... THIS IS SO EXPENSIVE ...
IF YOU WON'T WEAR IT, WE'LL JUST HAVE TO THROW IT AWAY.
しれっ
SHIRE (BLASÉ)
WHAT !?
YOU DON'T WANT TO?

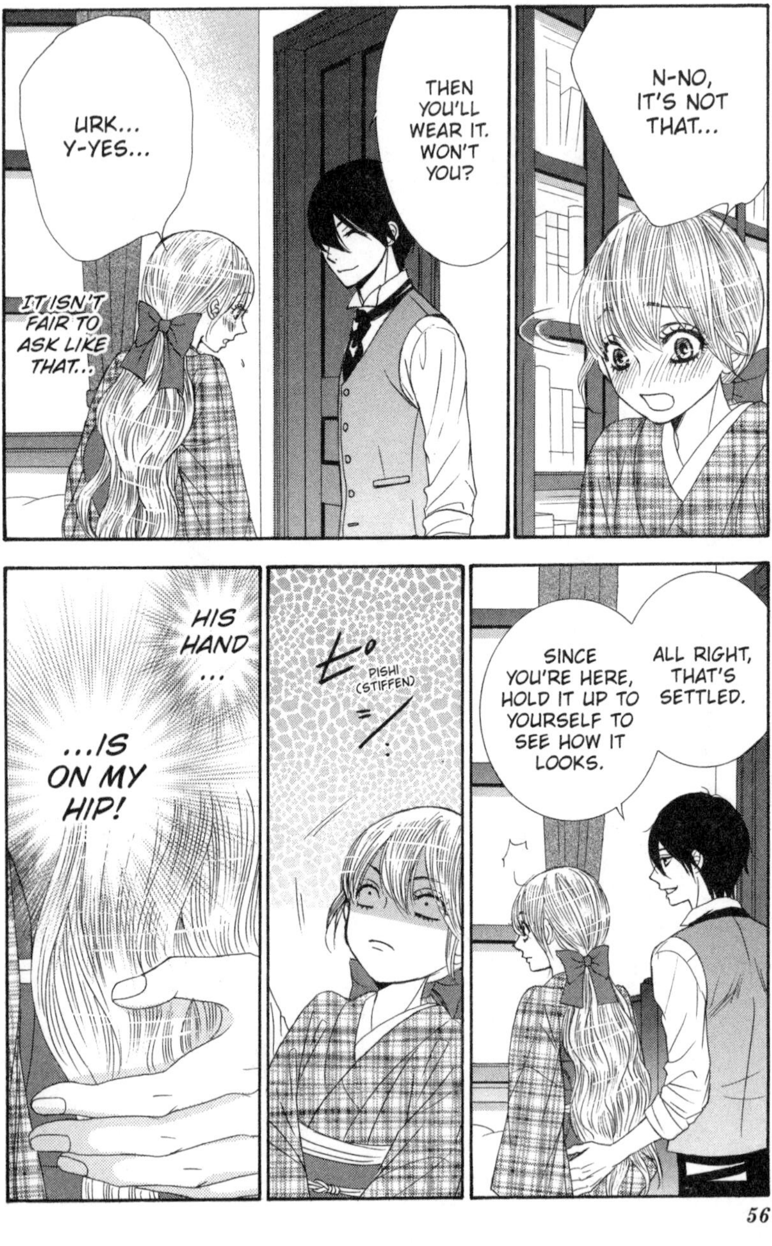
N-NO, IT'S NOT THAT...
THEN YOU'LL WEAR IT. WON'T YOU?
URK... Y-YES...
IT ISN'T FAIR TO ASK LIKE THAT...
ALL RIGHT, THAT'S SETTLED.
SINCE YOU'RE HERE, HOLD IT UP TO YOURSELF TO SEE HOW IT LOOKS.
PISHI (STIFFEN)
HIS HAND...
...IS ON MY HIP!

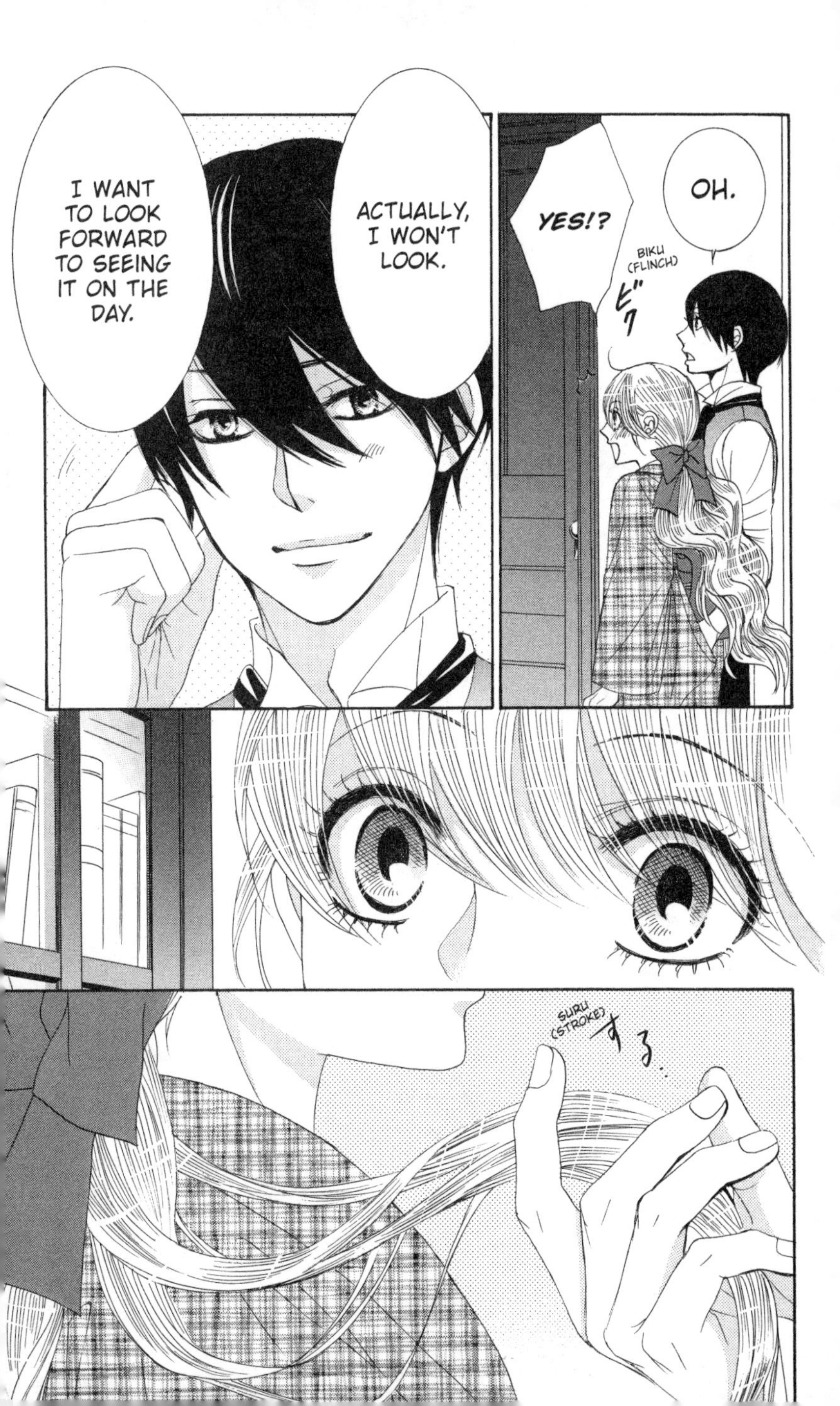
OH.
YES!?
BIKU (FLINCH)
ビク
ACTUALLY, I WON'T LOOK.
I WANT TO LOOK FORWARD TO SEEING IT ON THE DAY.
SURU (STROKE)
する

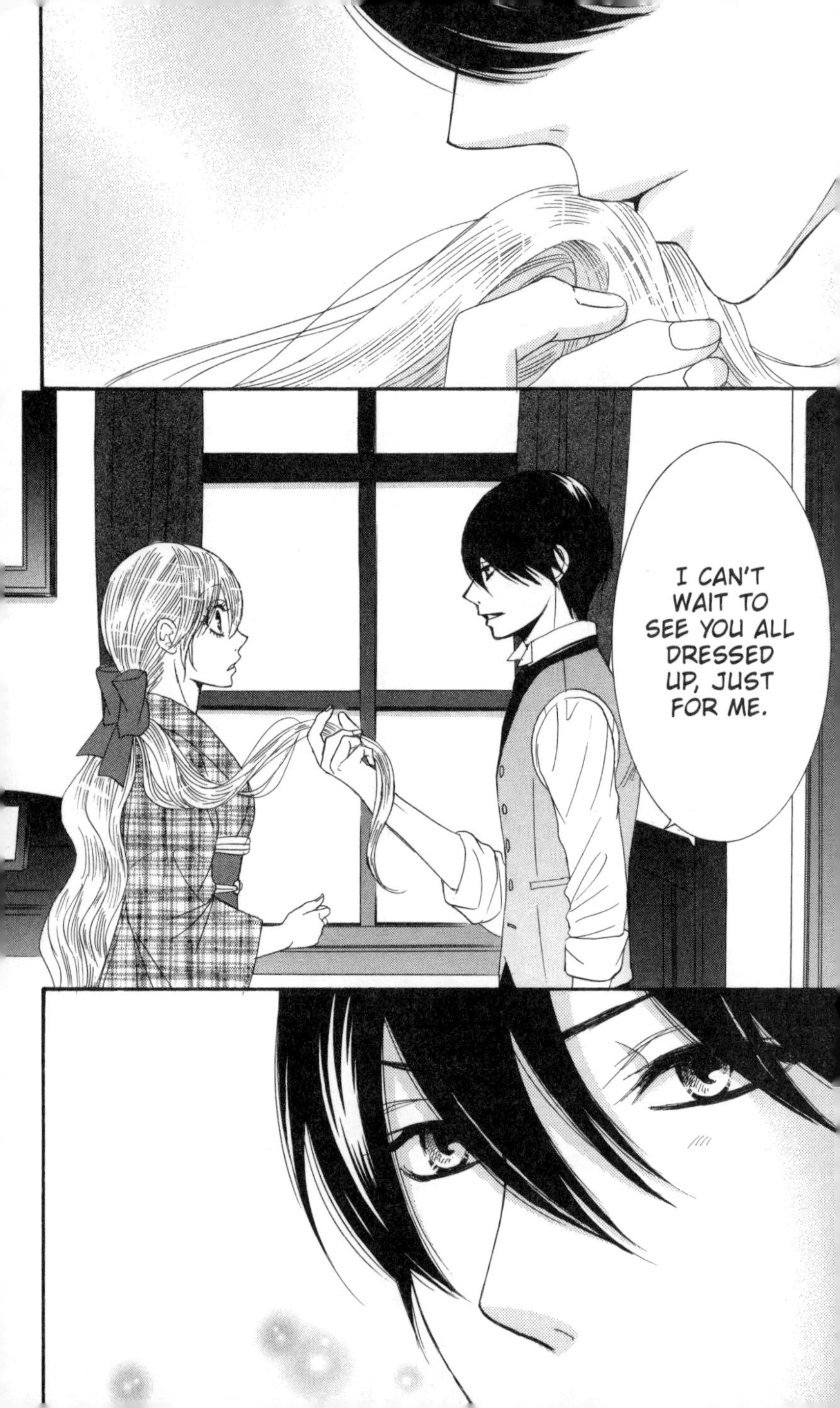
I CAN'T WAIT TO SEE YOU ALL DRESSED UP, JUST FOR ME.

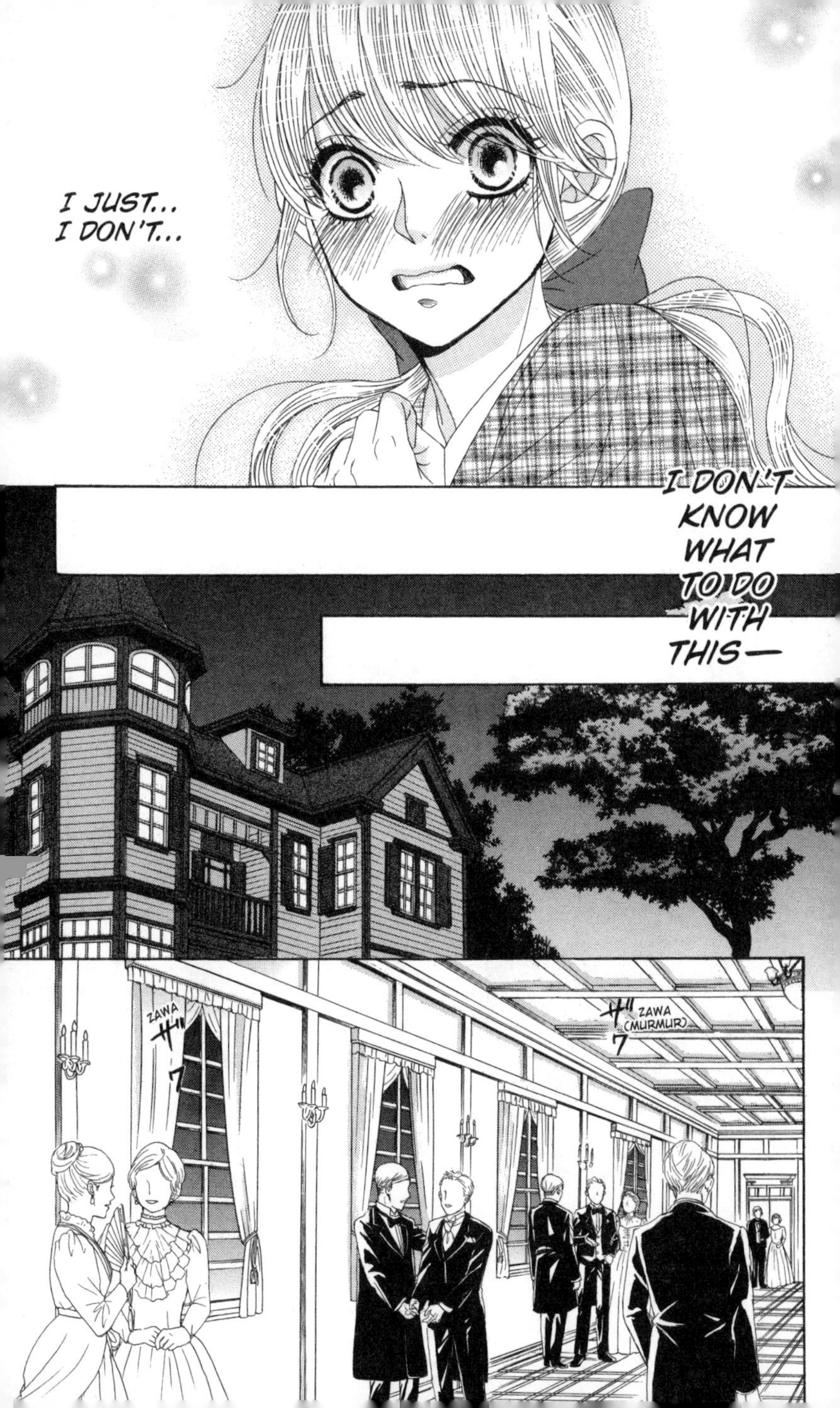
I JUST... I DON'T...
I DON'T KNOW WHAT TO DO WITH THIS—
ZAWA (MURMUR)
ZAWA

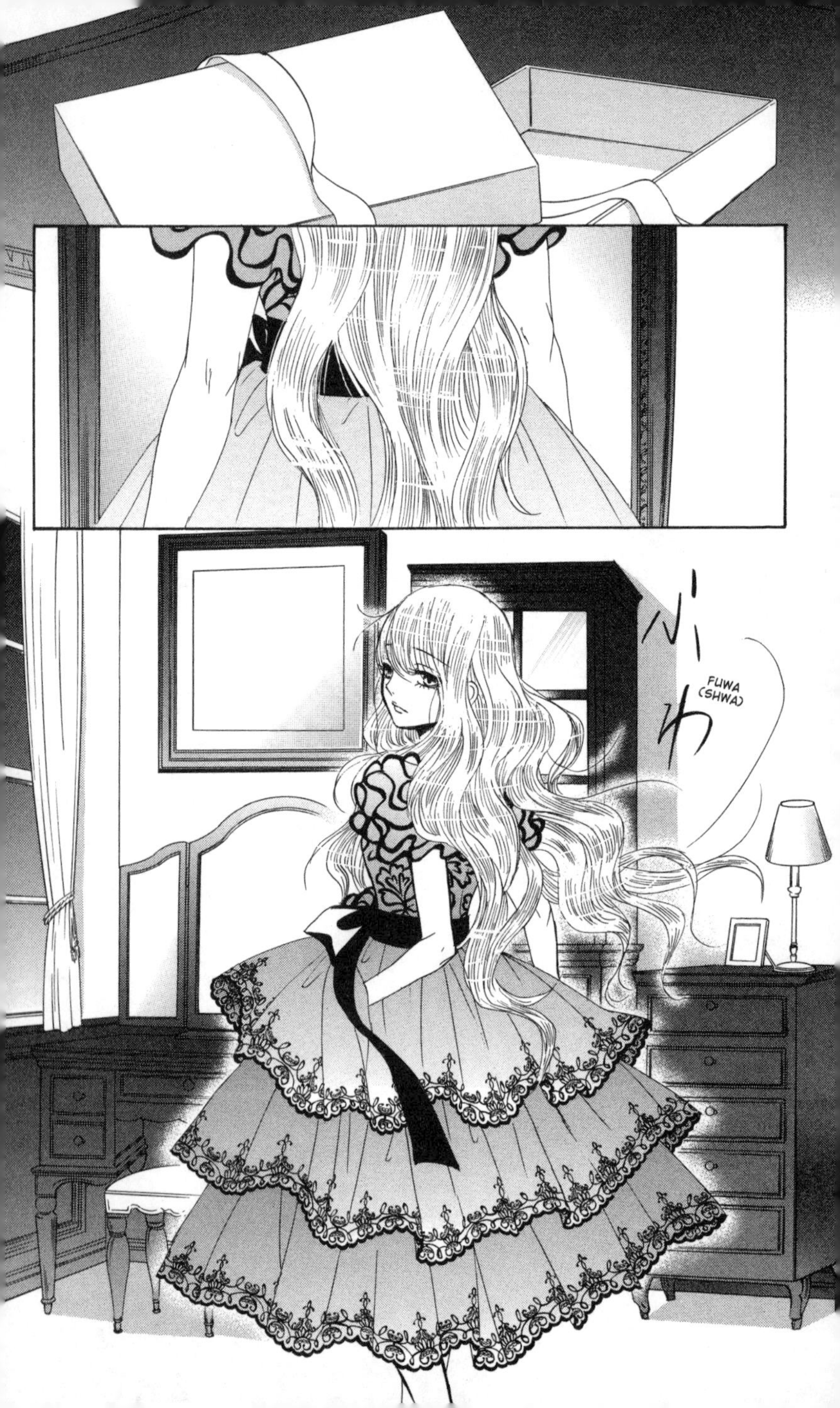
ふわ
FUWA (SHWA)

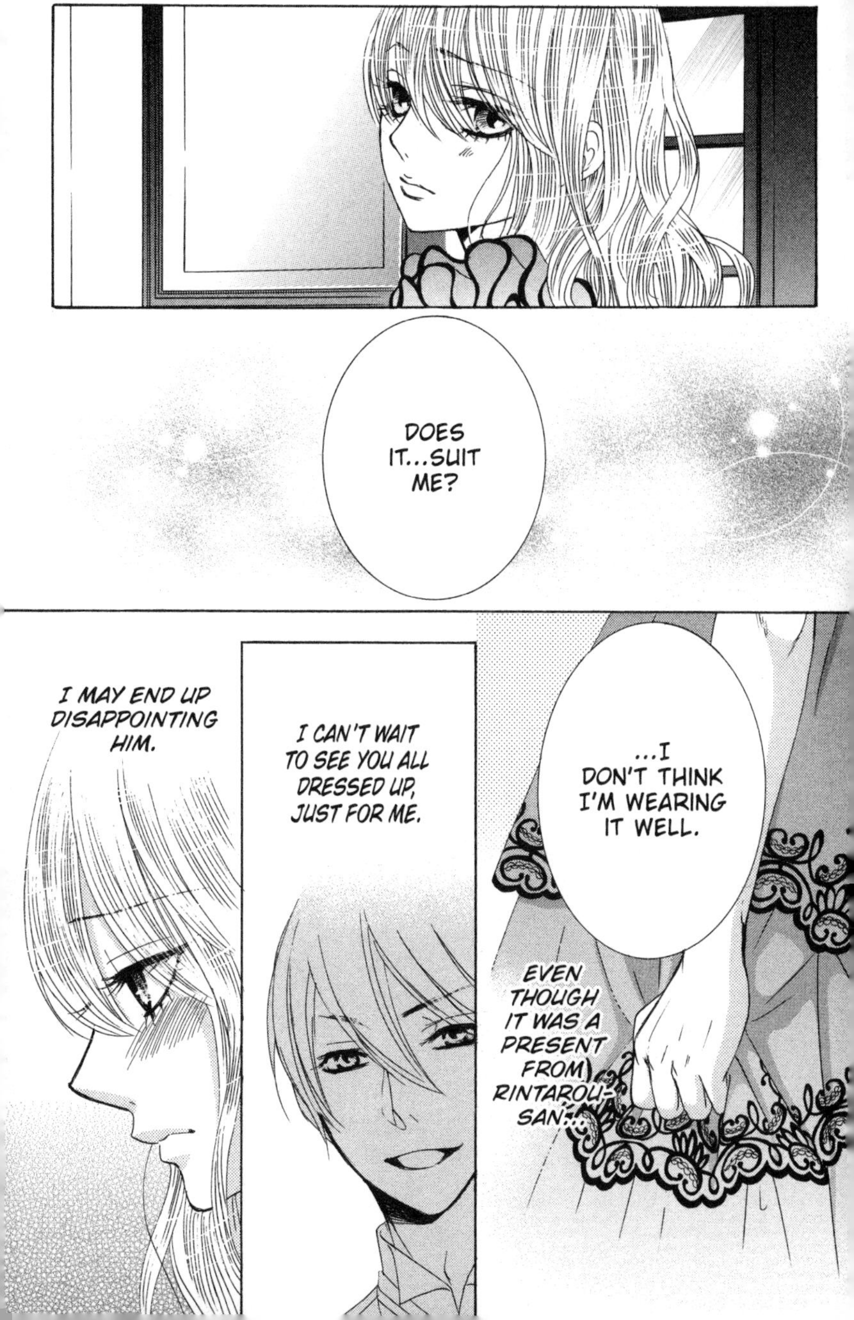
DOES IT...SUIT ME?
...I DON'T THINK I'M WEARING IT WELL.
EVEN THOUGH IT WAS A PRESENT FROM RINTAROU-SAN...
I CAN'T WAIT TO SEE YOU ALL DRESSED UP, JUST FOR ME.
I MAY END UP DISAPPOINTING HIM.

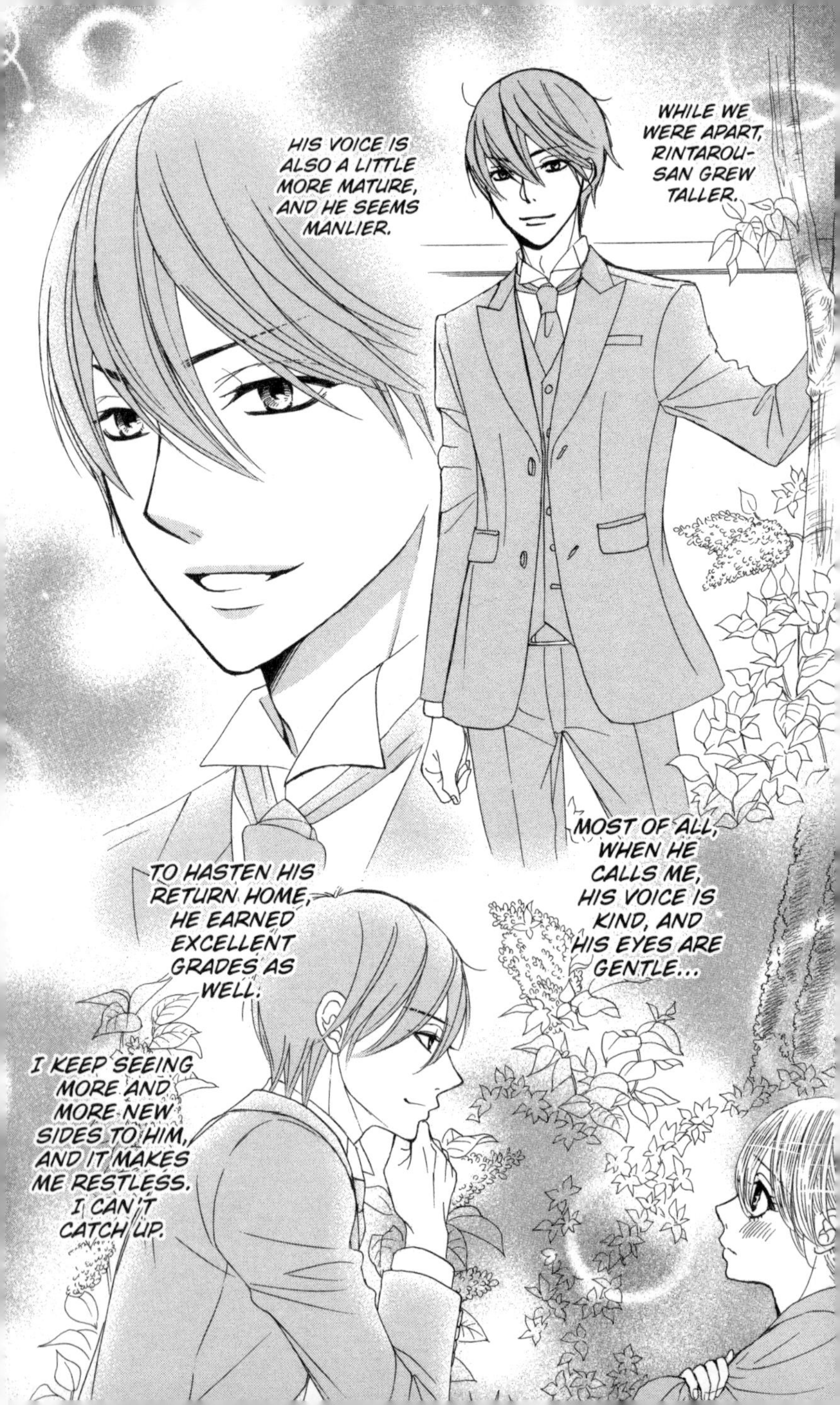
WHILE WE WERE APART, RINTAROU-SAN GREW TALLER.
HIS VOICE IS ALSO A LITTLE MORE MATURE, AND HE SEEMS MANLIER.
MOST OF ALL, WHEN HE CALLS ME, HIS VOICE IS KIND, AND HIS EYES ARE GENTLE...
TO HASTEN HIS RETURN HOME, HE EARNED EXCELLENT GRADES AS WELL.
I KEEP SEEING MORE AND MORE NEW SIDES TO HIM, AND IT MAKES ME RESTLESS. I CAN'T CATCH UP.

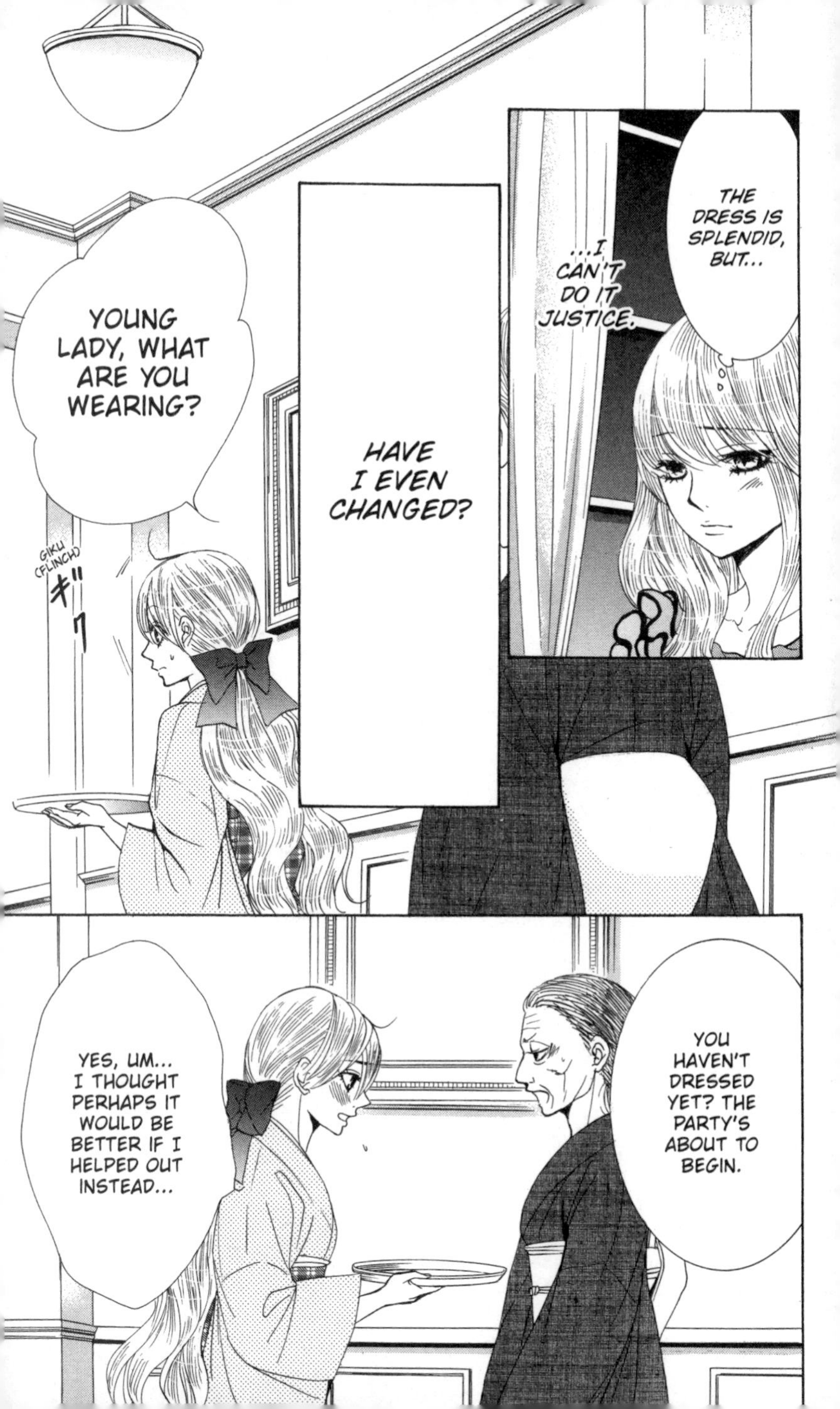
THE DRESS IS SPLENDID, BUT...
...I CAN'T DO IT JUSTICE.
HAVE I EVEN CHANGED?
YOUNG LADY, WHAT ARE YOU WEARING?
GIKU (FLINCH)
ギク
YOU HAVEN'T DRESSED YET? THE PARTY'S ABOUT TO BEGIN.
YES, UM... I THOUGHT PERHAPS IT WOULD BE BETTER IF I HELPED OUT INSTEAD...

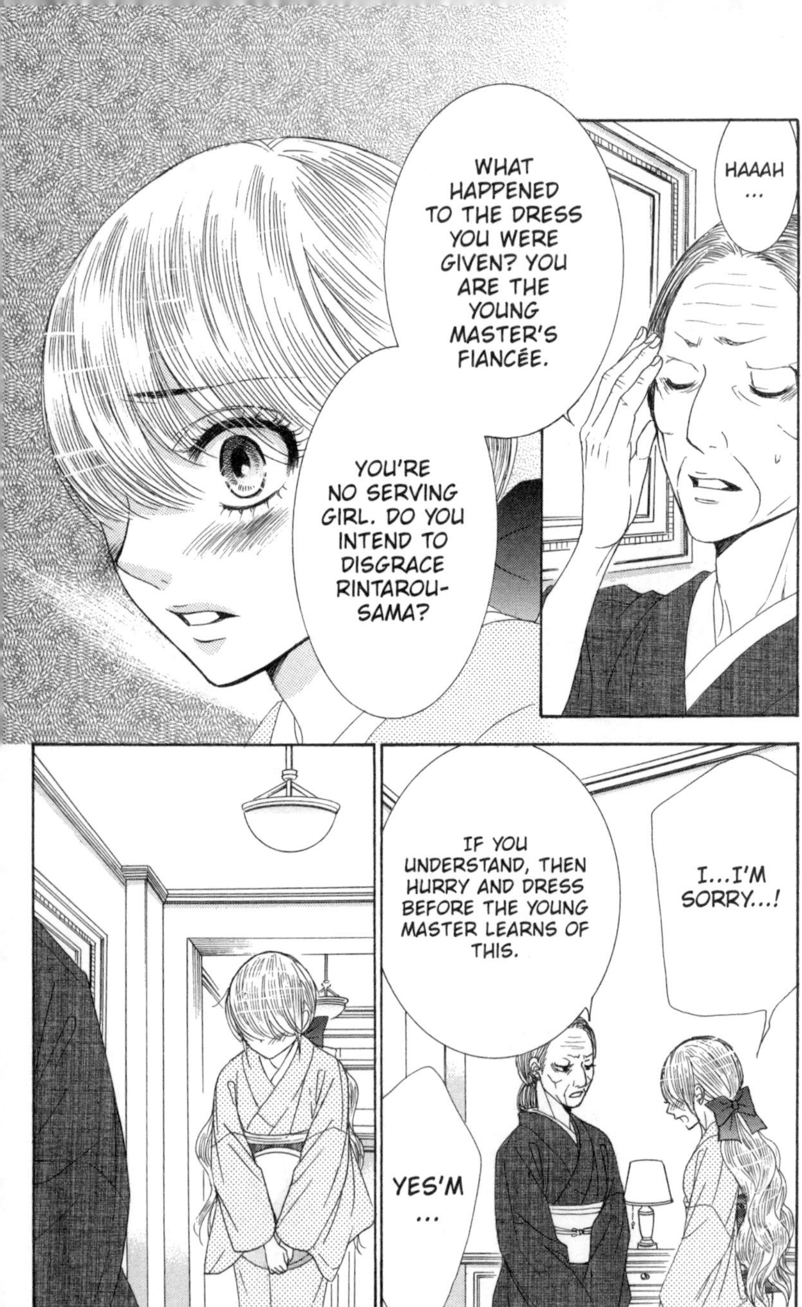
HAAAH...
WHAT HAPPENED TO THE DRESS YOU WERE GIVEN? YOU ARE THE YOUNG MASTER'S FIANCÉE.
YOU'RE NO SERVING GIRL. DO YOU INTEND TO DISGRACE RINTAROU-SAMA?
I...I'M SORRY...!
IF YOU UNDERSTAND, THEN HURRY AND DRESS BEFORE THE YOUNG MASTER LEARNS OF THIS.
YES'M...

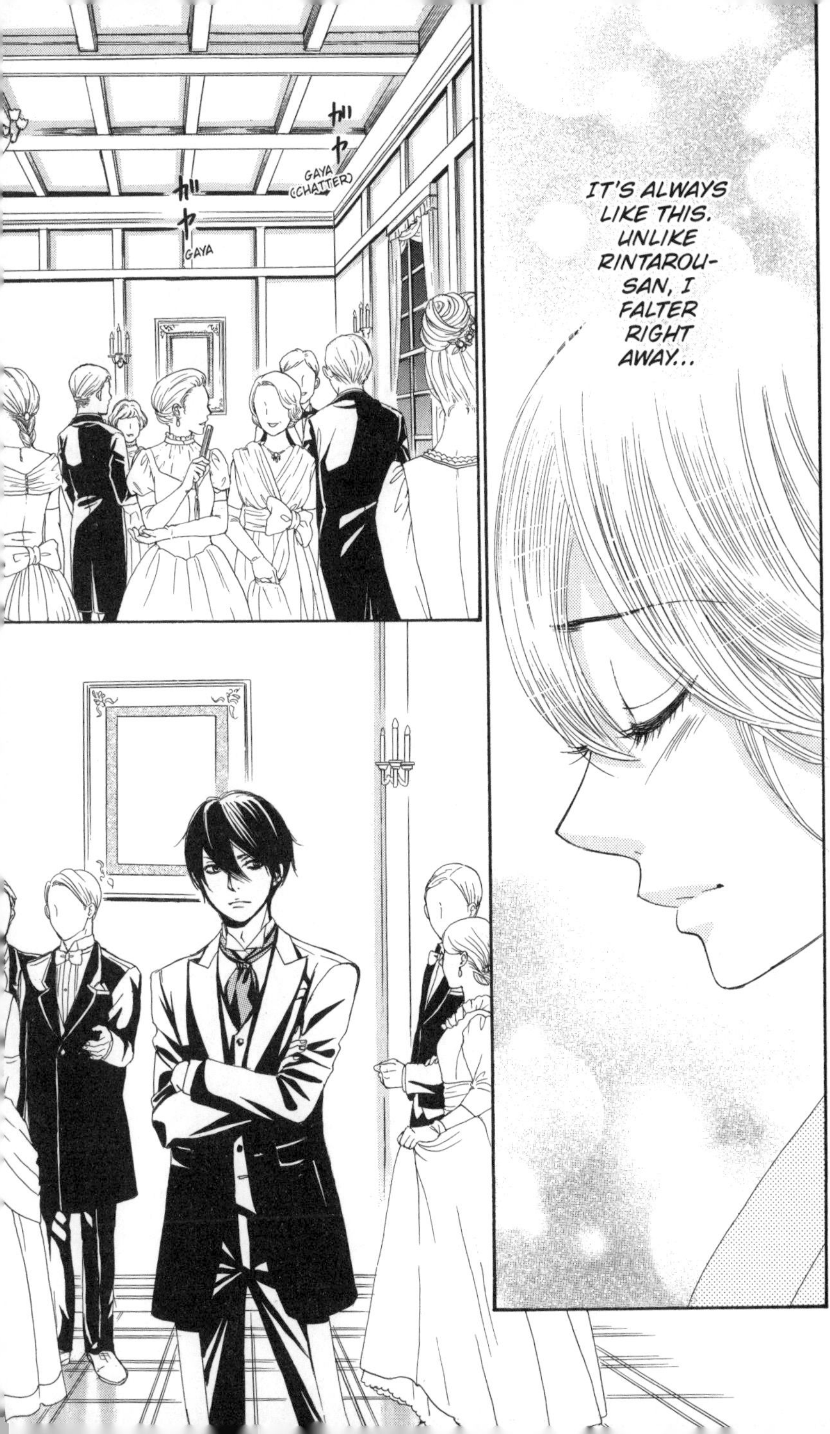

IT'S ALWAYS LIKE THIS. UNLIKE RINTAROU-SAN, I FALTER RIGHT AWAY...
ガヤ
GAYA (CHATTER)
ガヤ
GAYA

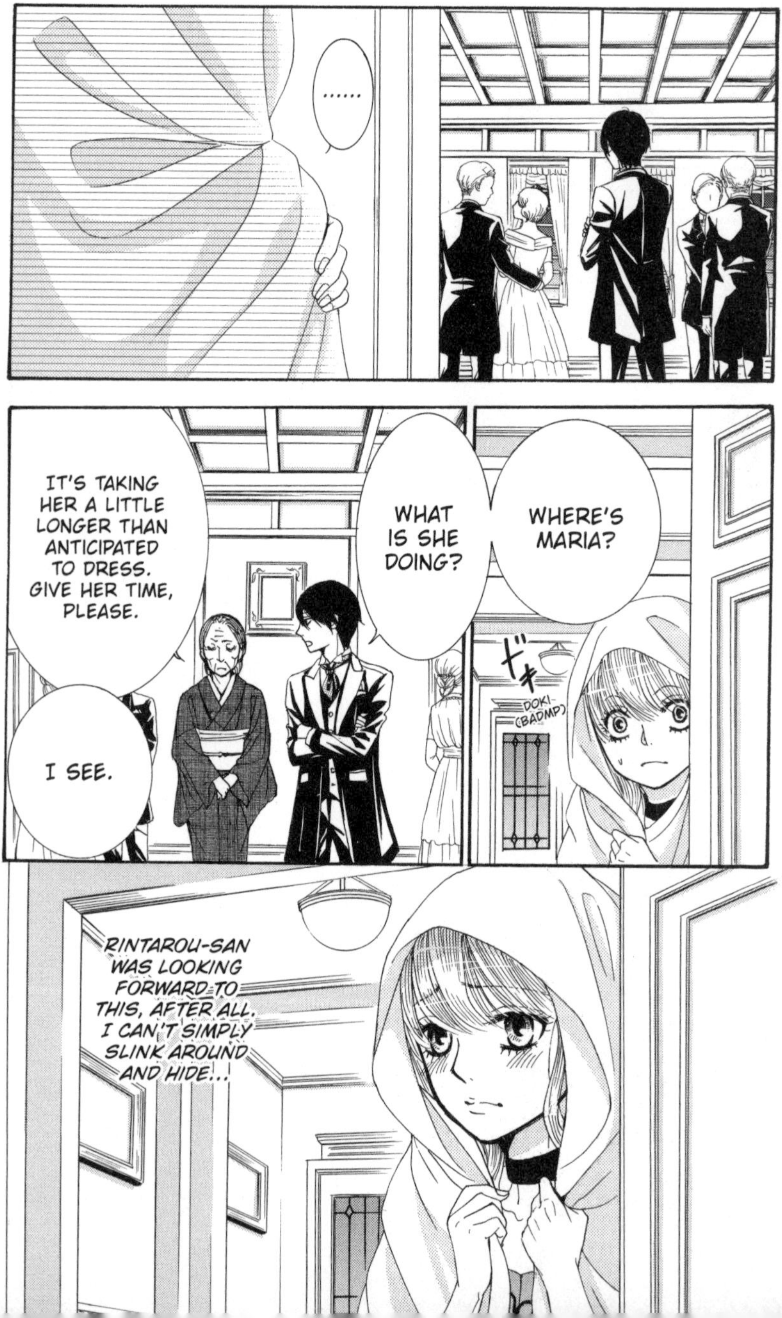

......
WHERE'S MARIA?
ドキ
DOKI (BADMP)
WHAT IS SHE DOING?
IT'S TAKING HER A LITTLE LONGER THAN ANTICIPATED TO DRESS. GIVE HER TIME, PLEASE.
I SEE.
RINTAROU-SAN WAS LOOKING FORWARD TO THIS, AFTER ALL. I CAN'T SIMPLY SLINK AROUND AND HIDE...

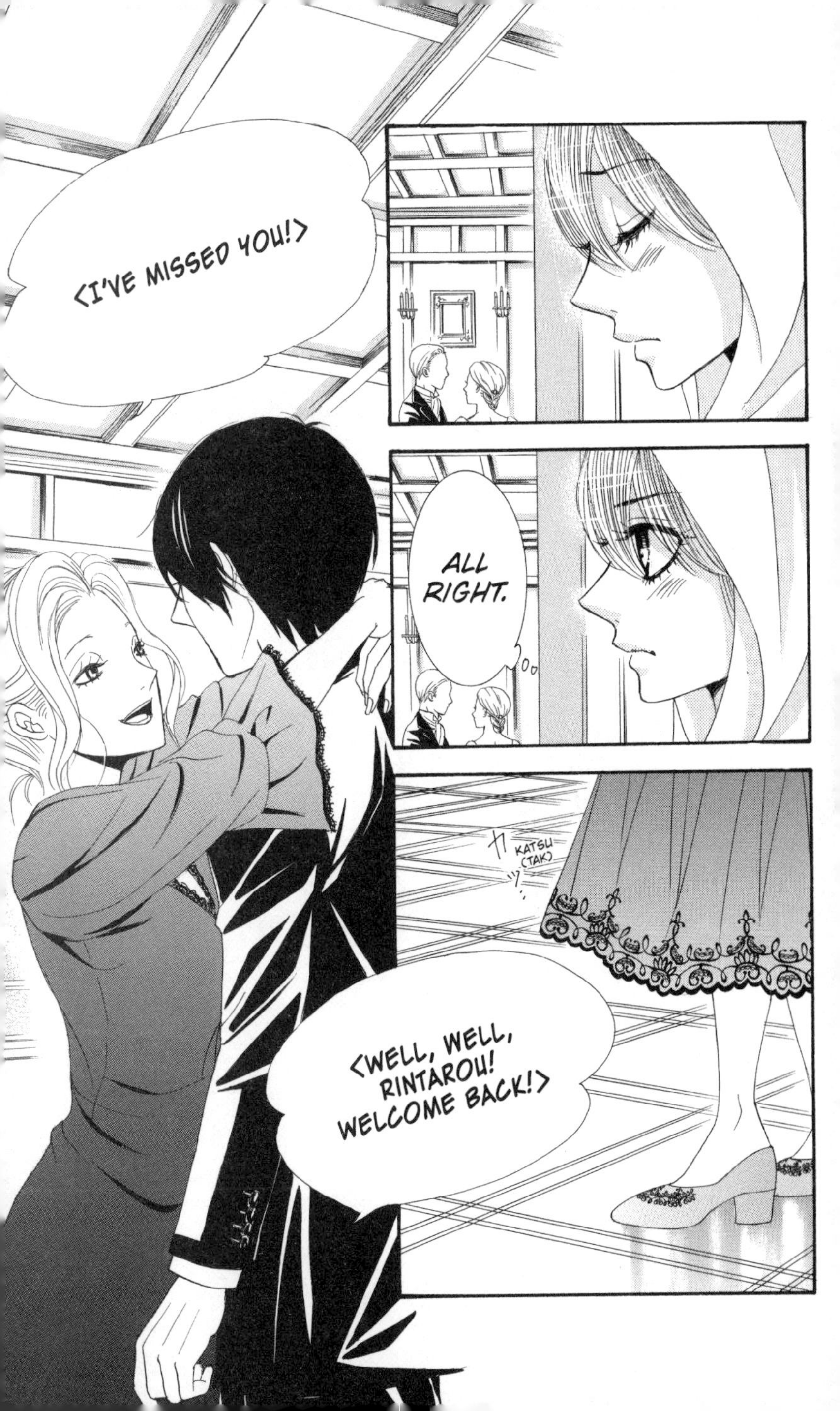
ALL RIGHT.
KATSU (TAK)
<WELL, WELL, RINTAROU! WELCOME BACK!>
<I'VE MISSED YOU!>

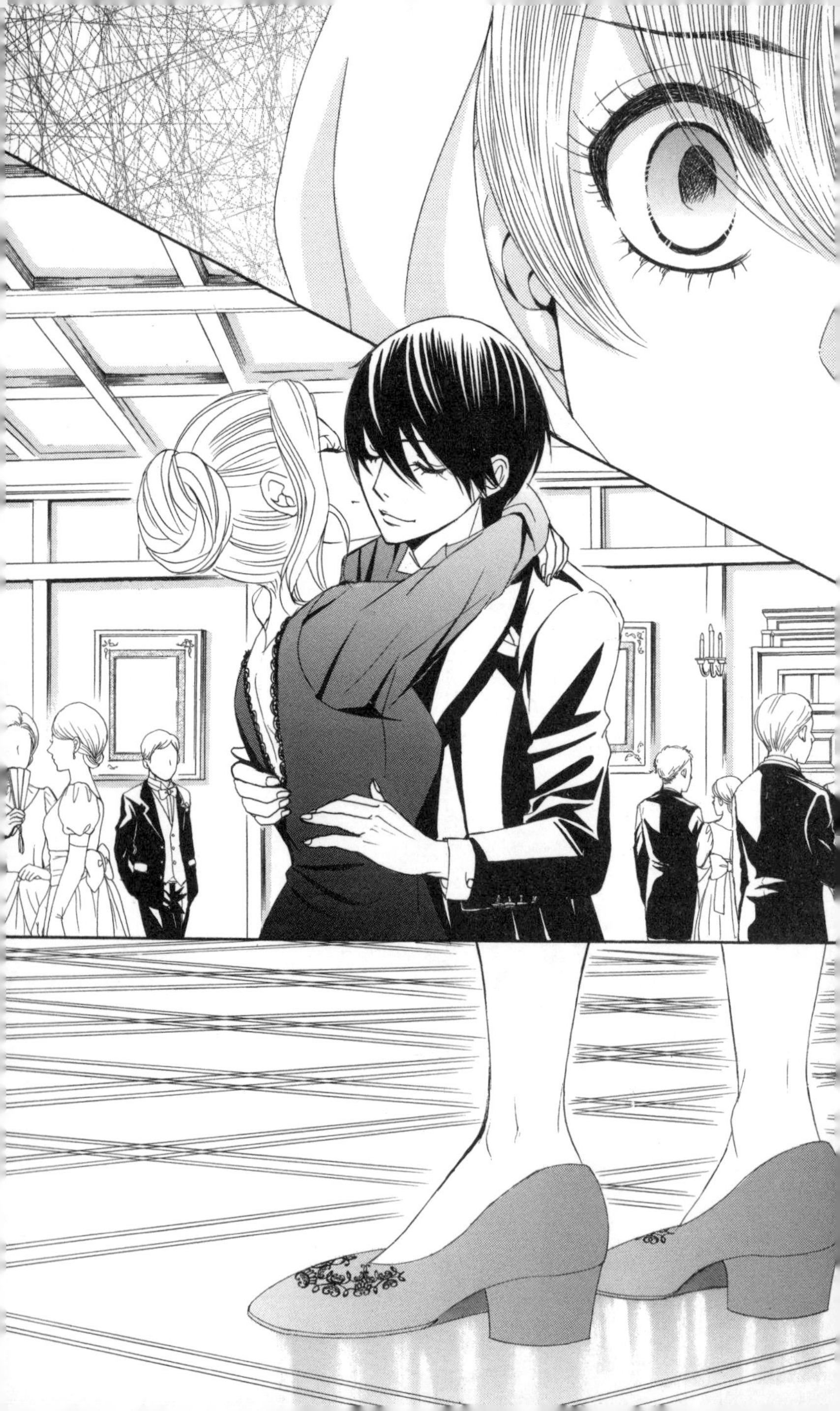

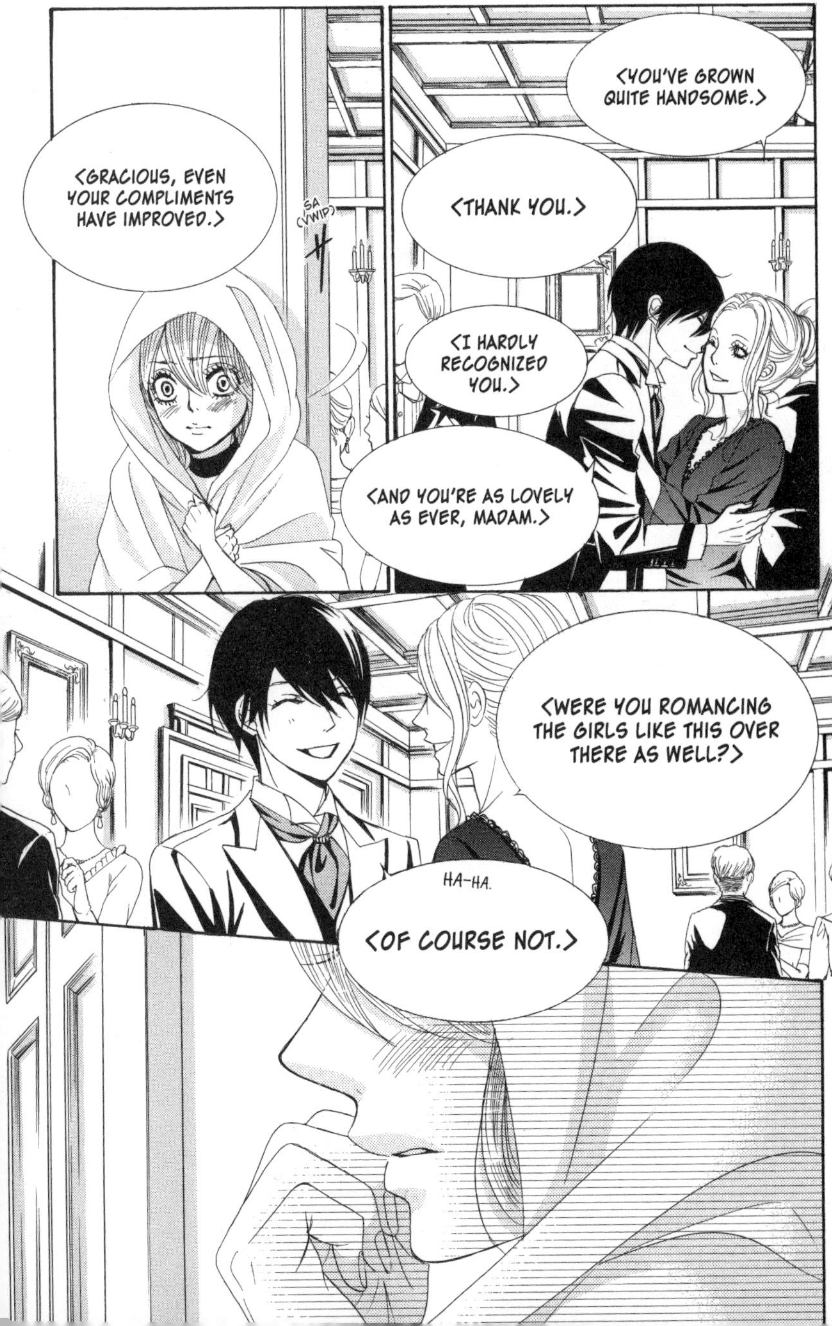
<YOU'VE GROWN QUITE HANDSOME.>
<THANK YOU.>
<I HARDLY RECOGNIZED YOU.>
<AND YOU'RE AS LOVELY AS EVER, MADAM.>
<GRACIOUS, EVEN YOUR COMPLIMENTS HAVE IMPROVED.>
SA (VWIP)
<WERE YOU ROMANCING THE GIRLS LIKE THIS OVER THERE AS WELL?>
HA-HA.
<OF COURSE NOT.>

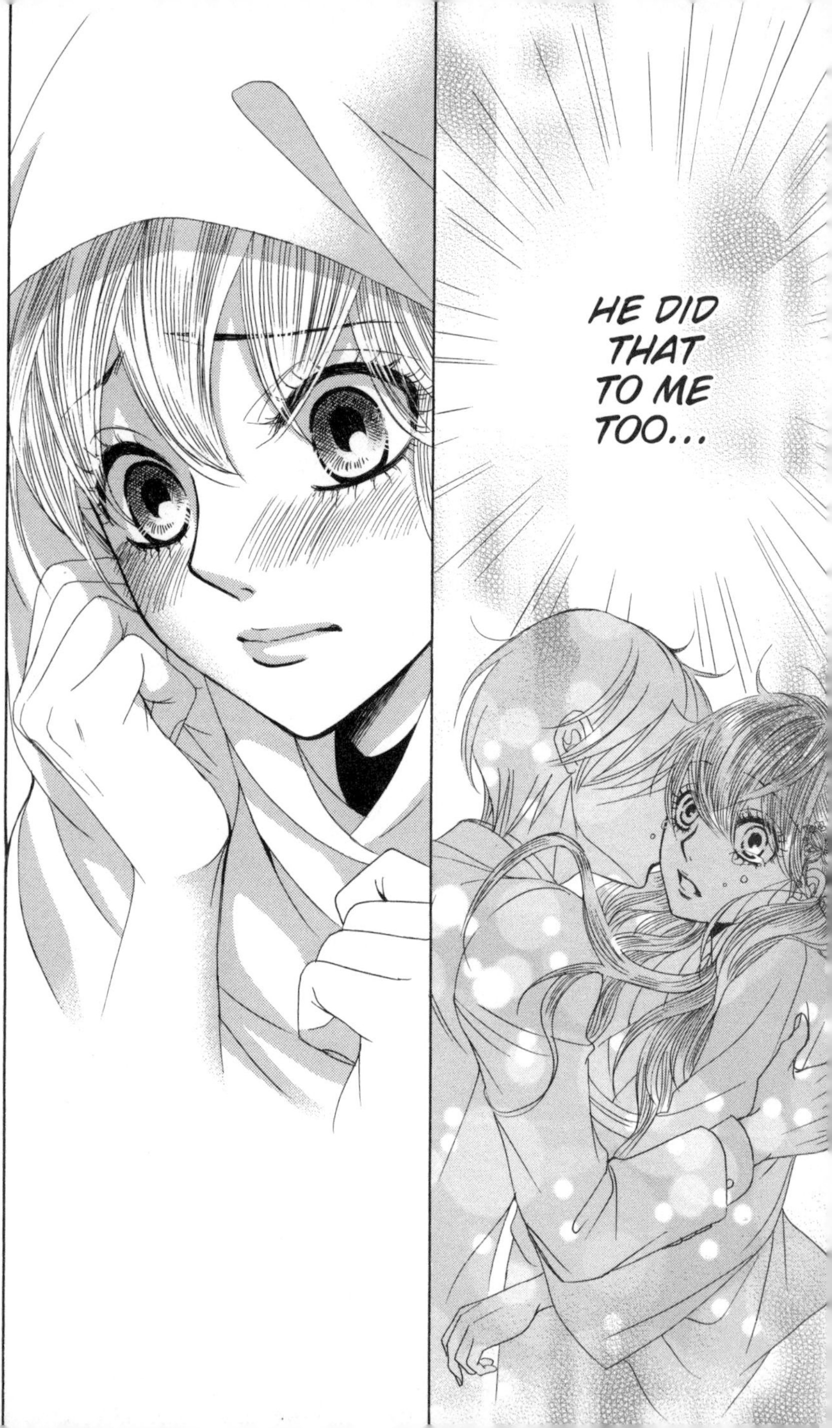
HE DID THAT TO ME TOO...

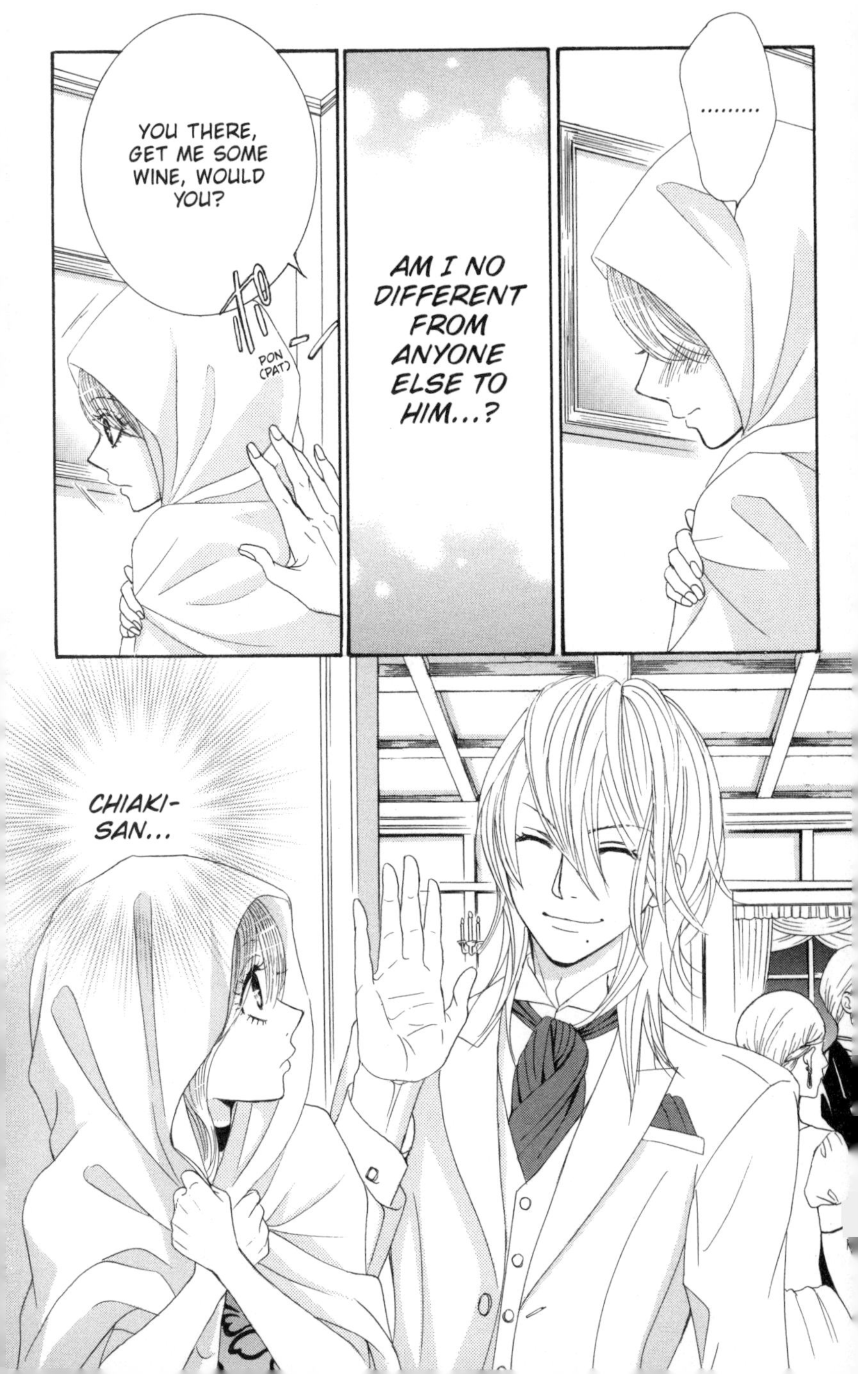
....
AM I NO DIFFERENT FROM ANYONE ELSE TO HIM...?
YOU THERE, GET ME SOME WINE, WOULD YOU?
PON (PAT)
CHIAKI-SAN...

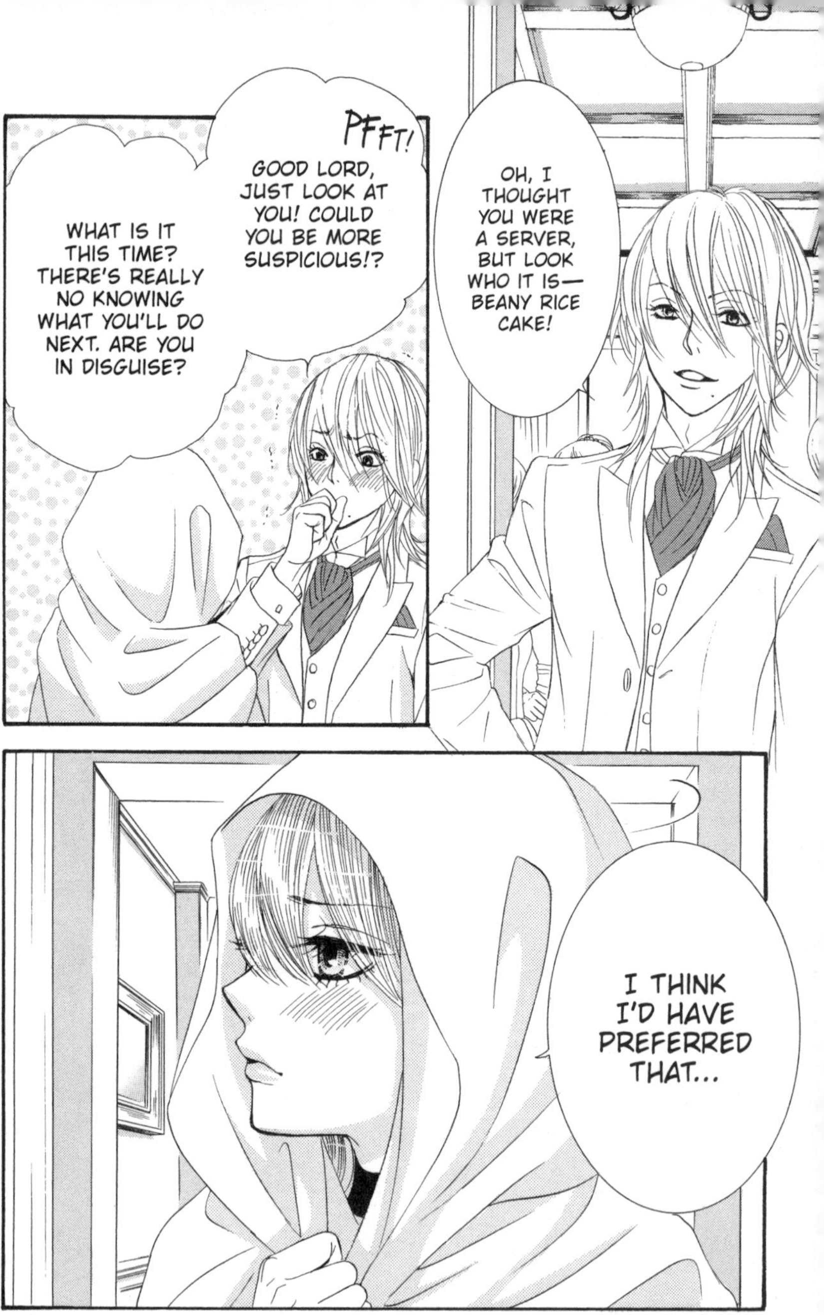
OH, I THOUGHT YOU WERE A SERVER, BUT LOOK WHO IT IS—BEANY RICE CAKE!
PFFT!
GOOD LORD, JUST LOOK AT YOU! COULD YOU BE MORE SUSPICIOUS!?
WHAT IS IT THIS TIME? THERE'S REALLY NO KNOWING WHAT YOU'LL DO NEXT. ARE YOU IN DISGUISE?
I THINK I'D HAVE PREFERRED THAT...

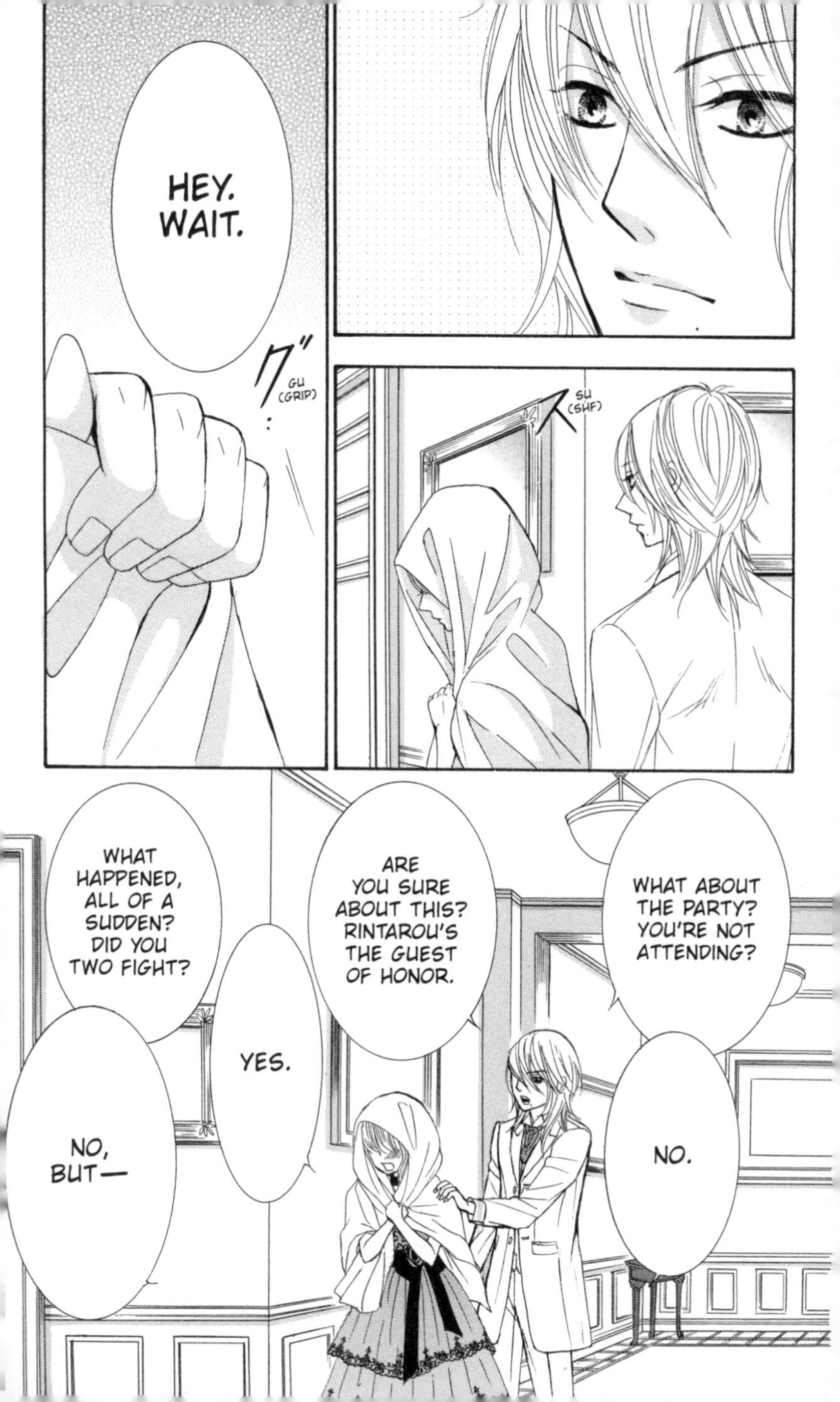
SU (SHF)
HEY. WAIT.
GU (GRIP)
WHAT ABOUT THE PARTY? YOU'RE NOT ATTENDING?
NO.
ARE YOU SURE ABOUT THIS? RINTAROU'S THE GUEST OF HONOR.
YES.
WHAT HAPPENED, ALL OF A SUDDEN? DID YOU TWO FIGHT?
NO, BUT—

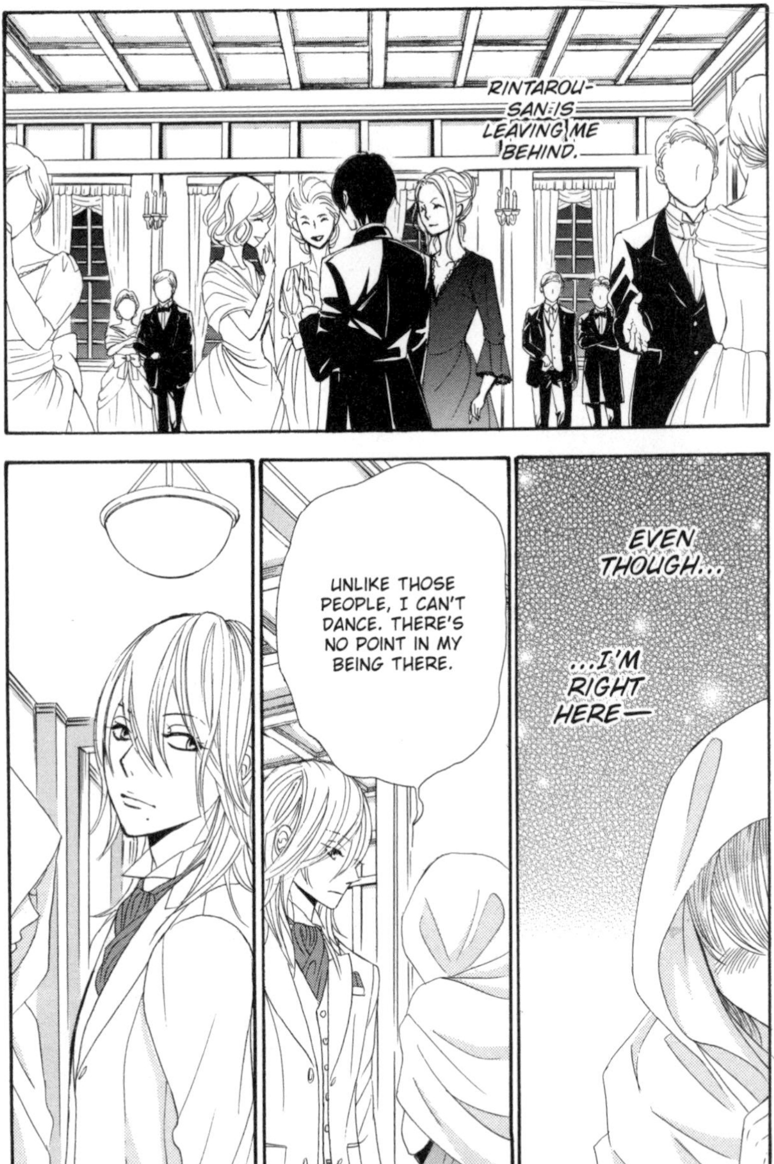
RINTAROU-SAN IS LEAVING ME BEHIND.
EVEN THOUGH...
...I'M RIGHT HERE—
UNLIKE THOSE PEOPLE, I CAN'T DANCE. THERE'S NO POINT IN MY BEING THERE.

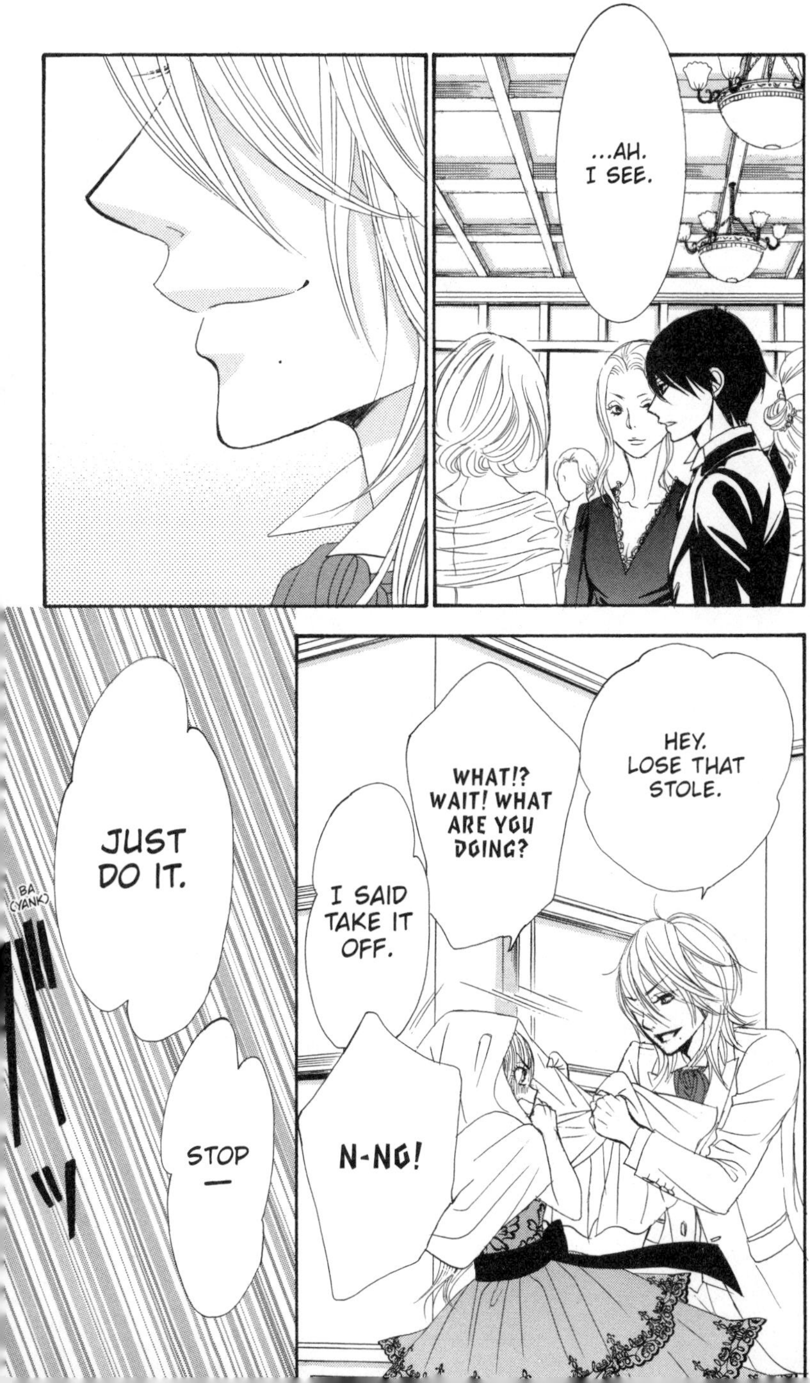
...AH. I SEE.
HEY. LOSE THAT STOLE.
WHAT!? WAIT! WHAT ARE YOU DOING?
I SAID TAKE IT OFF.
N-NO!
JUST DO IT.
STOP—
BA (YANK)

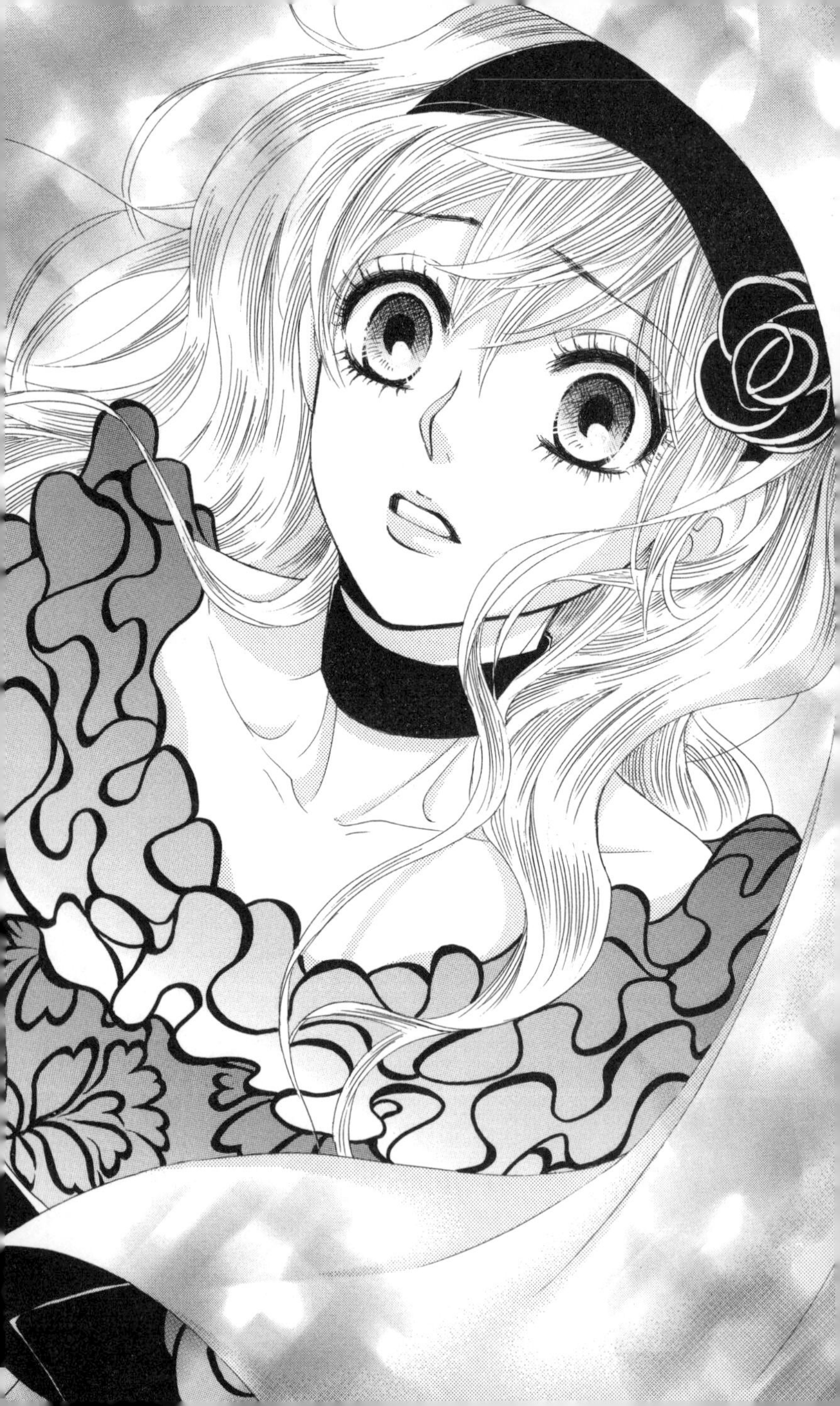

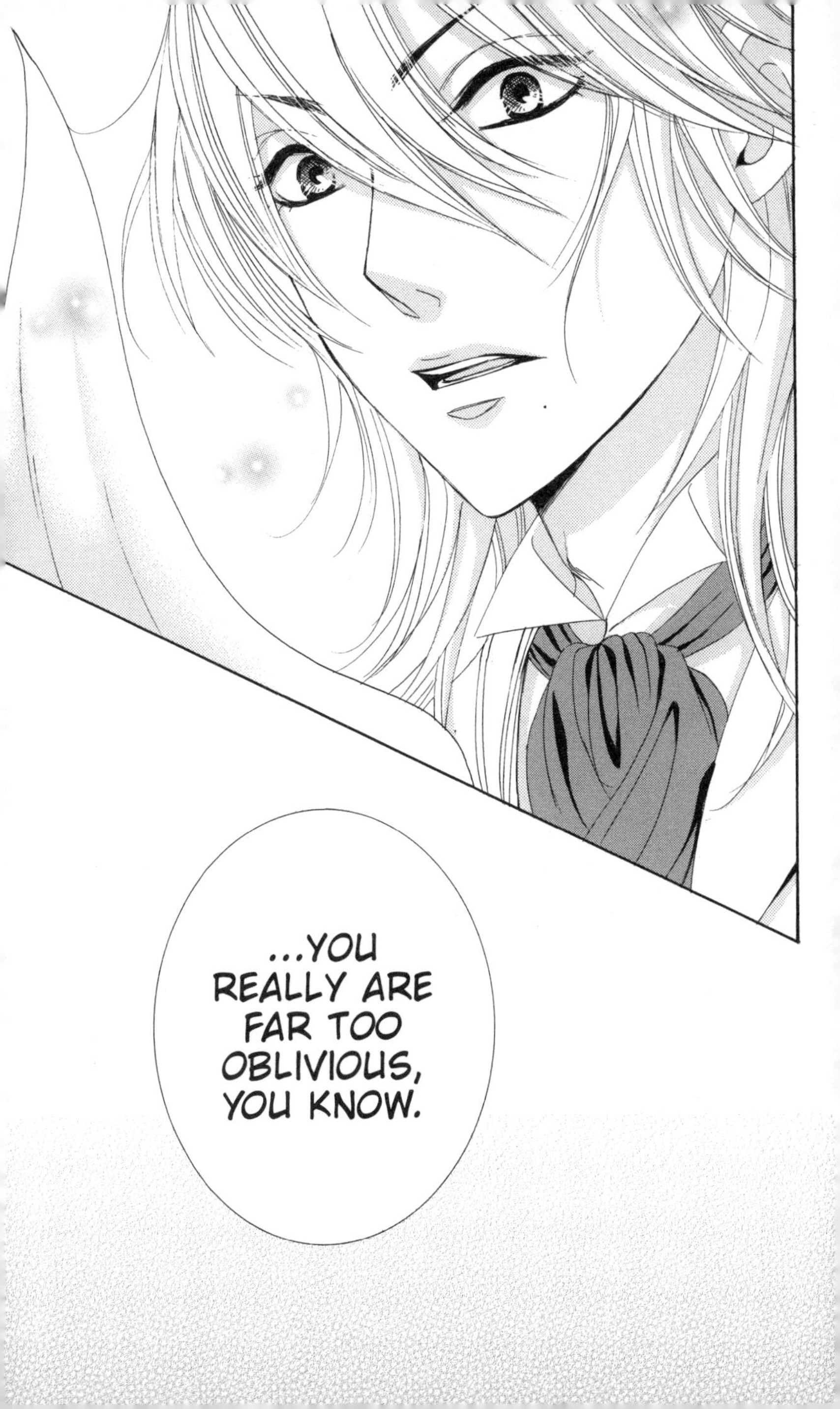
...YOU REALLY ARE FAR TOO OBLIVIOUS, YOU KNOW.

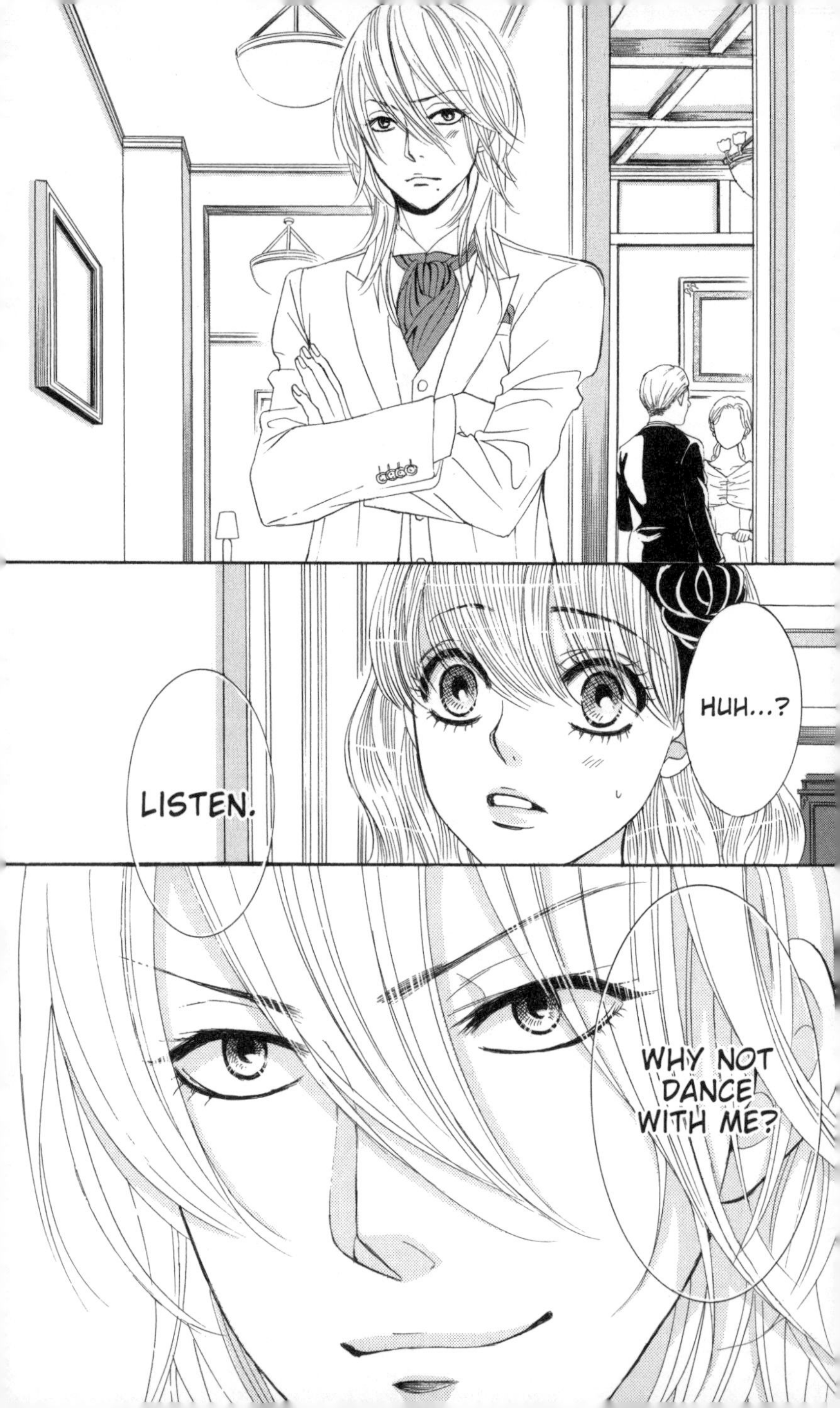
HUH...?
LISTEN.
WHY NOT DANCE WITH ME?

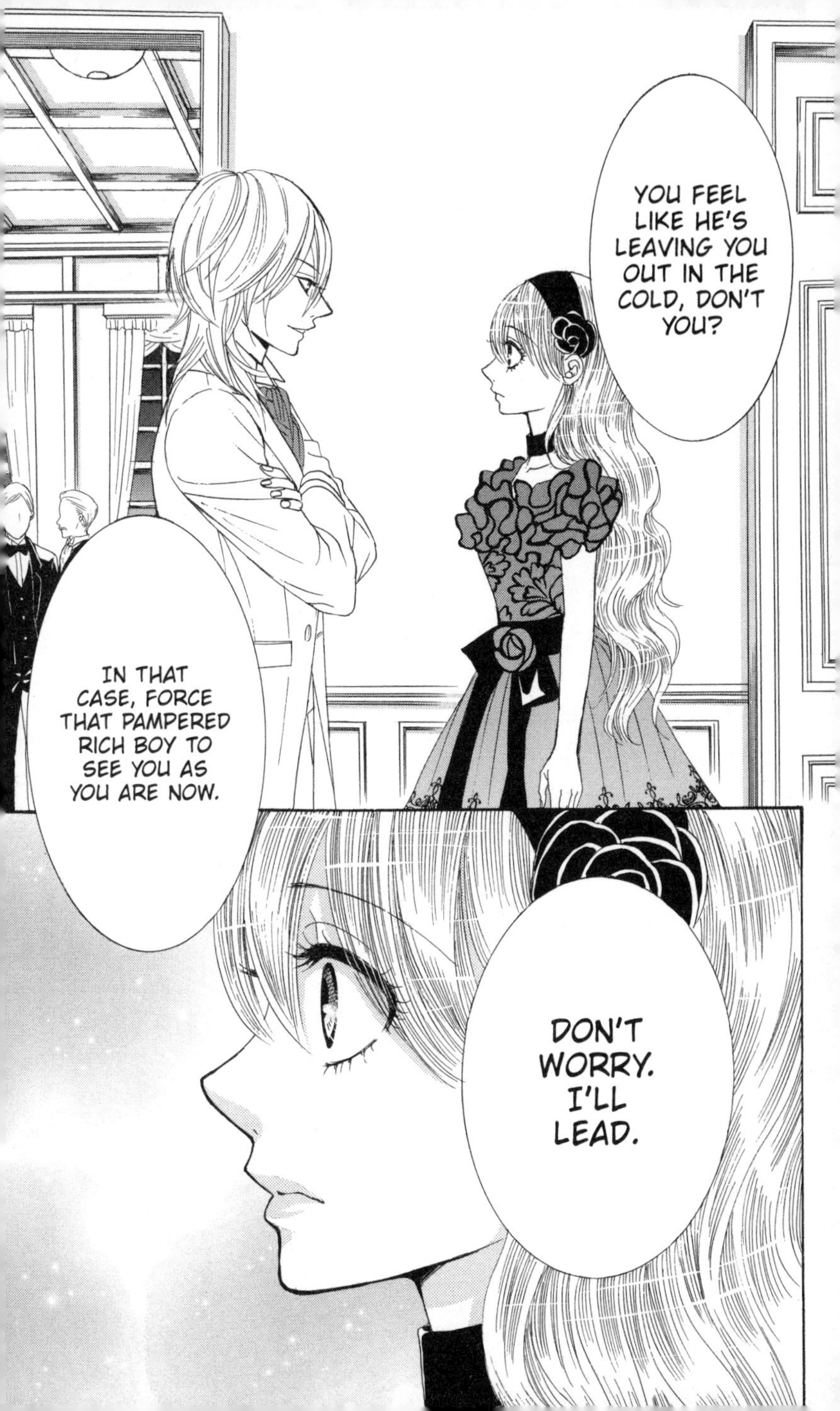
YOU FEEL LIKE HE'S LEAVING YOU OUT IN THE COLD, DON'T YOU?
IN THAT CASE, FORCE THAT PAMPERED RICH BOY TO SEE YOU AS YOU ARE NOW.
DON'T WORRY. I'LL LEAD.

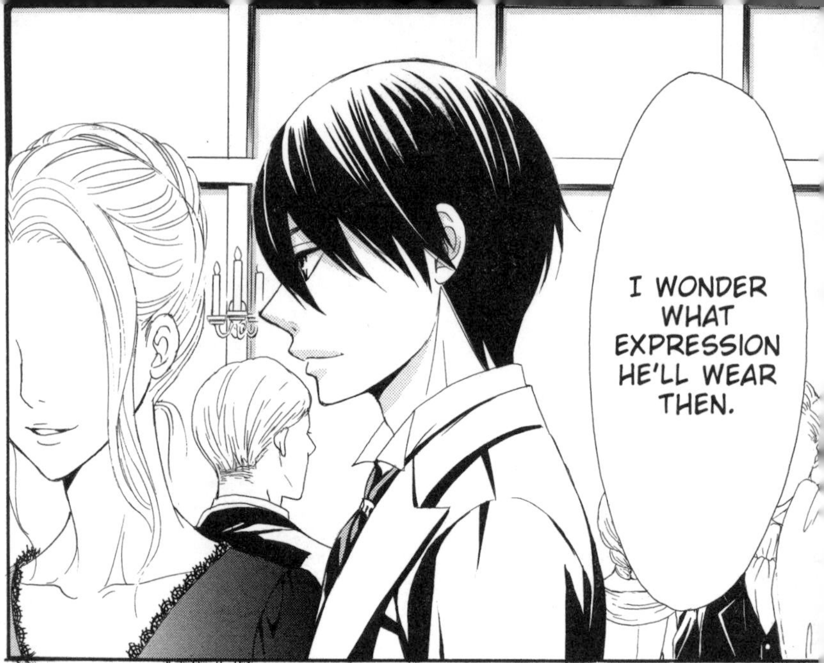
I WONDER WHAT EXPRESSION HE'LL WEAR THEN.
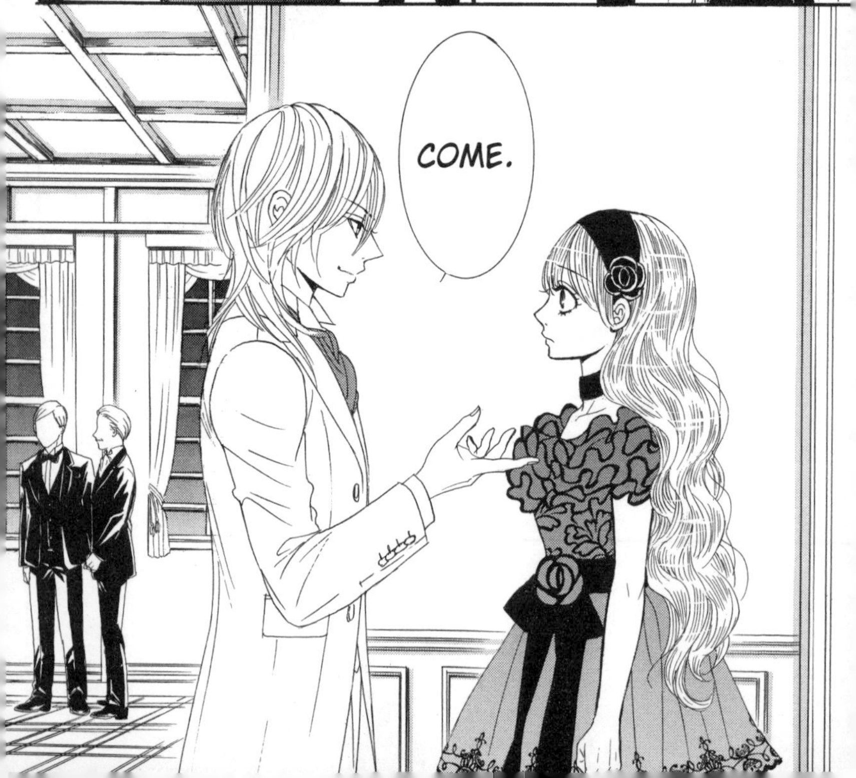
COME.

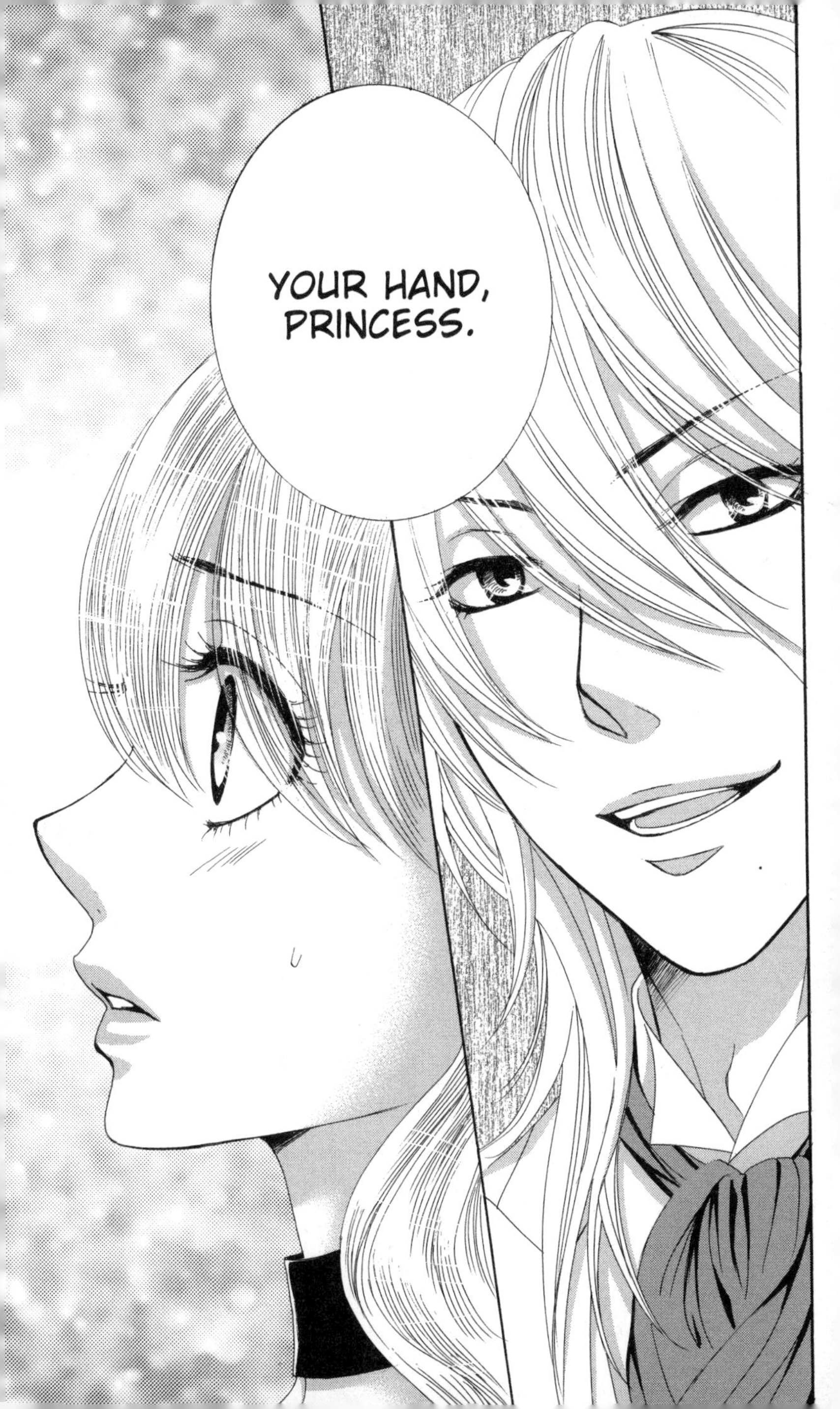
YOUR HAND, PRINCESS.

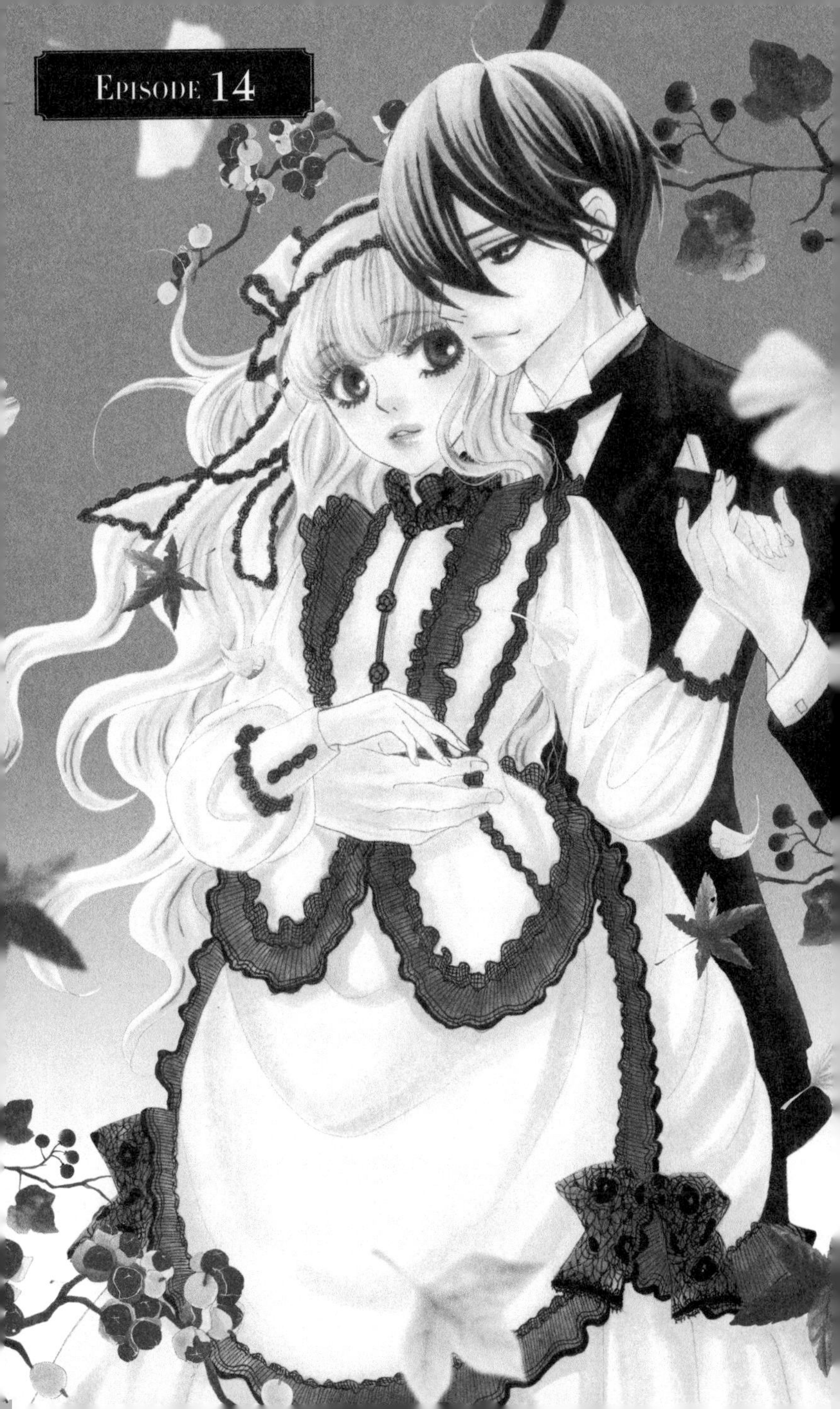
Episode 14

Golden Japanesque

A SPLENDID YOKOHAMA ROMANCE

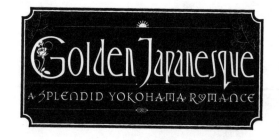

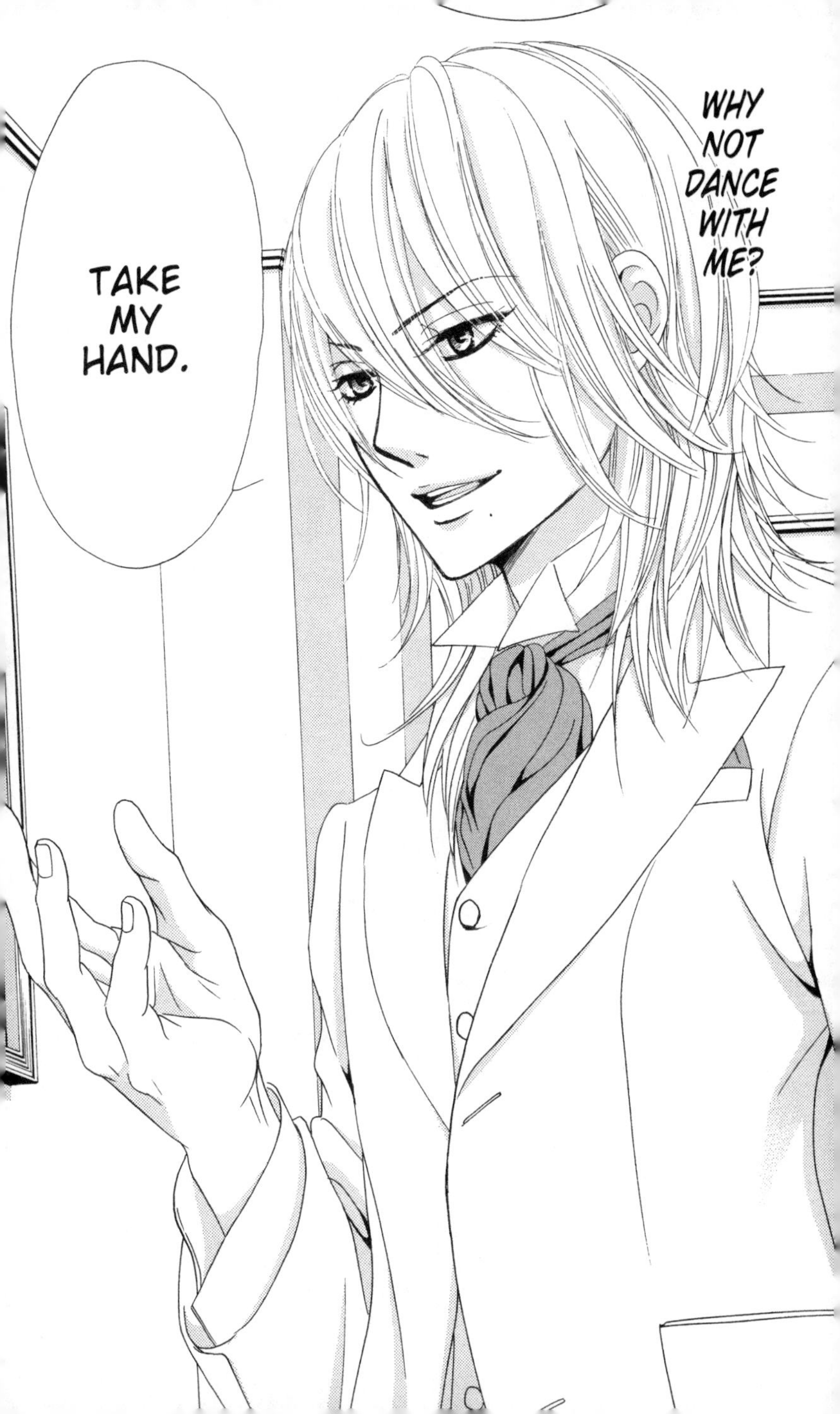
WHY NOT DANCE WITH ME?
TAKE MY HAND.

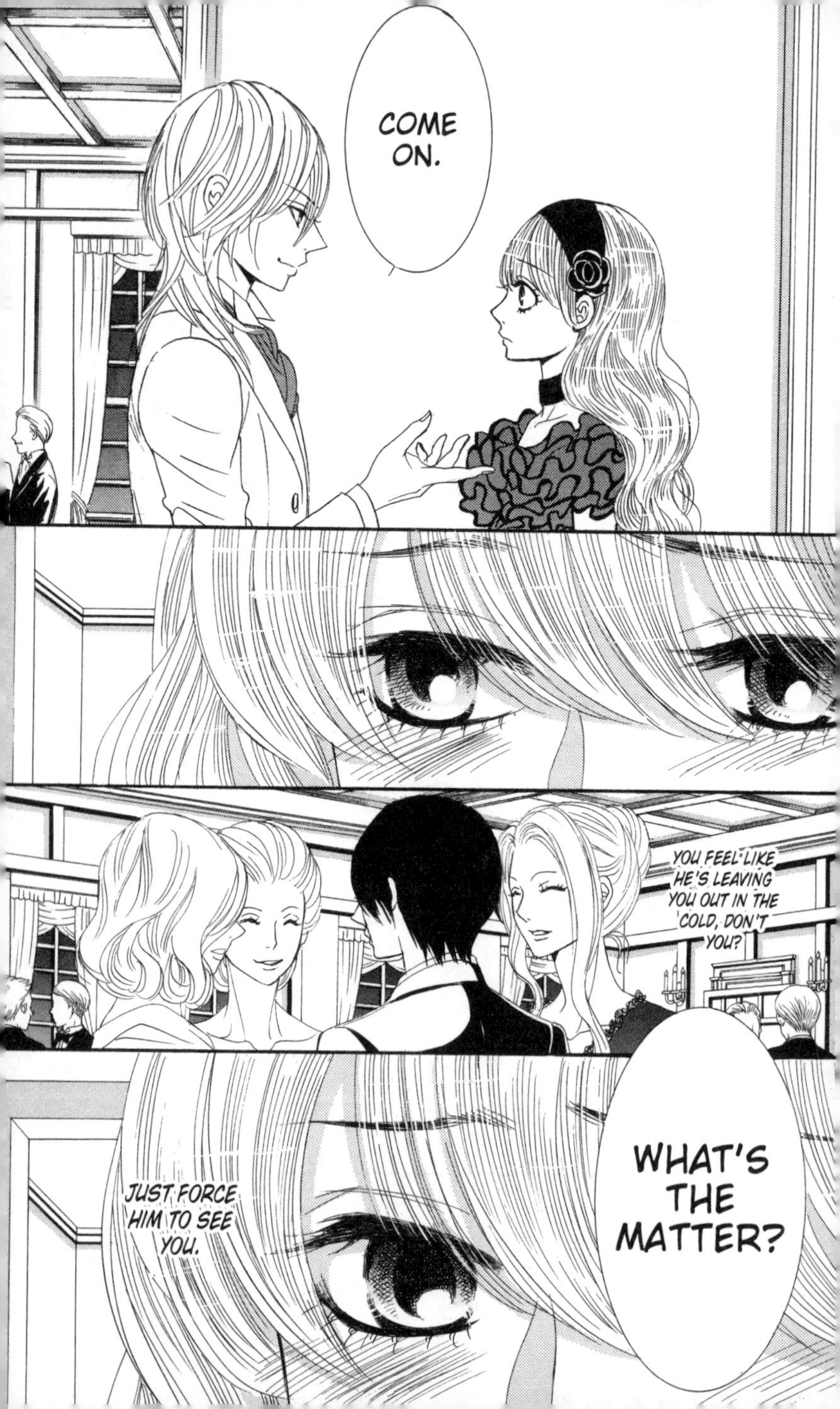
COME ON.
YOU FEEL LIKE HE'S LEAVING YOU OUT IN THE COLD, DON'T YOU?
WHAT'S THE MATTER?
JUST FORCE HIM TO SEE YOU.

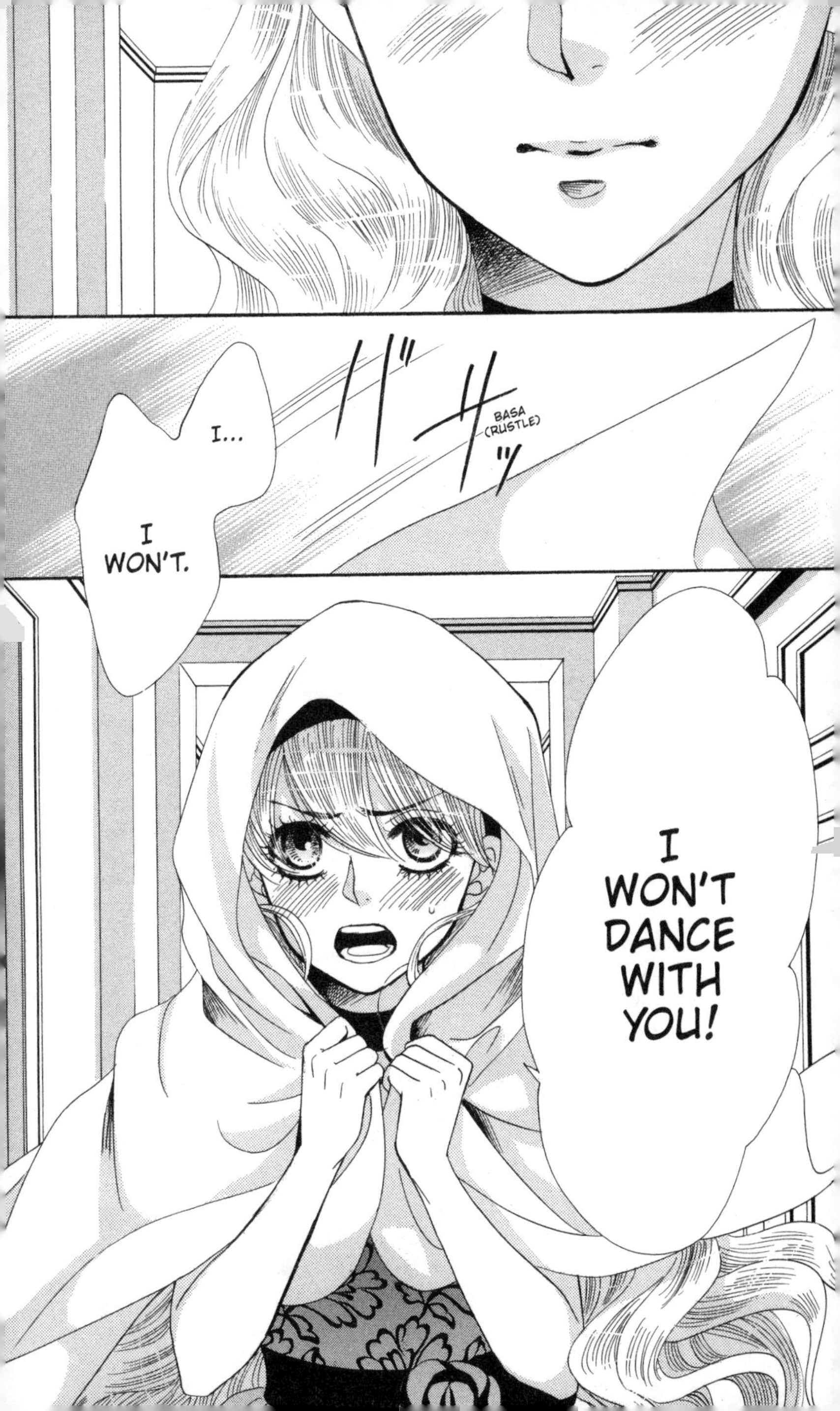
ザッ
BASA (RUSTLE)
I...
I WON'T.
I WON'T DANCE WITH YOU!

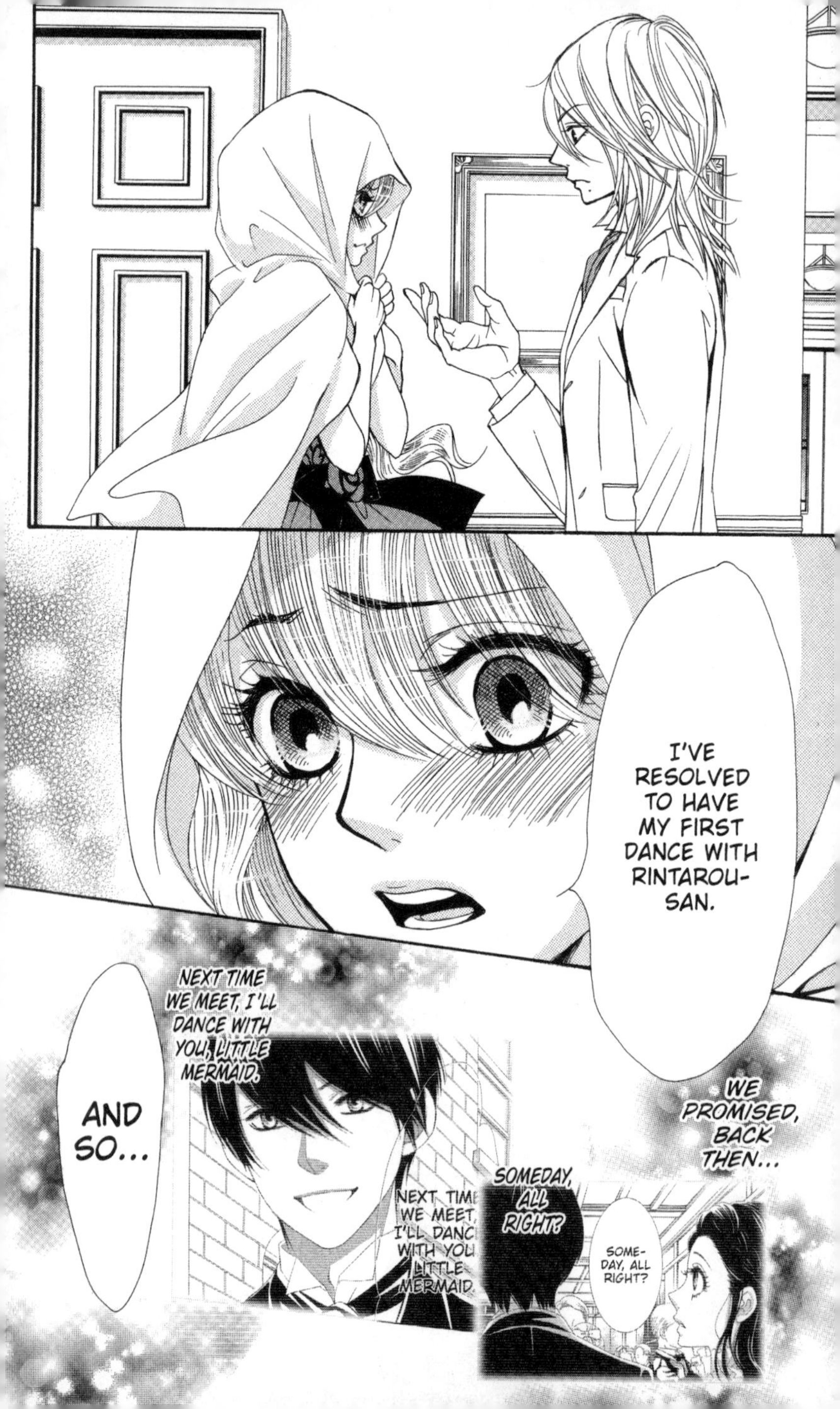

I'VE RESOLVED TO HAVE MY FIRST DANCE WITH RINTAROU-SAN.
WE PROMISED, BACK THEN...
SOMEDAY, ALL RIGHT?
SOME-DAY, ALL RIGHT?
NEXT TIME WE MEET, I'LL DANCE WITH YOU, LITTLE MERMAID.
NEXT TIME WE MEET, I'LL DANCE WITH YOU, LITTLE MERMAID.
AND SO...

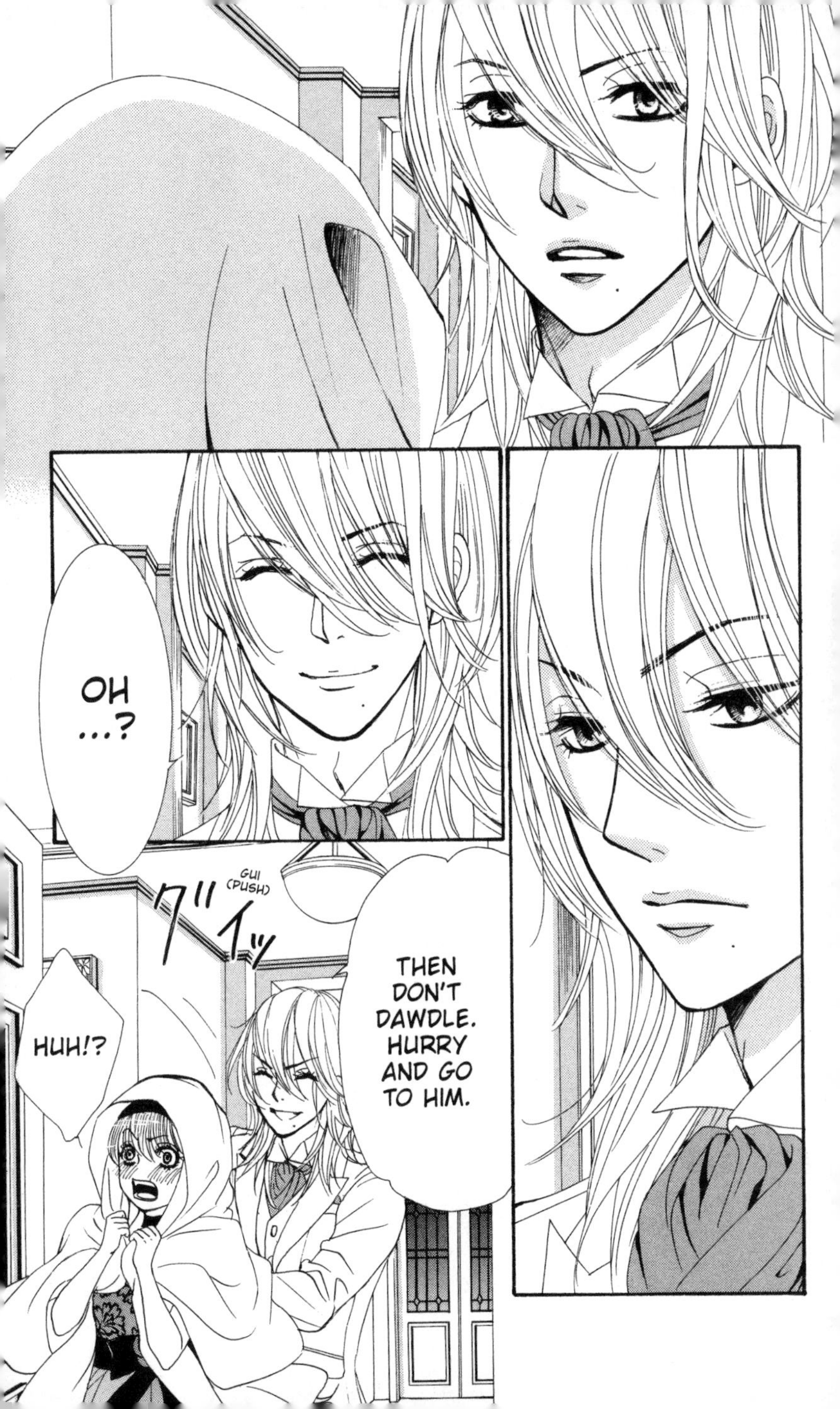
OH ...?
THEN DON'T DAWDLE. HURRY AND GO TO HIM.
GUI (PUSH)
HUH!?

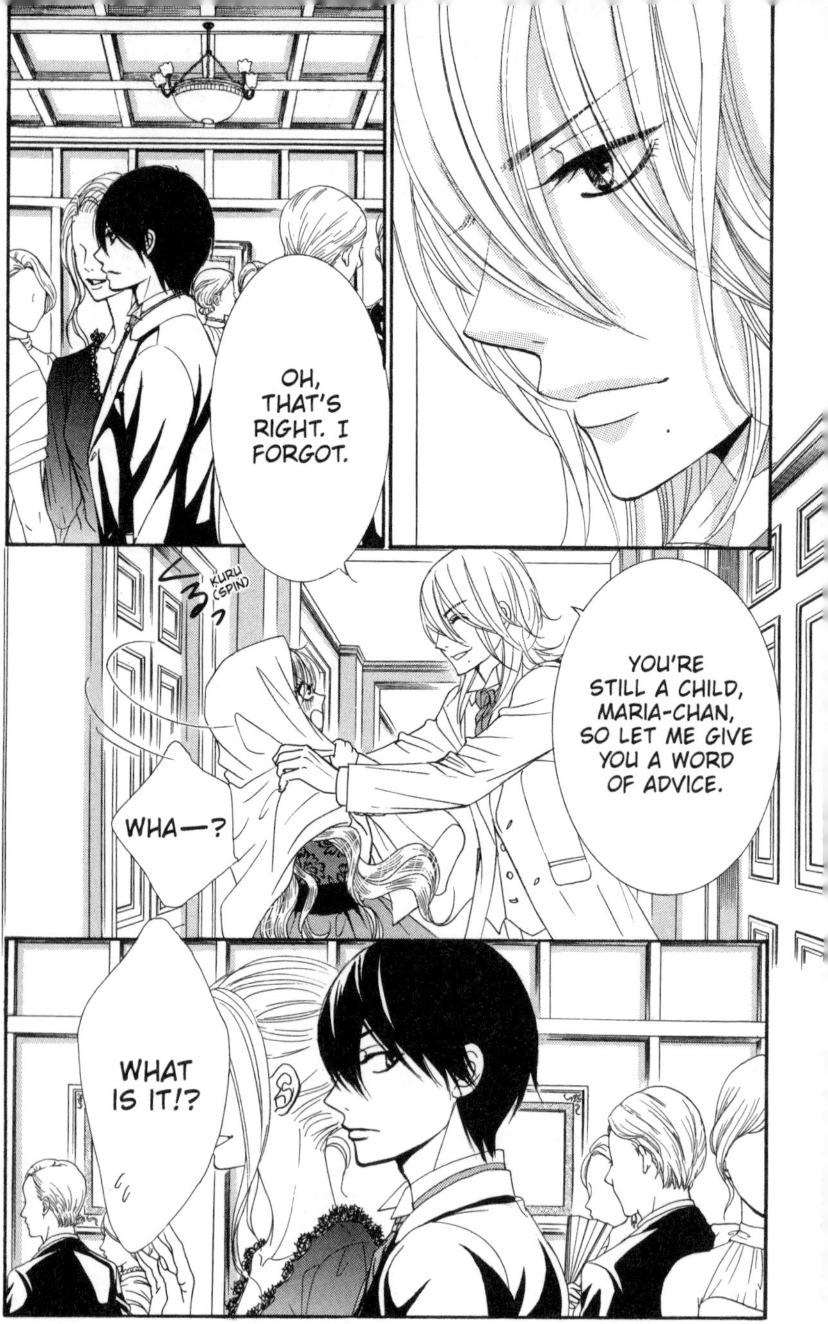
OH, THAT'S RIGHT. I FORGOT.
YOU'RE STILL A CHILD, MARIA-CHAN, SO LET ME GIVE YOU A WORD OF ADVICE.
KURU (SPIN)
WHA—?
WHAT IS IT!?

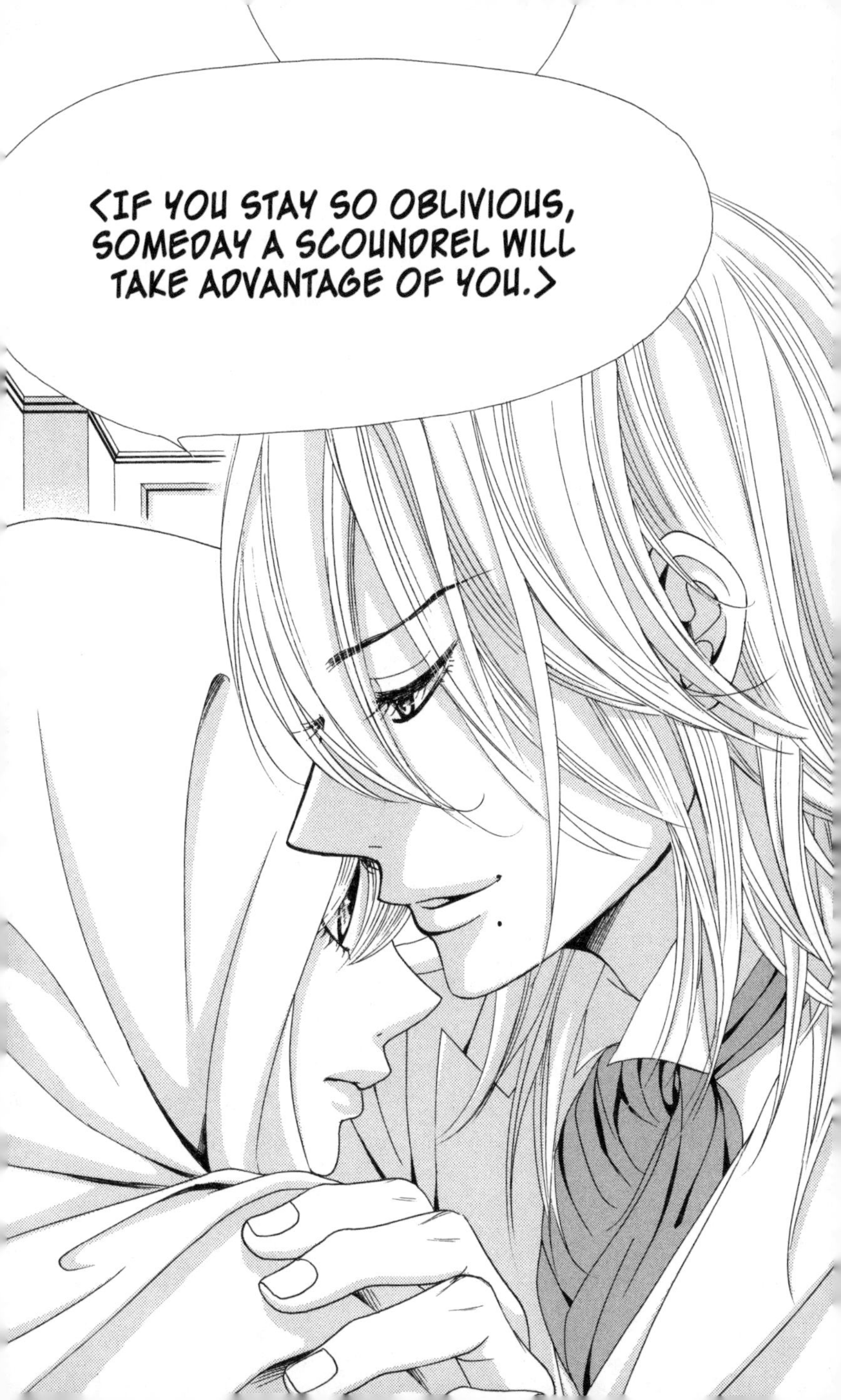
<IF YOU STAY SO OBLIVIOUS, SOMEDAY A SCOUNDREL WILL TAKE ADVANTAGE OF YOU.>

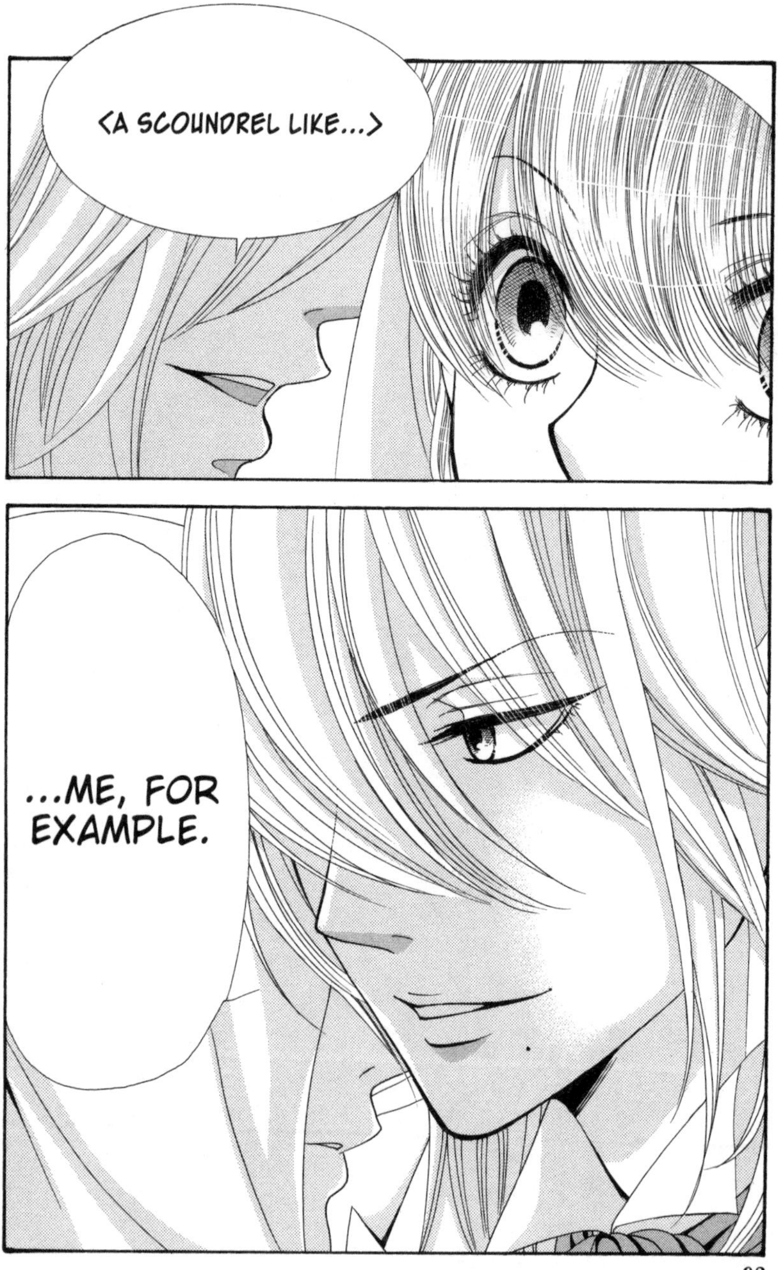
<A SCOUNDREL LIKE...>
...ME, FOR EXAMPLE.

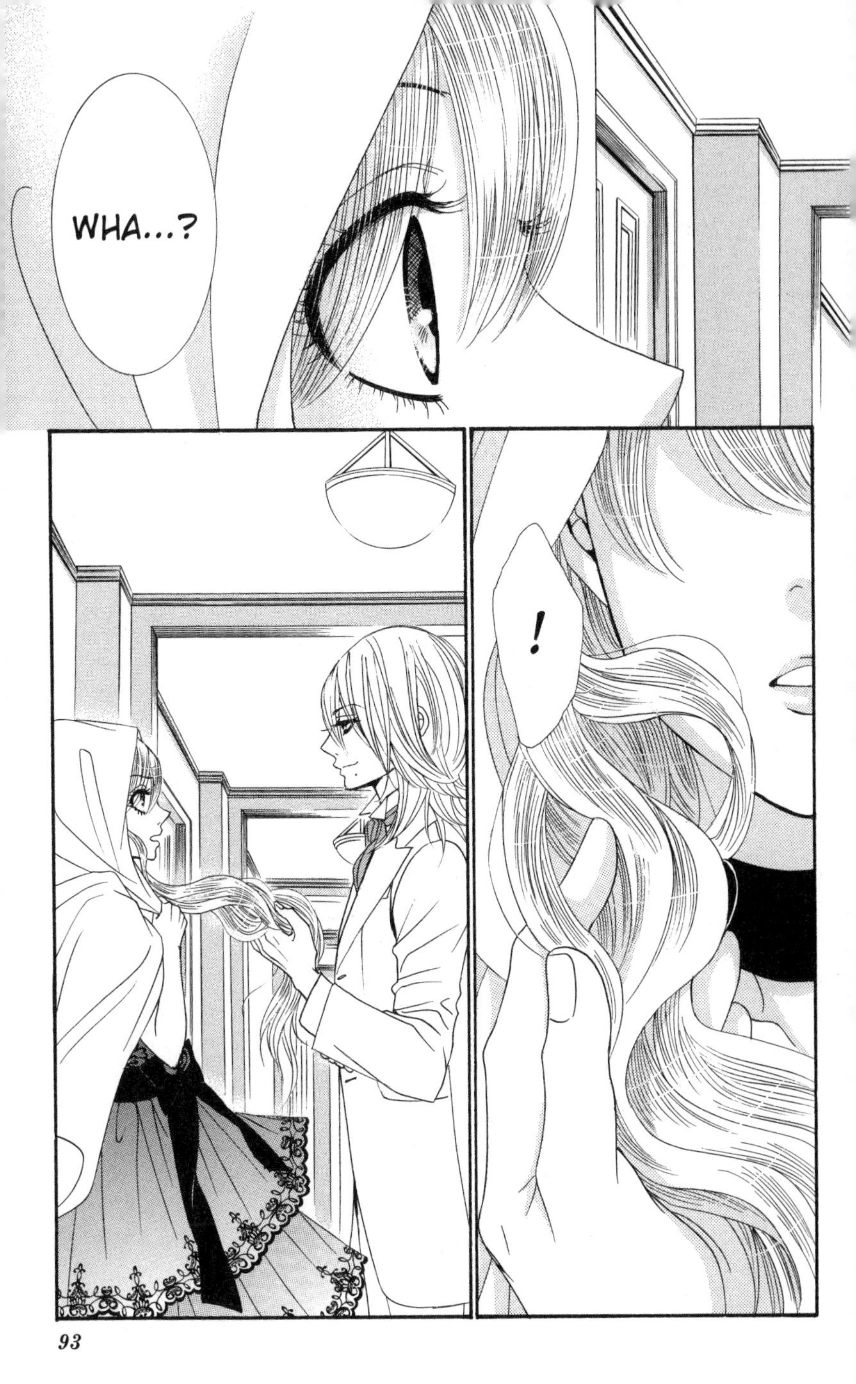
WHA...?
!

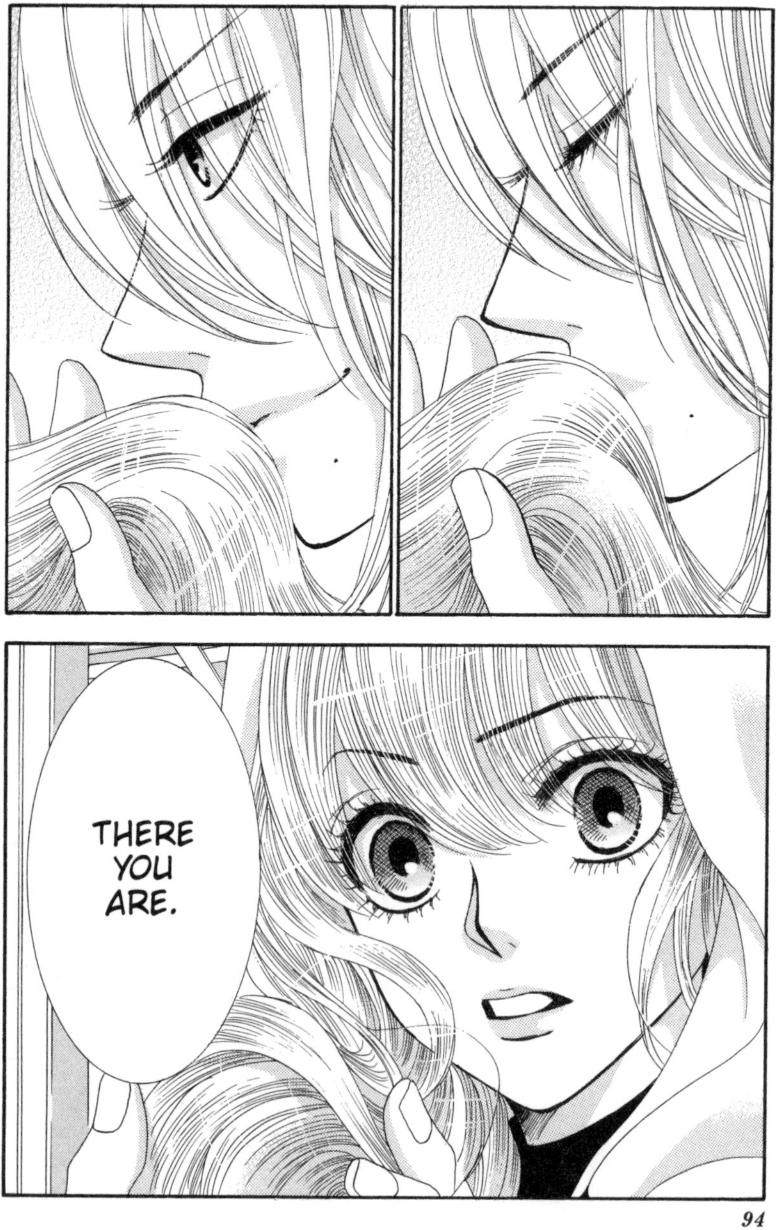
THERE YOU ARE.

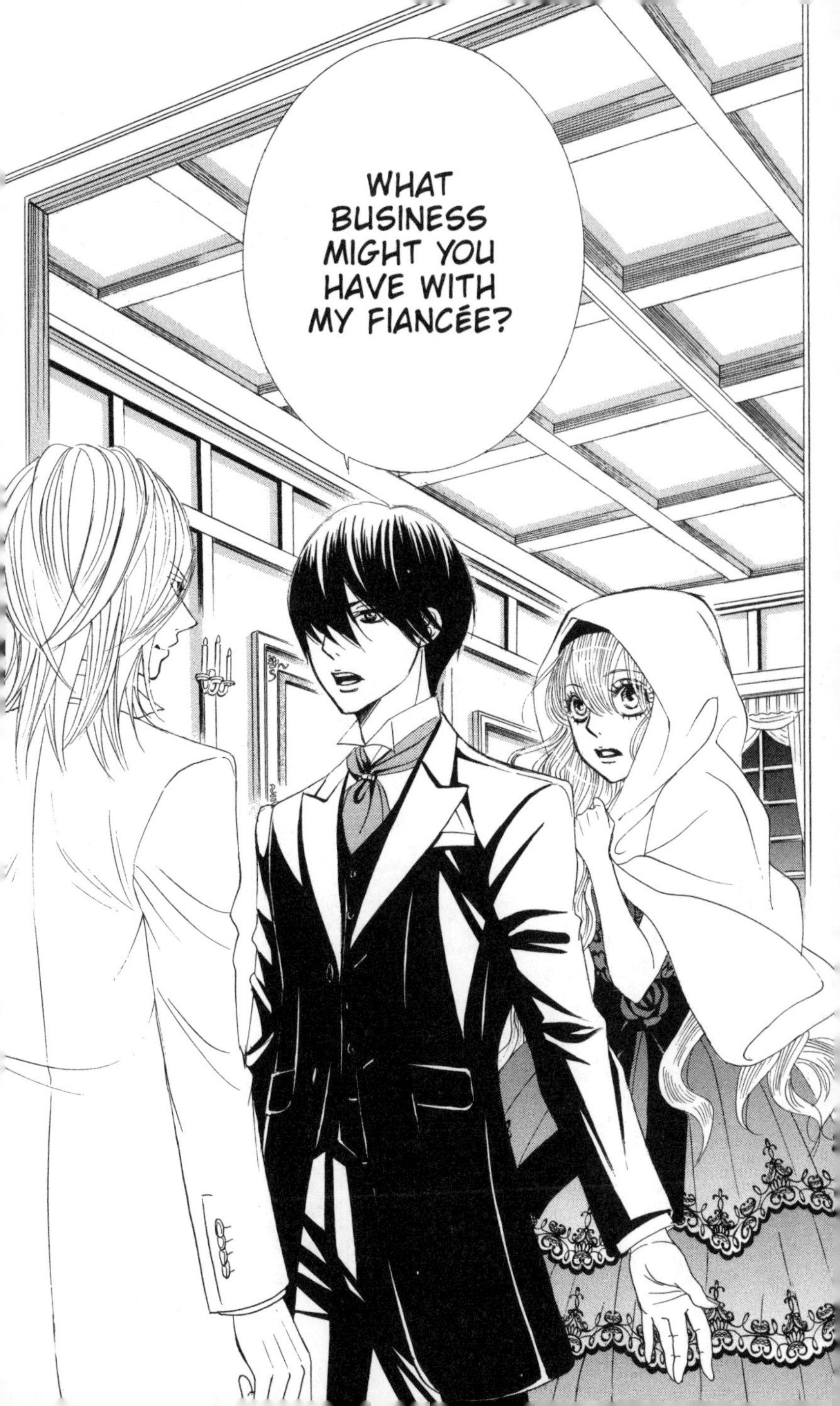
WHAT BUSINESS MIGHT YOU HAVE WITH MY FIANCÉE?

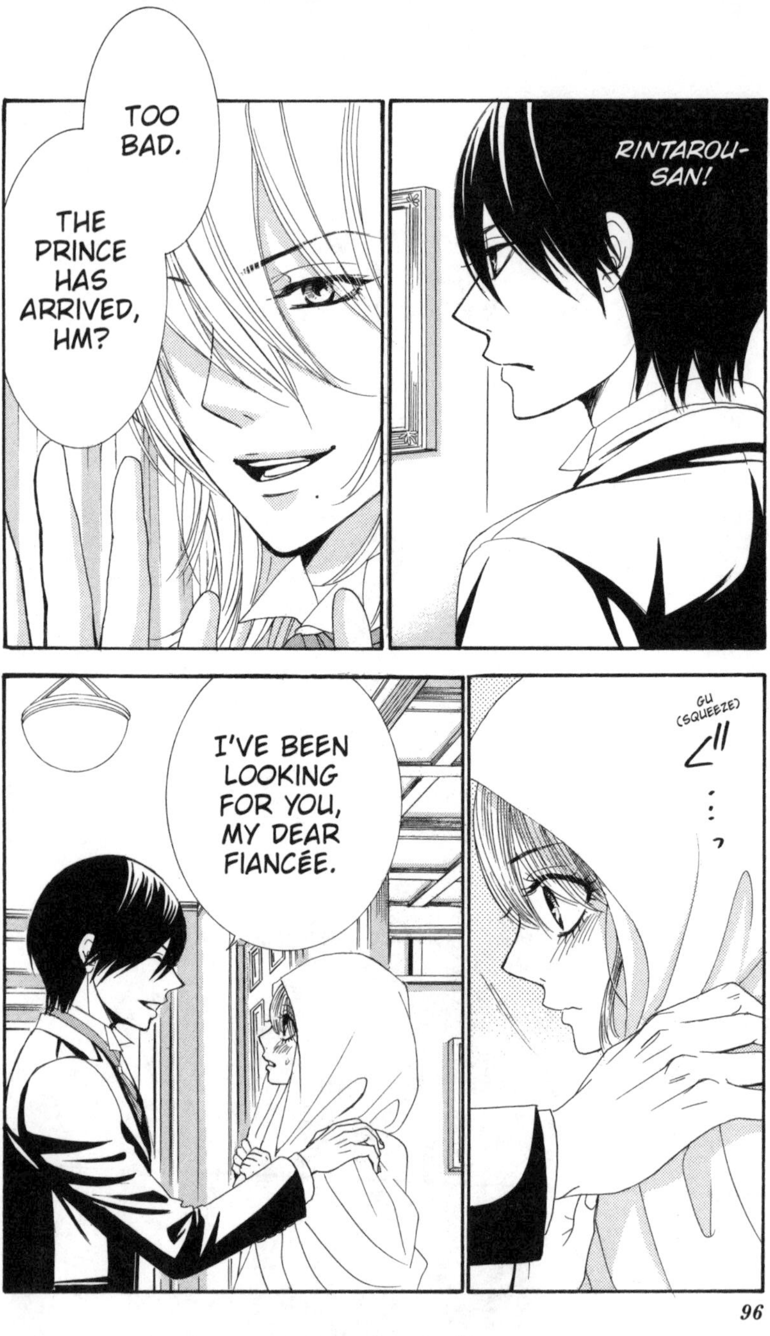
RINTAROU-SAN!
TOO BAD.
THE PRINCE HAS ARRIVED, HM?
GU (SQUEEZE)
...
I'VE BEEN LOOKING FOR YOU, MY DEAR FIANCÉE.

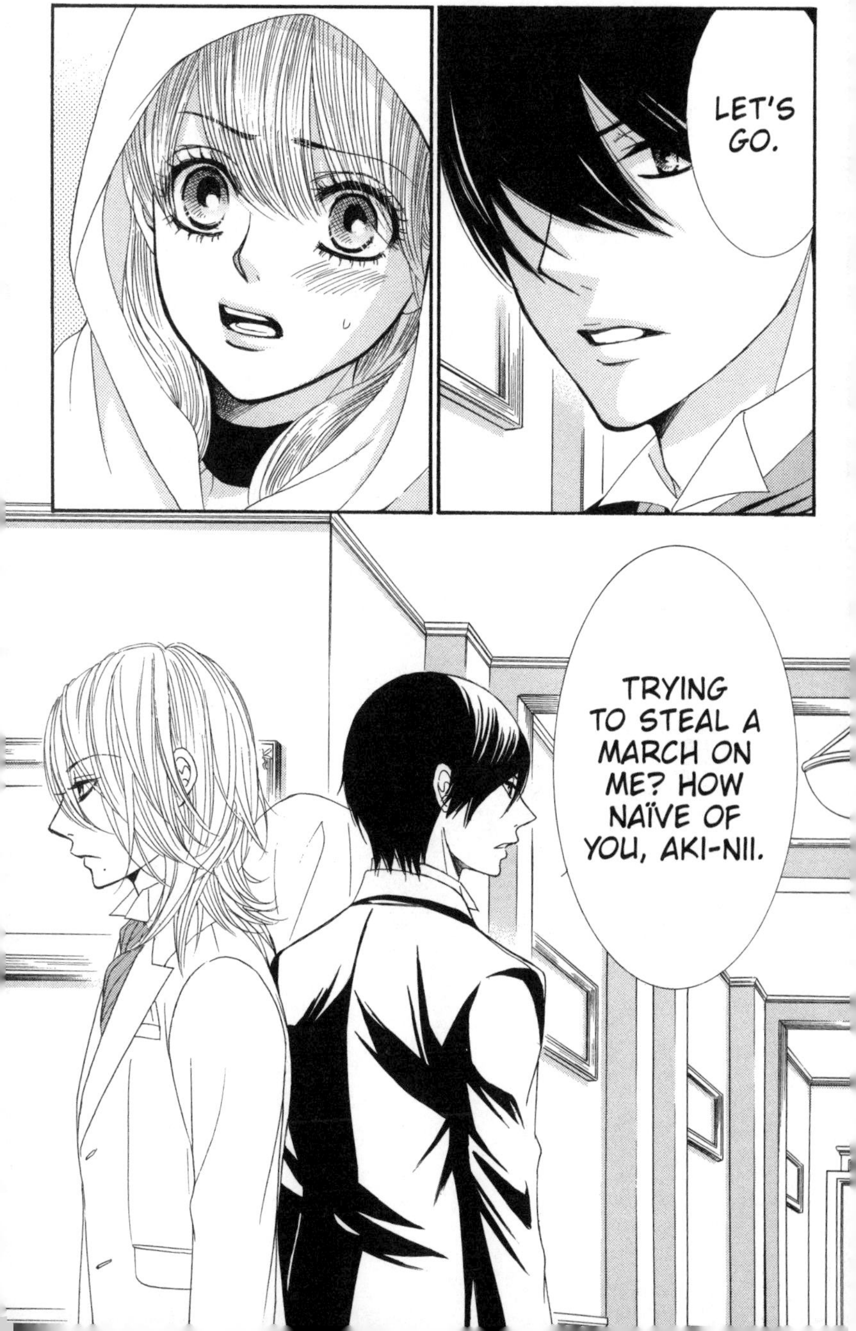
LET'S GO.
TRYING TO STEAL A MARCH ON ME? HOW NAÏVE OF YOU, AKI-NII.

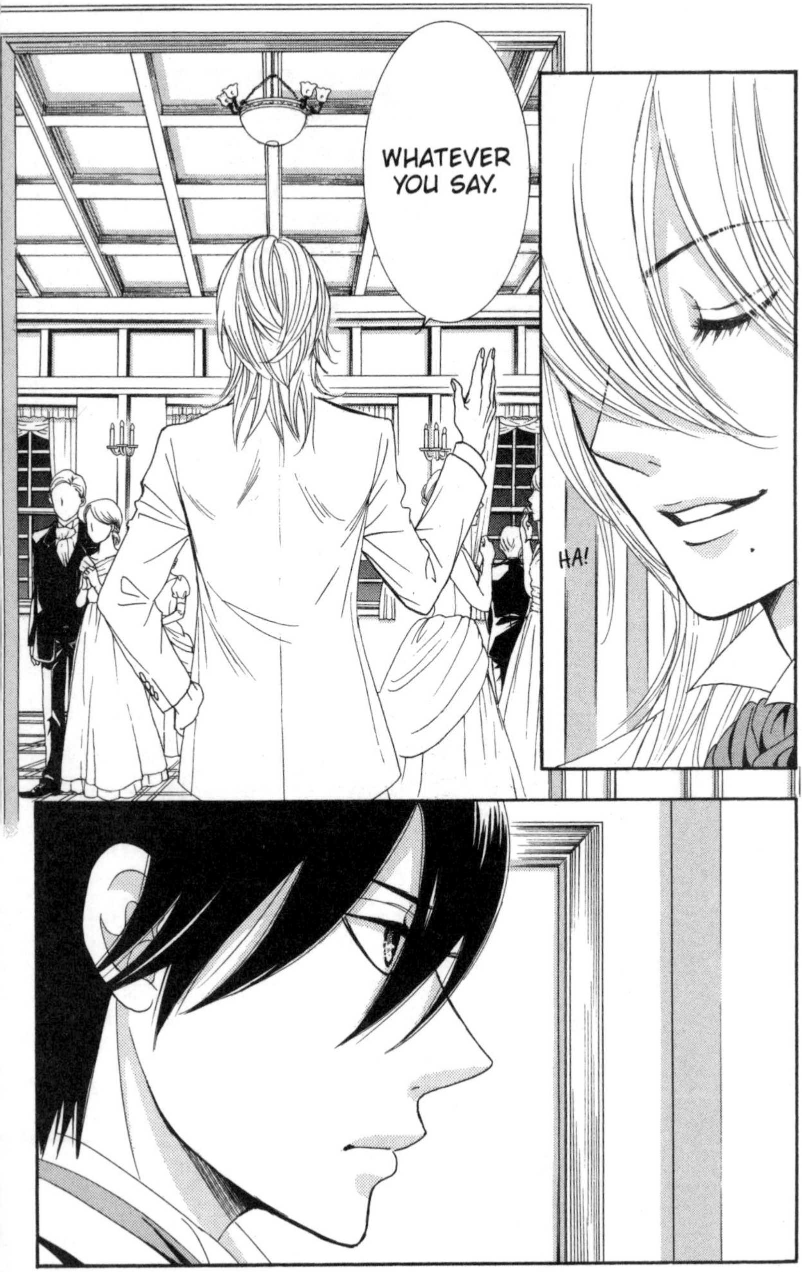
HA!
WHATEVER YOU SAY.

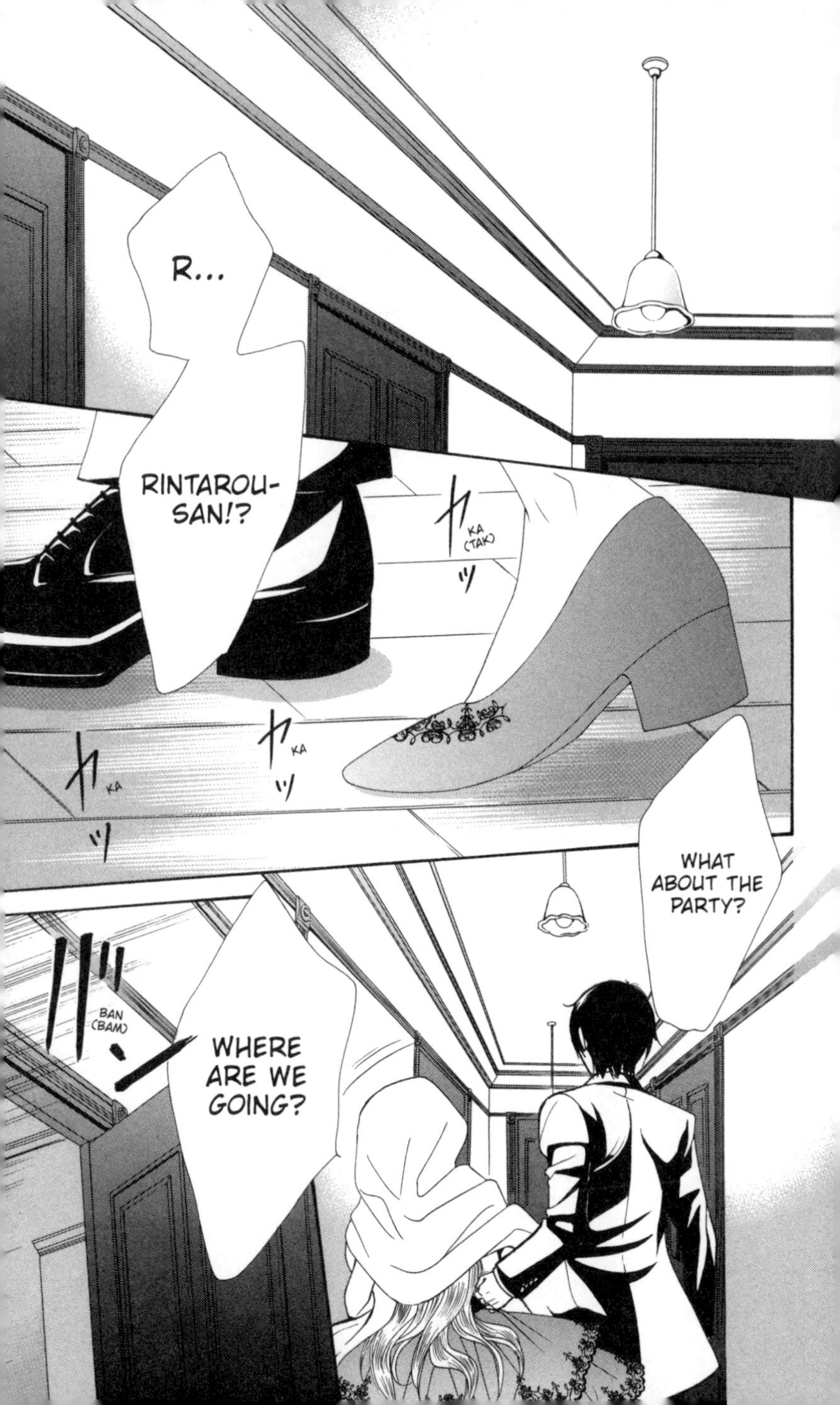

R...
RINTAROU-SAN!?
カ KA (TAK) ッ
カ KA ッ
カ KA ッ
WHAT ABOUT THE PARTY?
WHERE ARE WE GOING?
バ BAN (BAM) ン

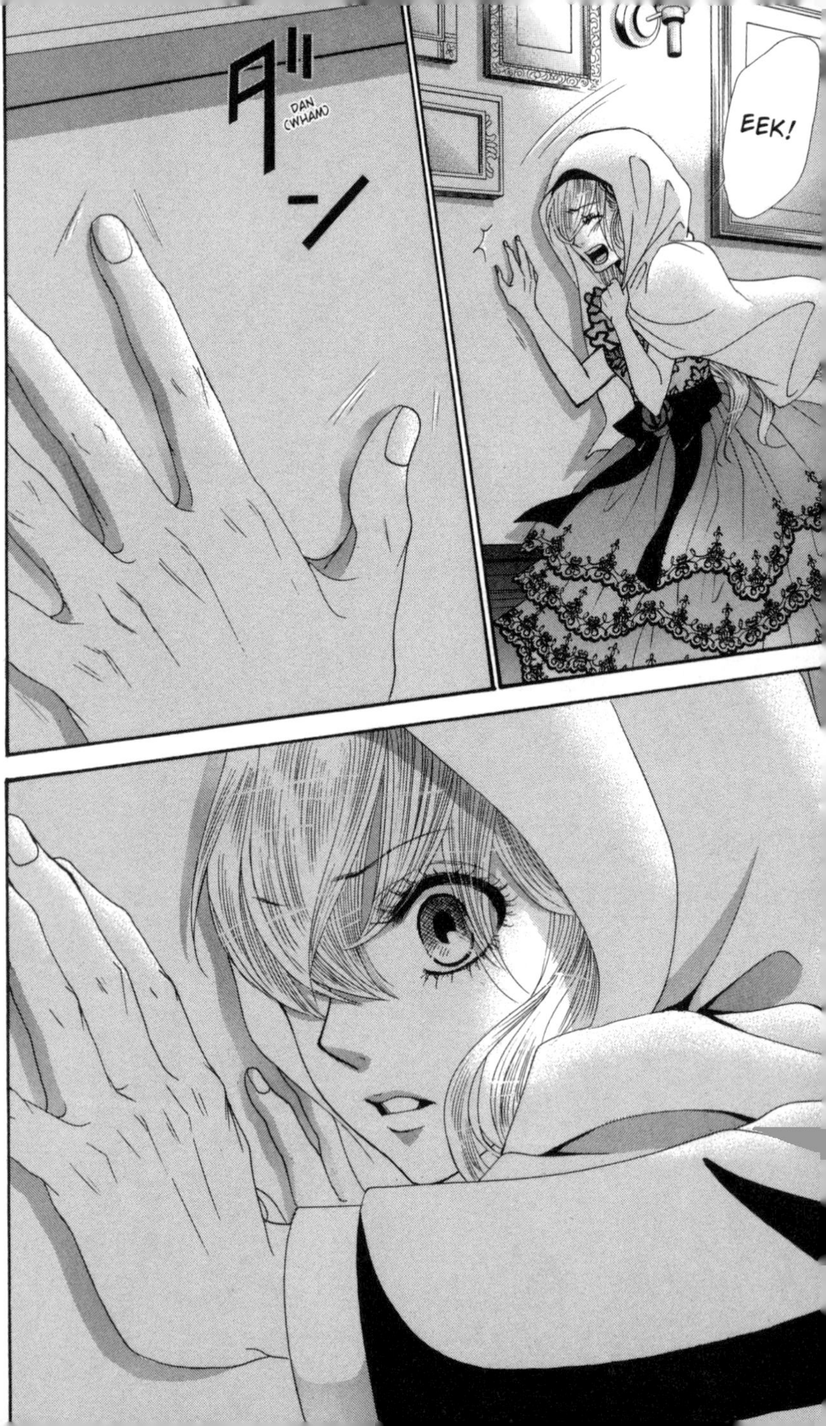
EEK!
ダン
DAN (WHAM)

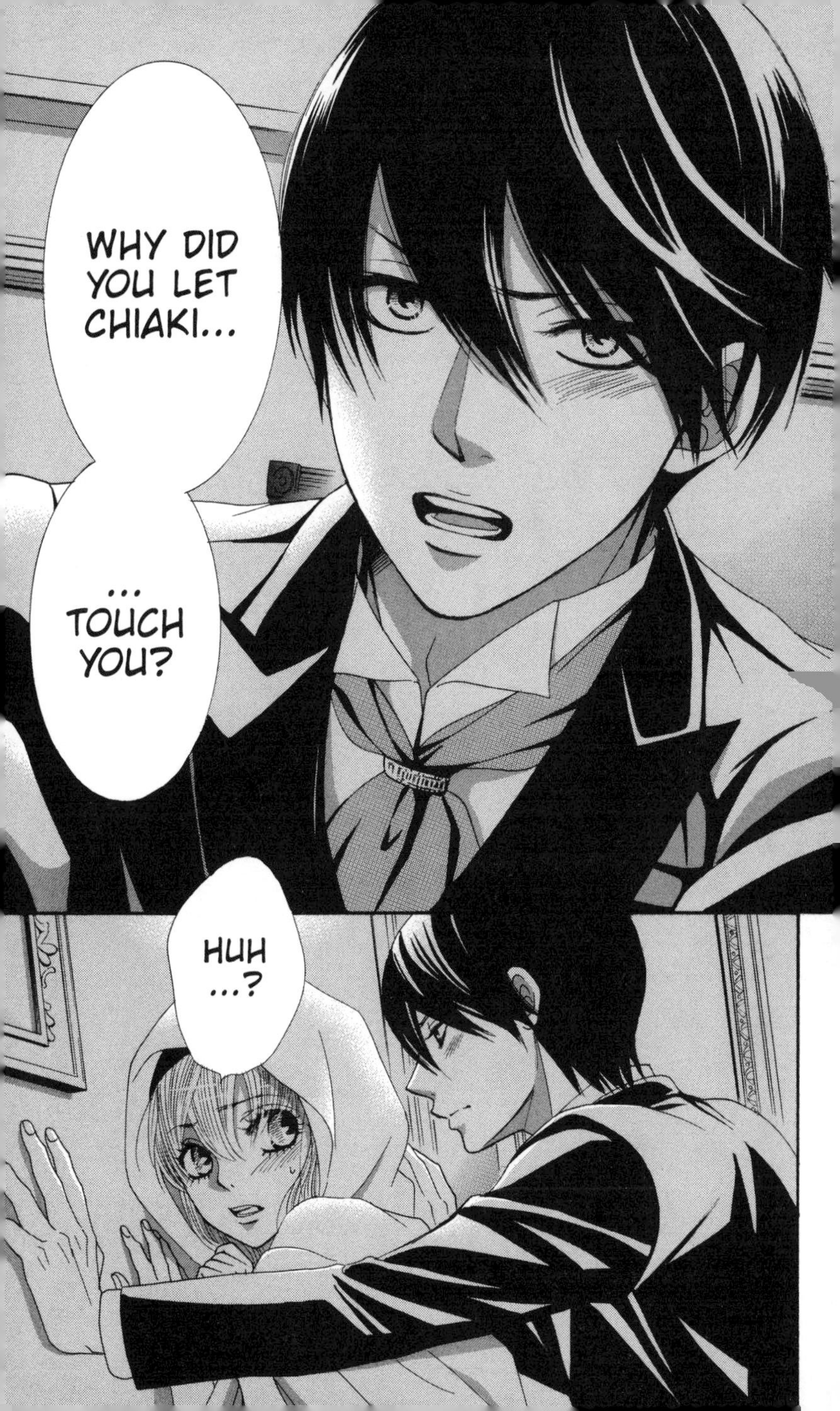
WHY DID YOU LET CHIAKI...
... TOUCH YOU?
HUH ...?

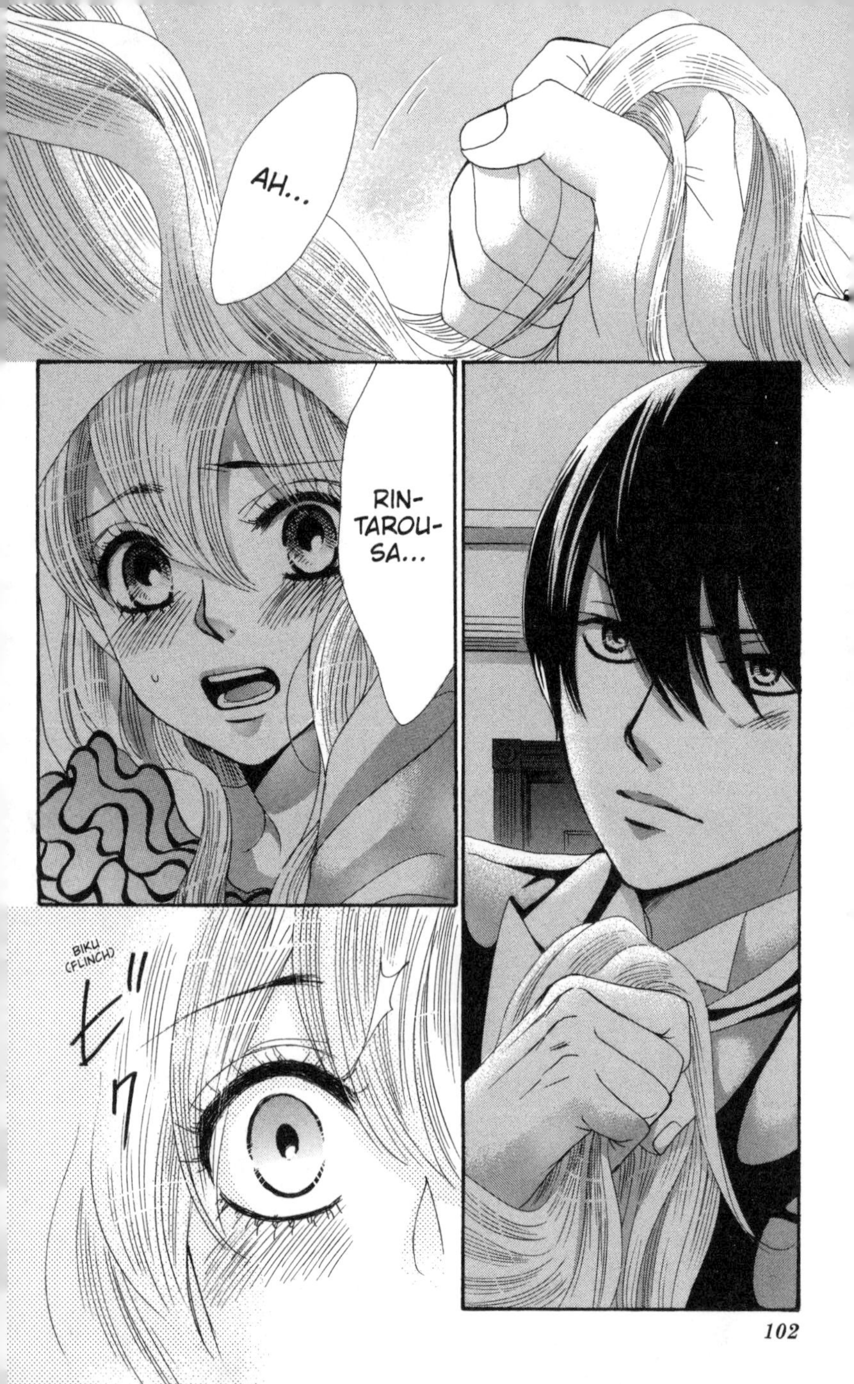
AH...
RIN-TAROU-SA...
BIKU (FLINCH)

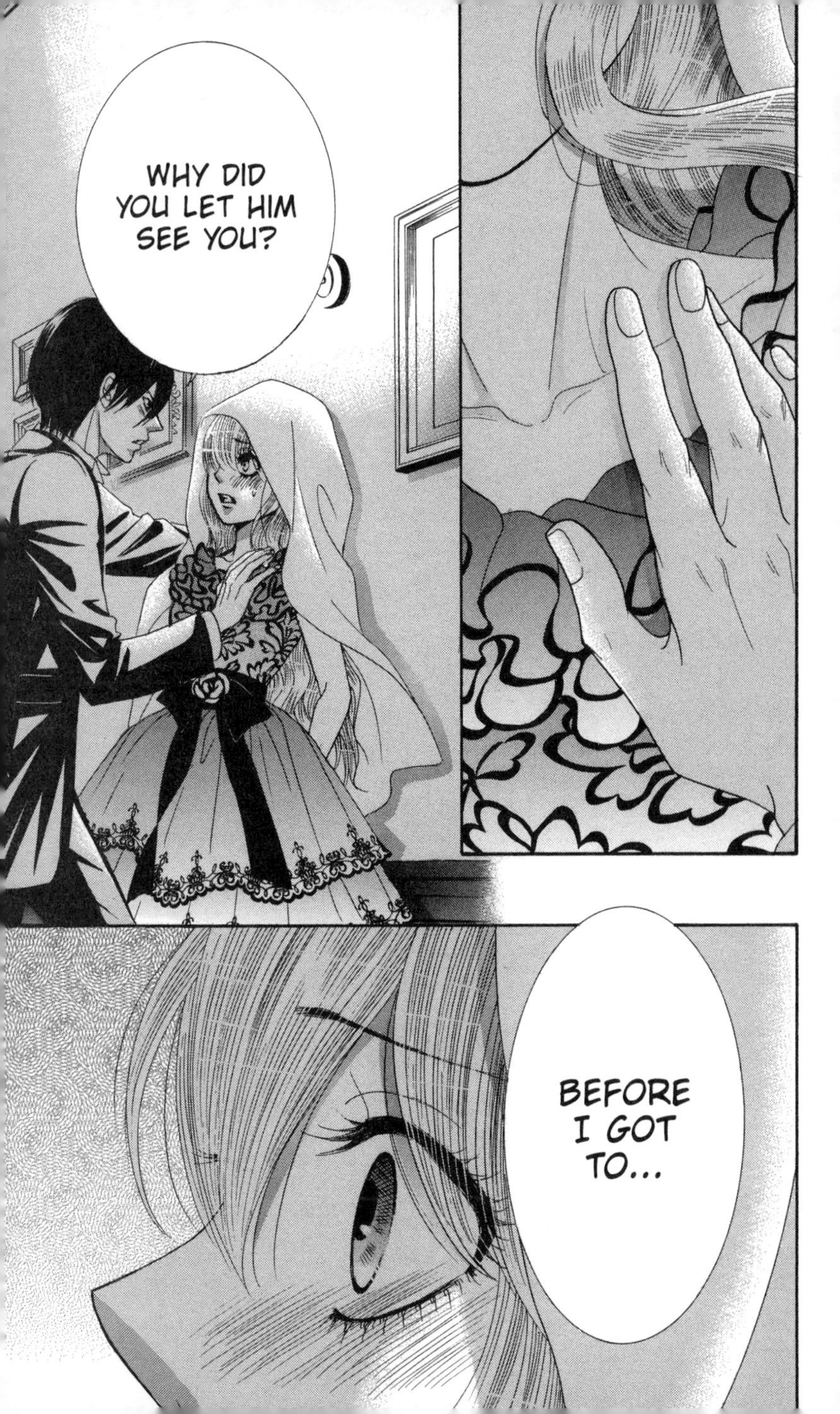
WHY DID YOU LET HIM SEE YOU?
BEFORE I GOT TO...

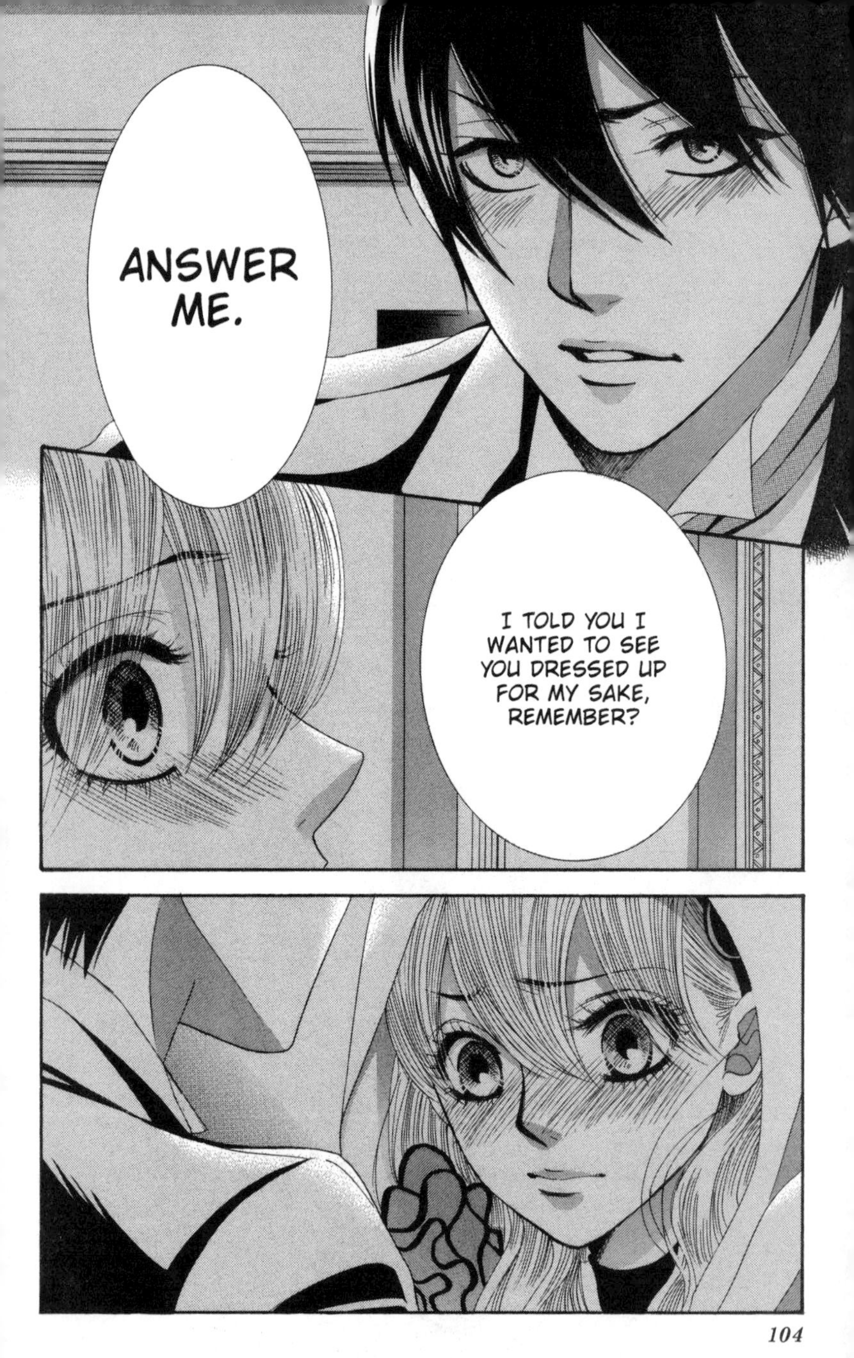
ANSWER ME.
I TOLD YOU I WANTED TO SEE YOU DRESSED UP FOR MY SAKE, REMEMBER?

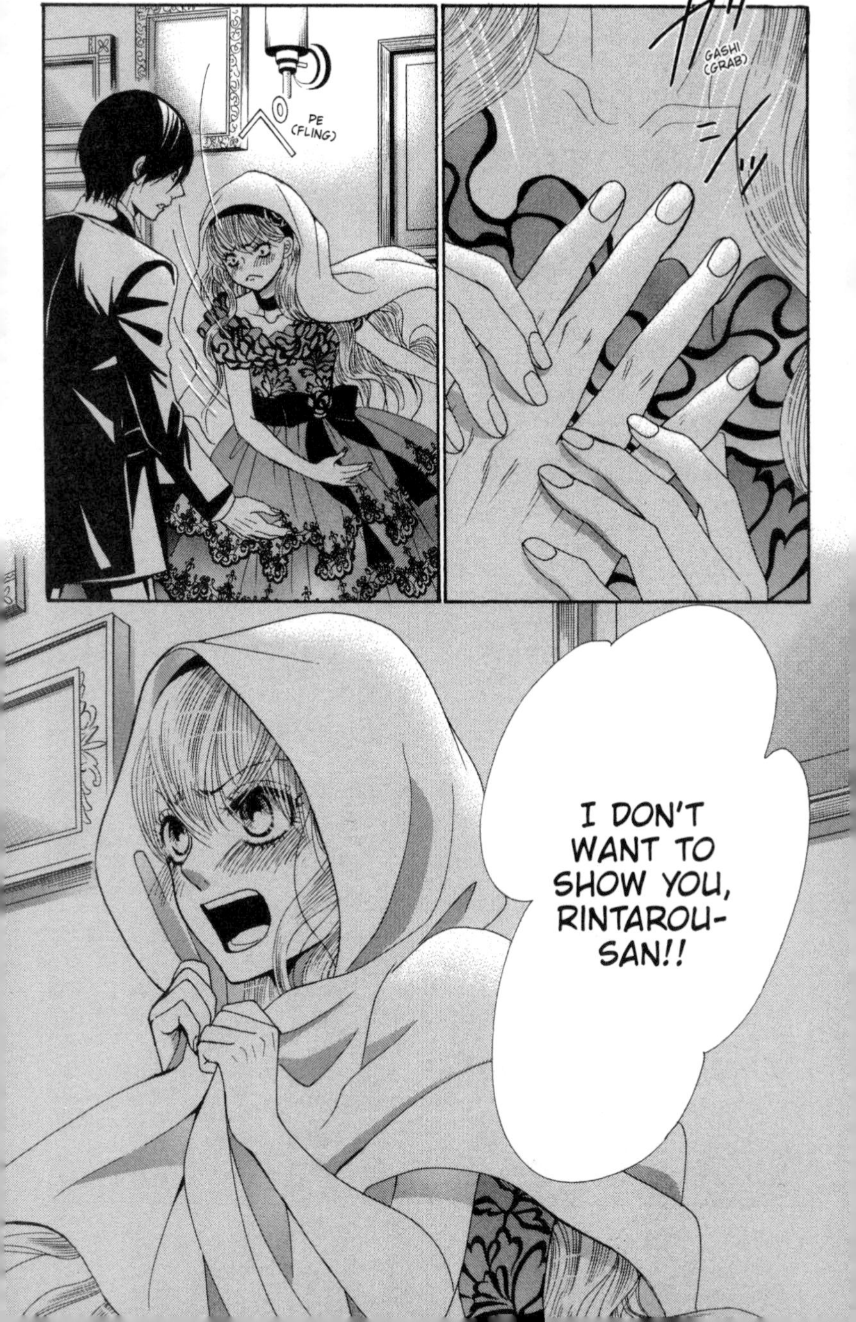
GASHI (GRAB)
PE (FLING)
I DON'T WANT TO SHOW YOU, RINTAROU-SAN!!

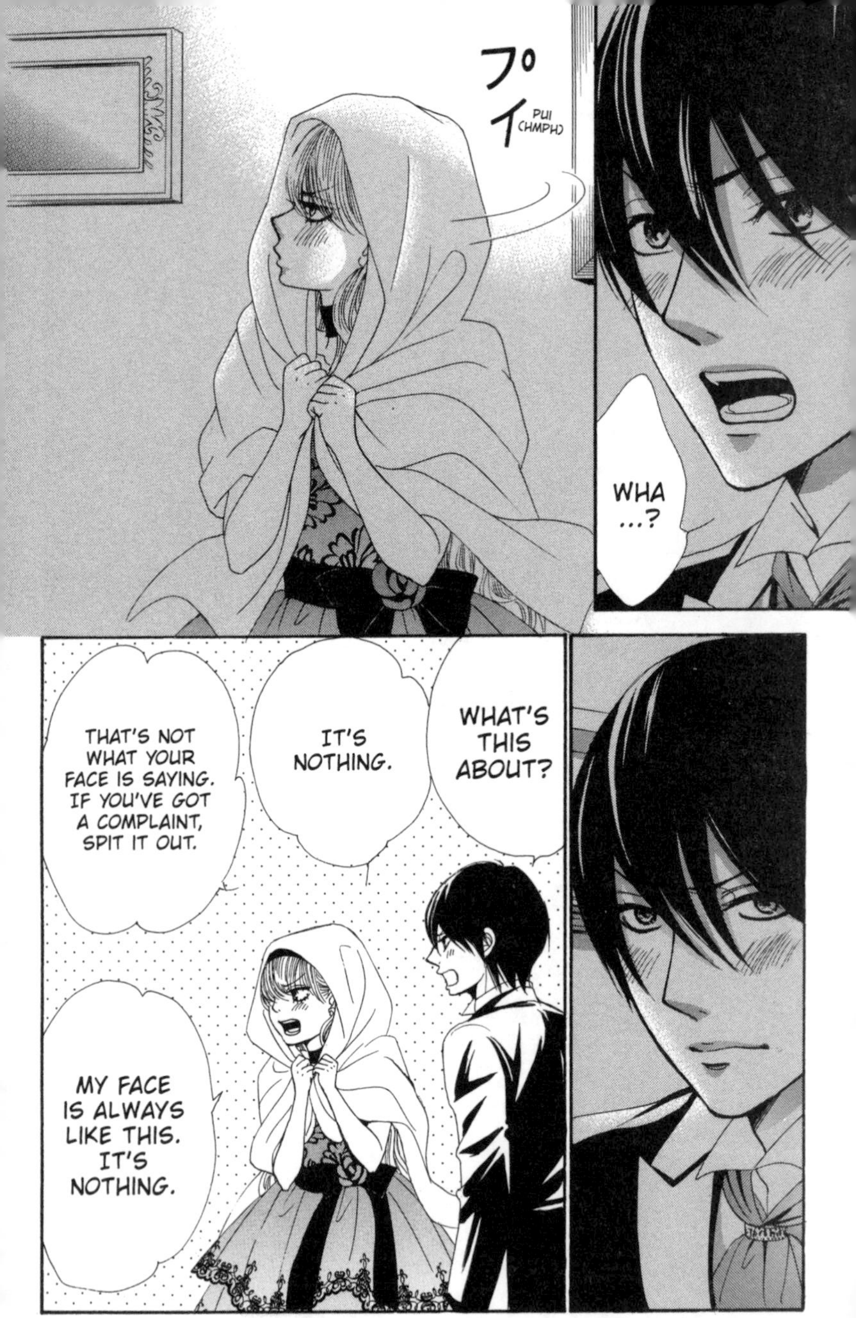
WHA ...?
プイ
PUI (HMPH)
WHAT'S THIS ABOUT?
IT'S NOTHING.
THAT'S NOT WHAT YOUR FACE IS SAYING. IF YOU'VE GOT A COMPLAINT, SPIT IT OUT.
MY FACE IS ALWAYS LIKE THIS. IT'S NOTHING.

AY—

AY OUN WANNOO.
(I DON'T WANT TO.)

….!

むに
MUNI
(PINCH)

LOOK AT ME!

LET GO OF ME.

I WILL ONCE YOU TELL ME WHY, PROPERLY.

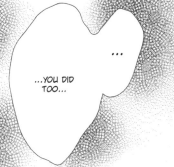

…

…YOU DID TOO…

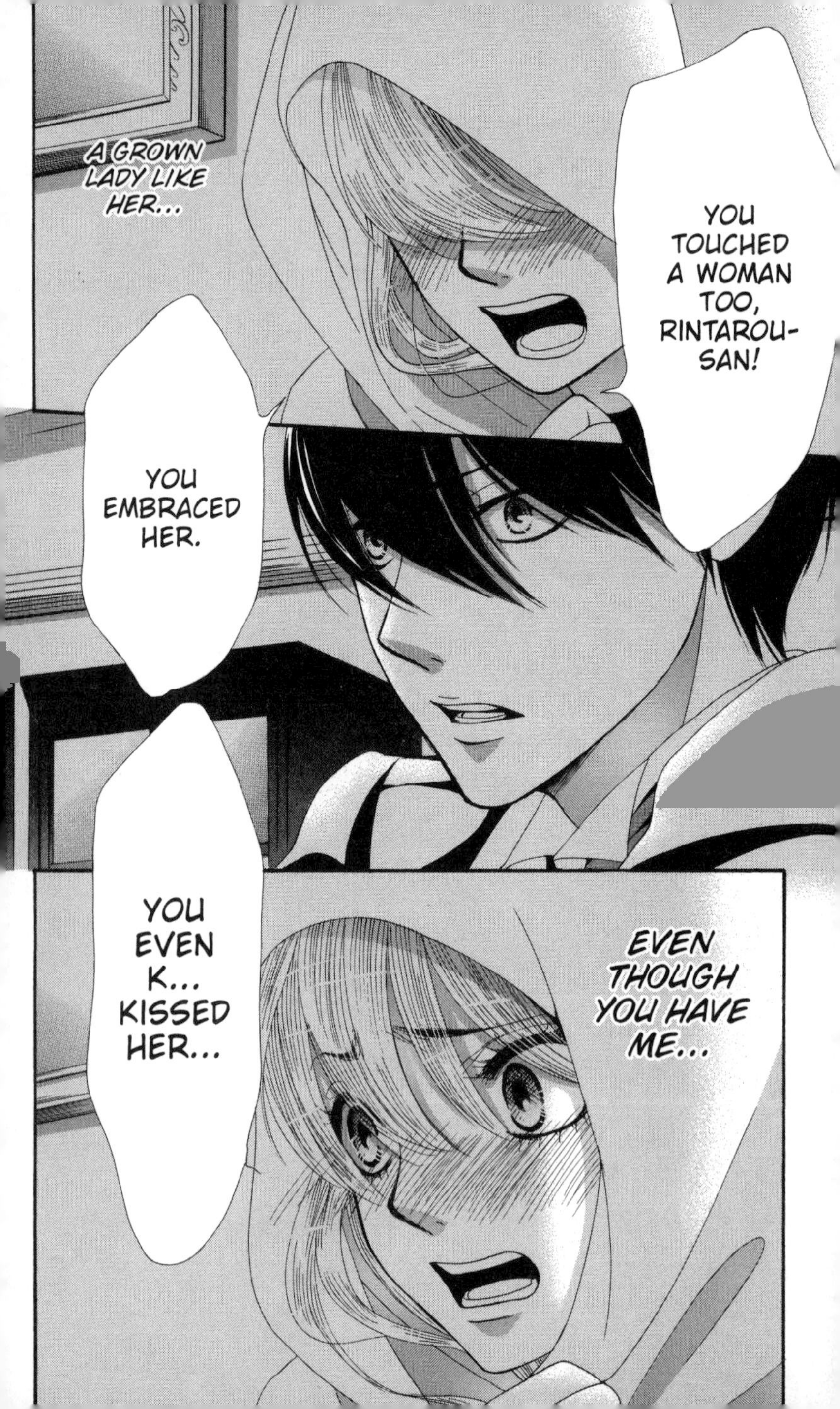
YOU TOUCHED A WOMAN TOO, RINTAROU-SAN!
A GROWN LADY LIKE HER...
YOU EMBRACED HER.
EVEN THOUGH YOU HAVE ME...
YOU EVEN K... KISSED HER...

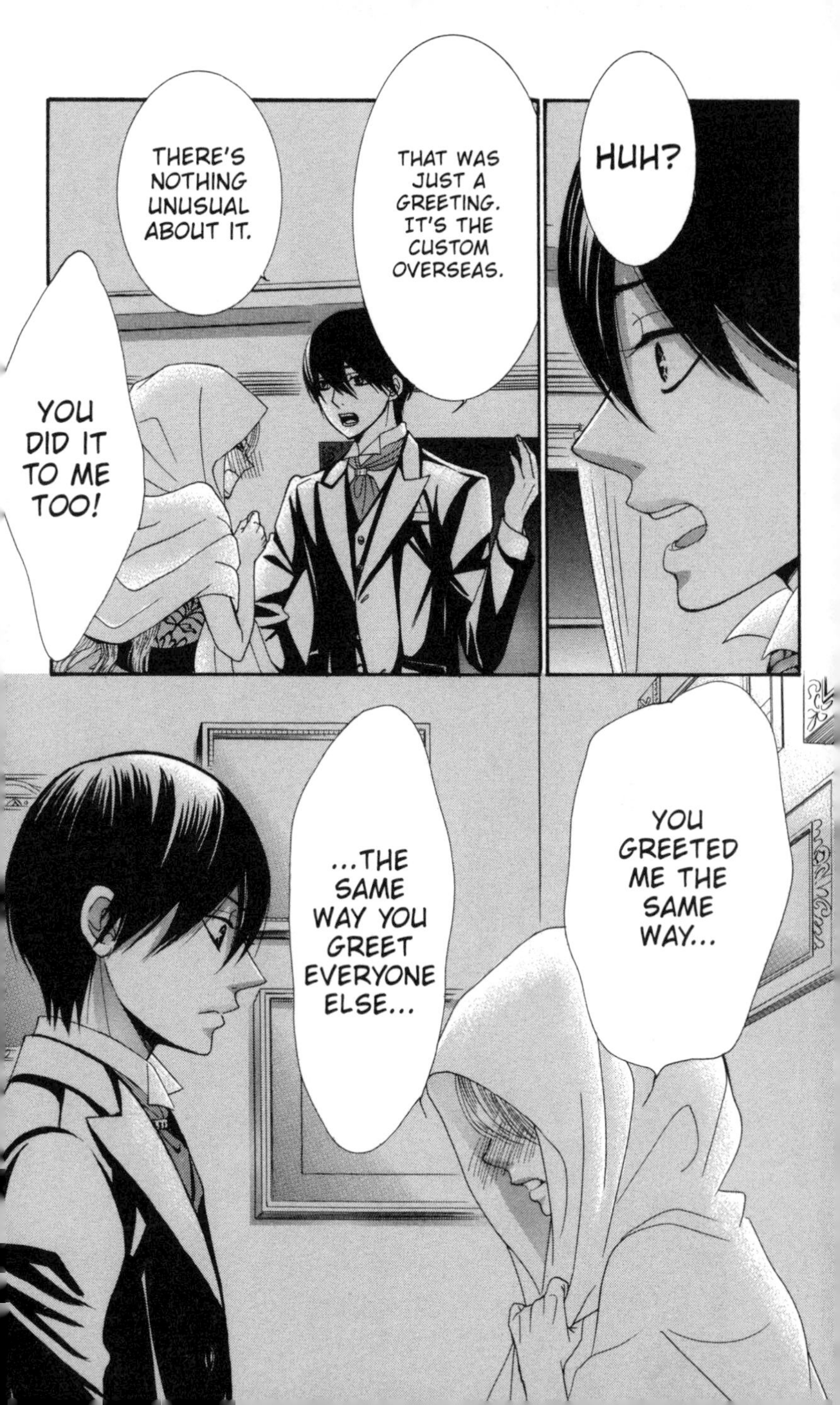
HUH?
THAT WAS JUST A GREETING. IT'S THE CUSTOM OVERSEAS.
THERE'S NOTHING UNUSUAL ABOUT IT.
YOU DID IT TO ME TOO!
YOU GREETED ME THE SAME WAY...
...THE SAME WAY YOU GREET EVERYONE ELSE...

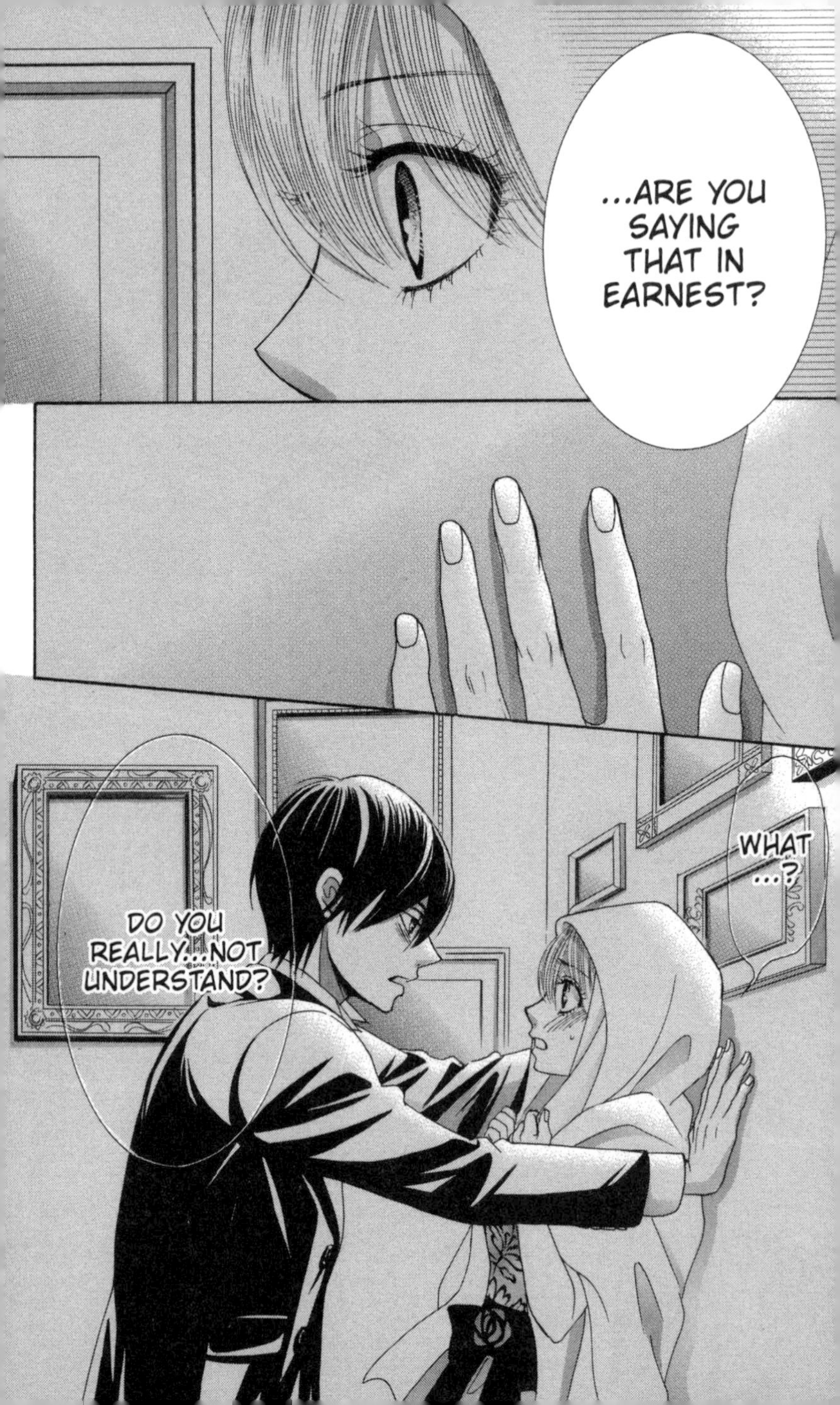
...ARE YOU SAYING THAT IN EARNEST?
WHAT ...?
DO YOU REALLY...NOT UNDERSTAND?

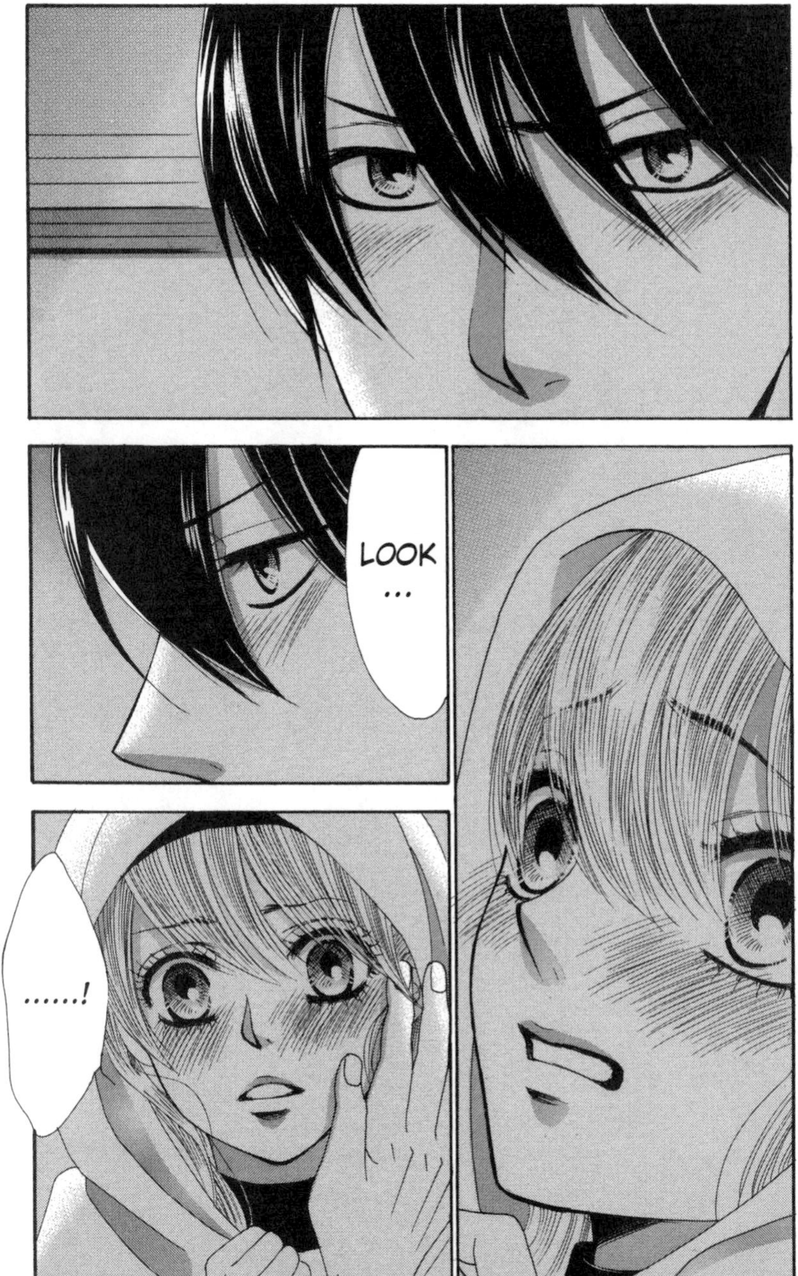

LOOK...
......!

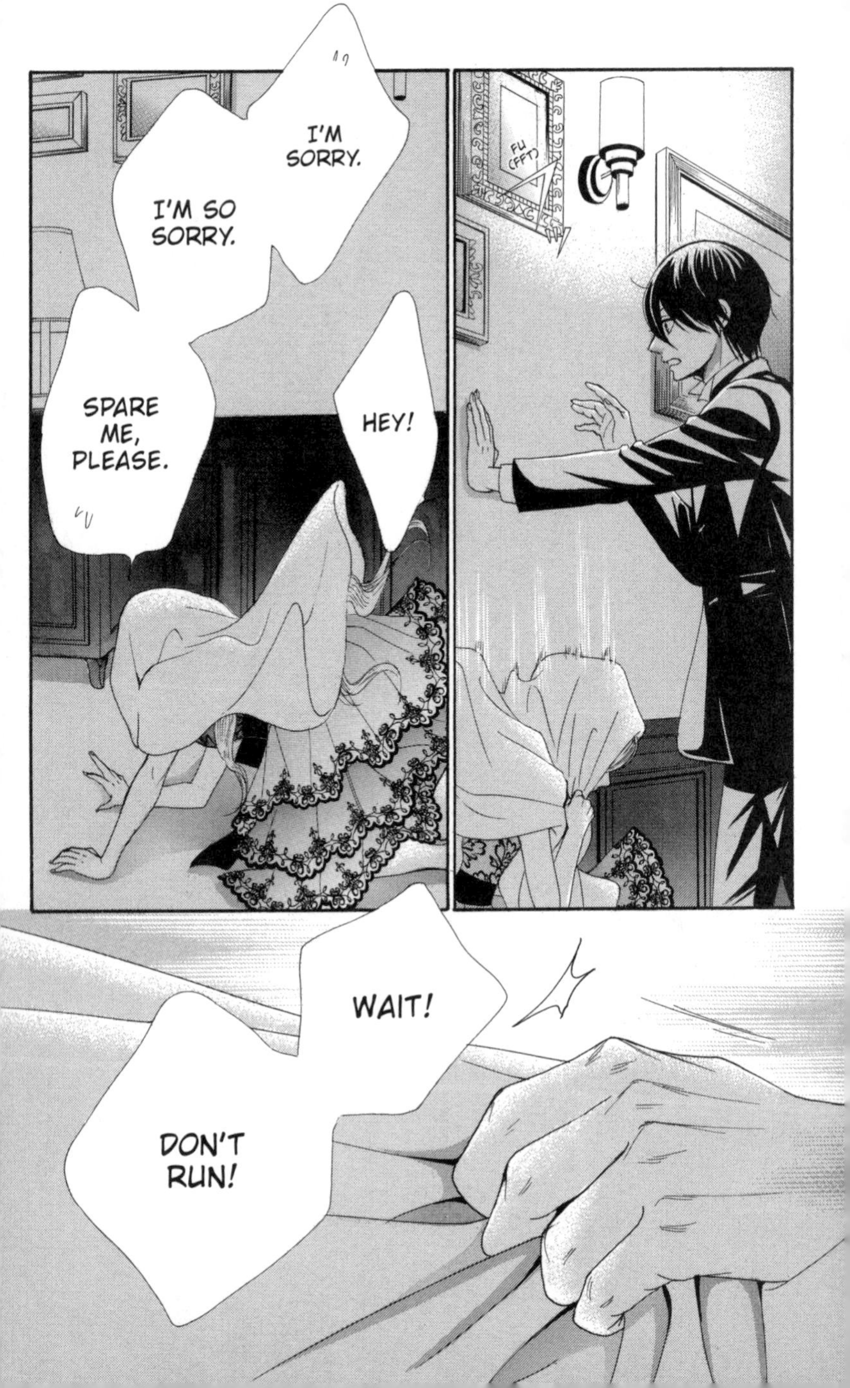
FU (FFT)
I'M SORRY.
I'M SO SORRY.
HEY!
SPARE ME, PLEASE.
WAIT!
DON'T RUN!

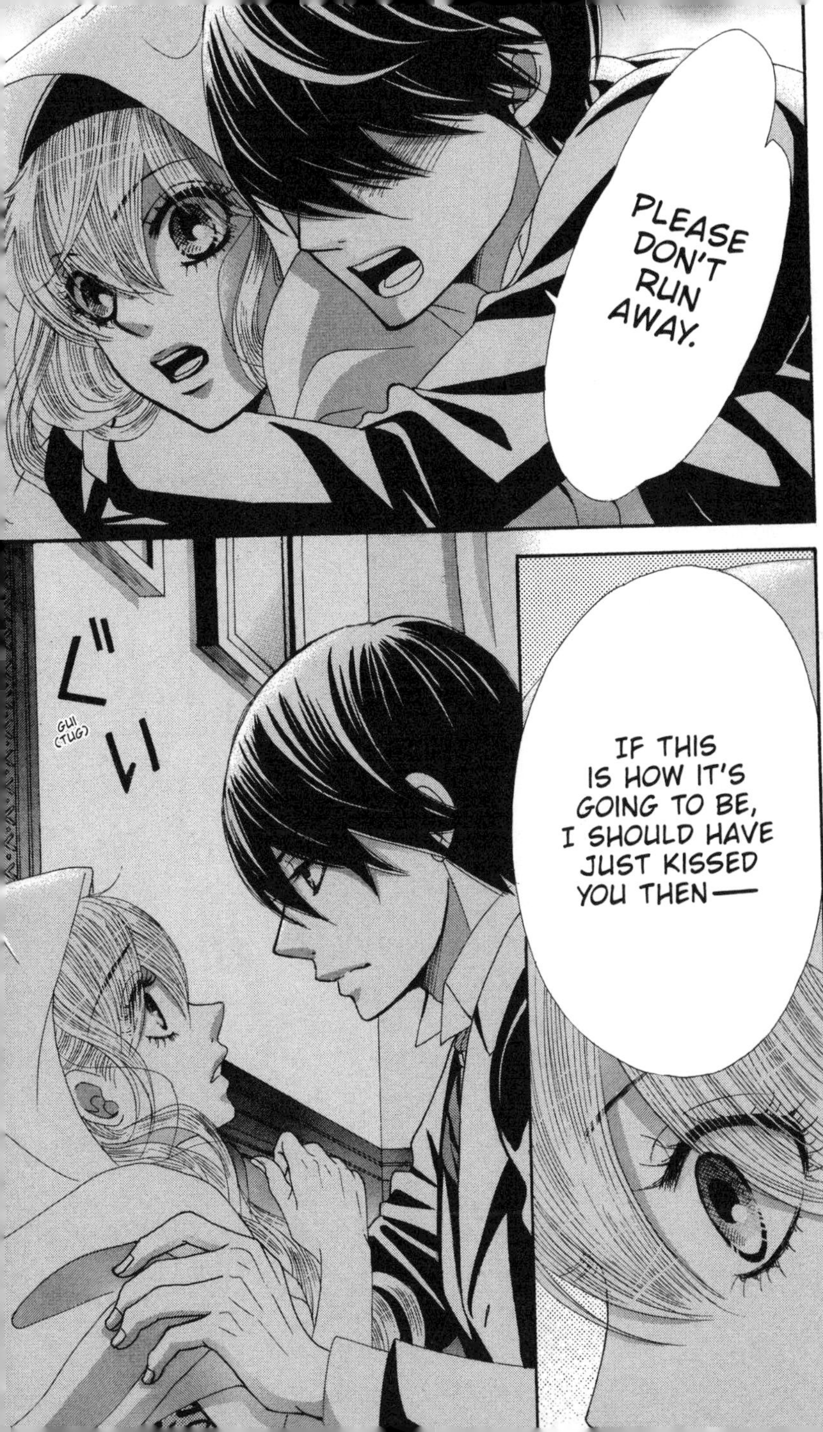
PLEASE DON'T RUN AWAY.
IF THIS IS HOW IT'S GOING TO BE, I SHOULD HAVE JUST KISSED YOU THEN—
じい
GUI (TUG)

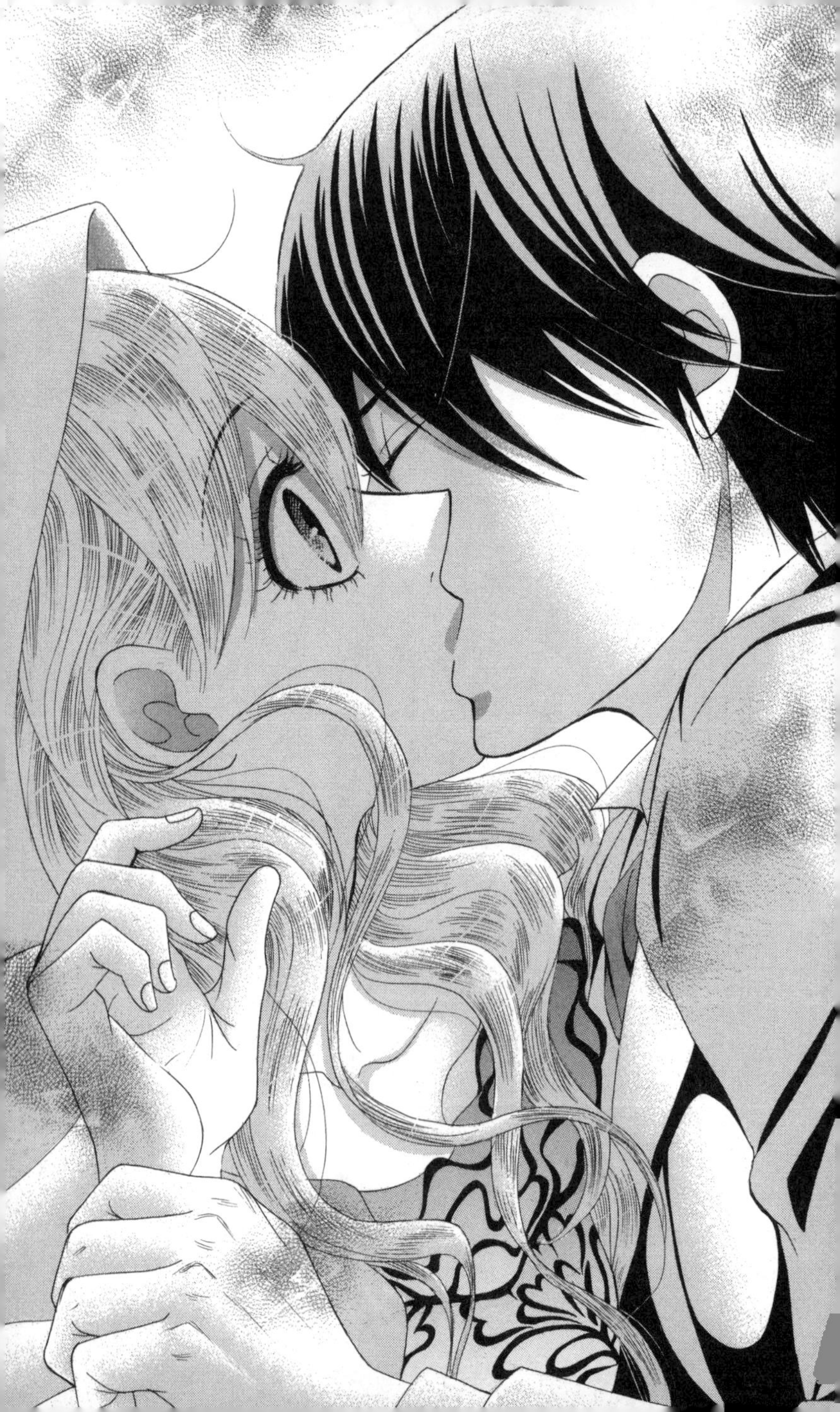

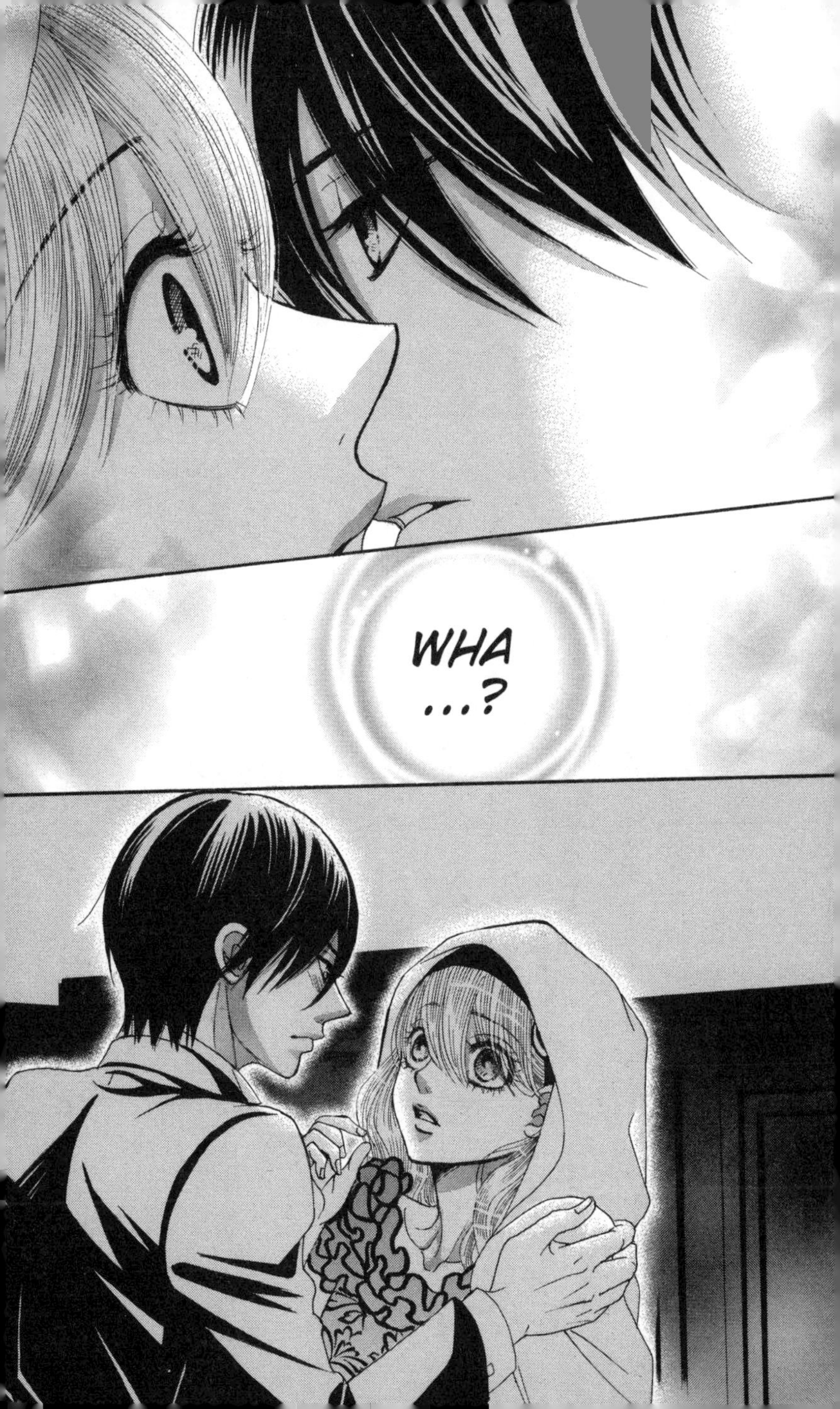
WHA
...?

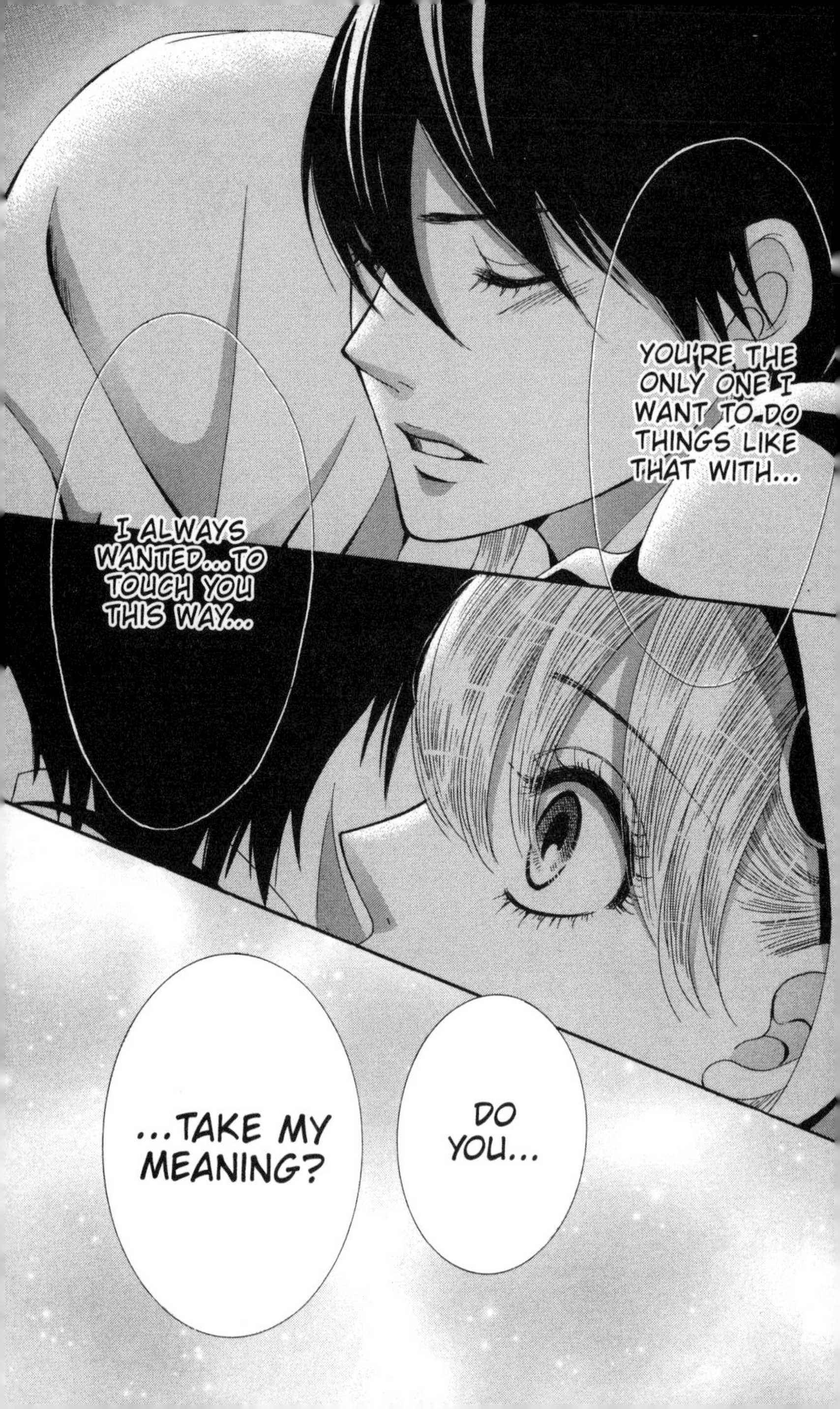
YOU'RE THE ONLY ONE I WANT TO DO THINGS LIKE THAT WITH...
I ALWAYS WANTED...TO TOUCH YOU THIS WAY...
DO YOU...
...TAKE MY MEANING?

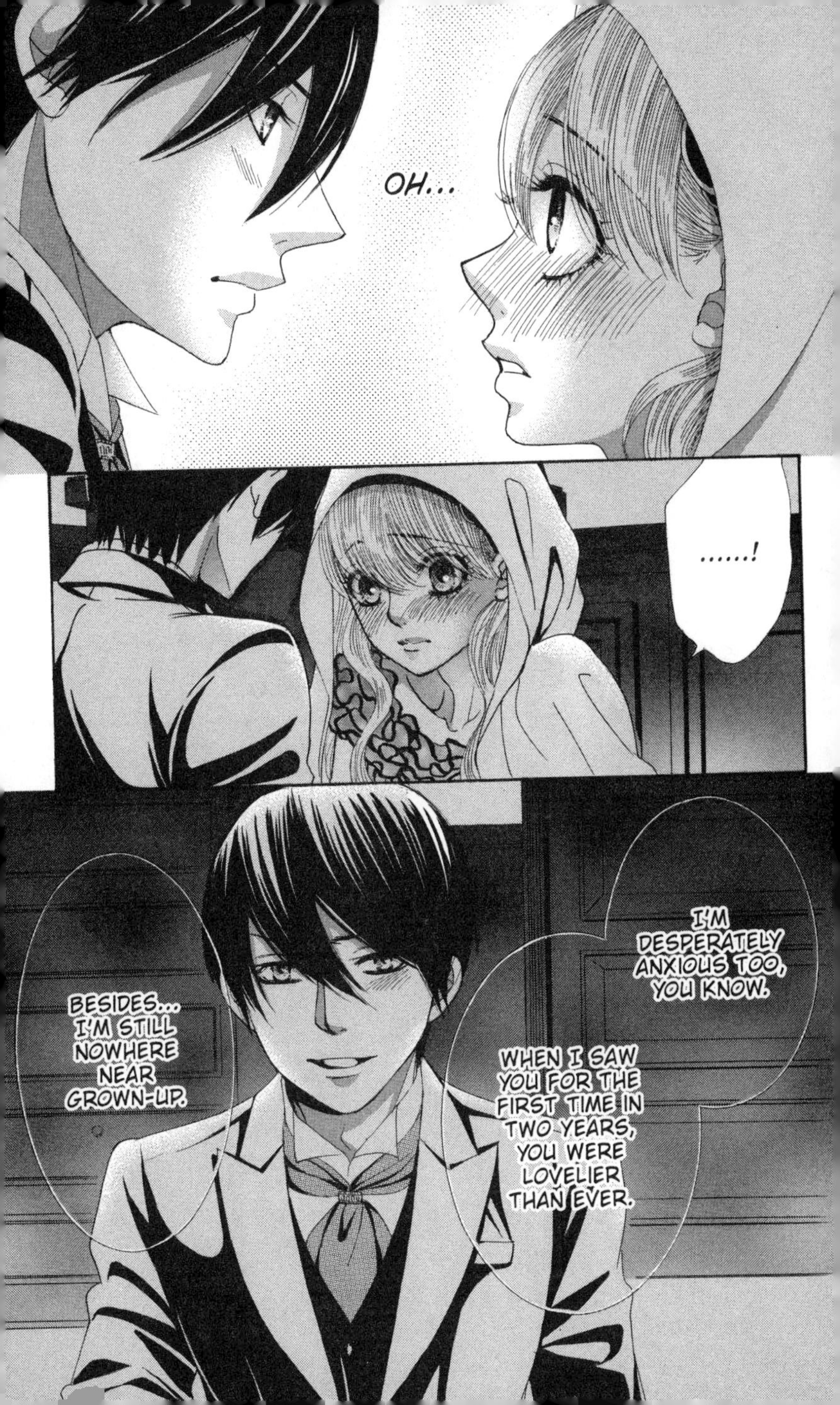
OH...
......!
I'M DESPERATELY ANXIOUS TOO, YOU KNOW.
WHEN I SAW YOU FOR THE FIRST TIME IN TWO YEARS, YOU WERE LOVELIER THAN EVER.
BESIDES... I'M STILL NOWHERE NEAR GROWN-UP.

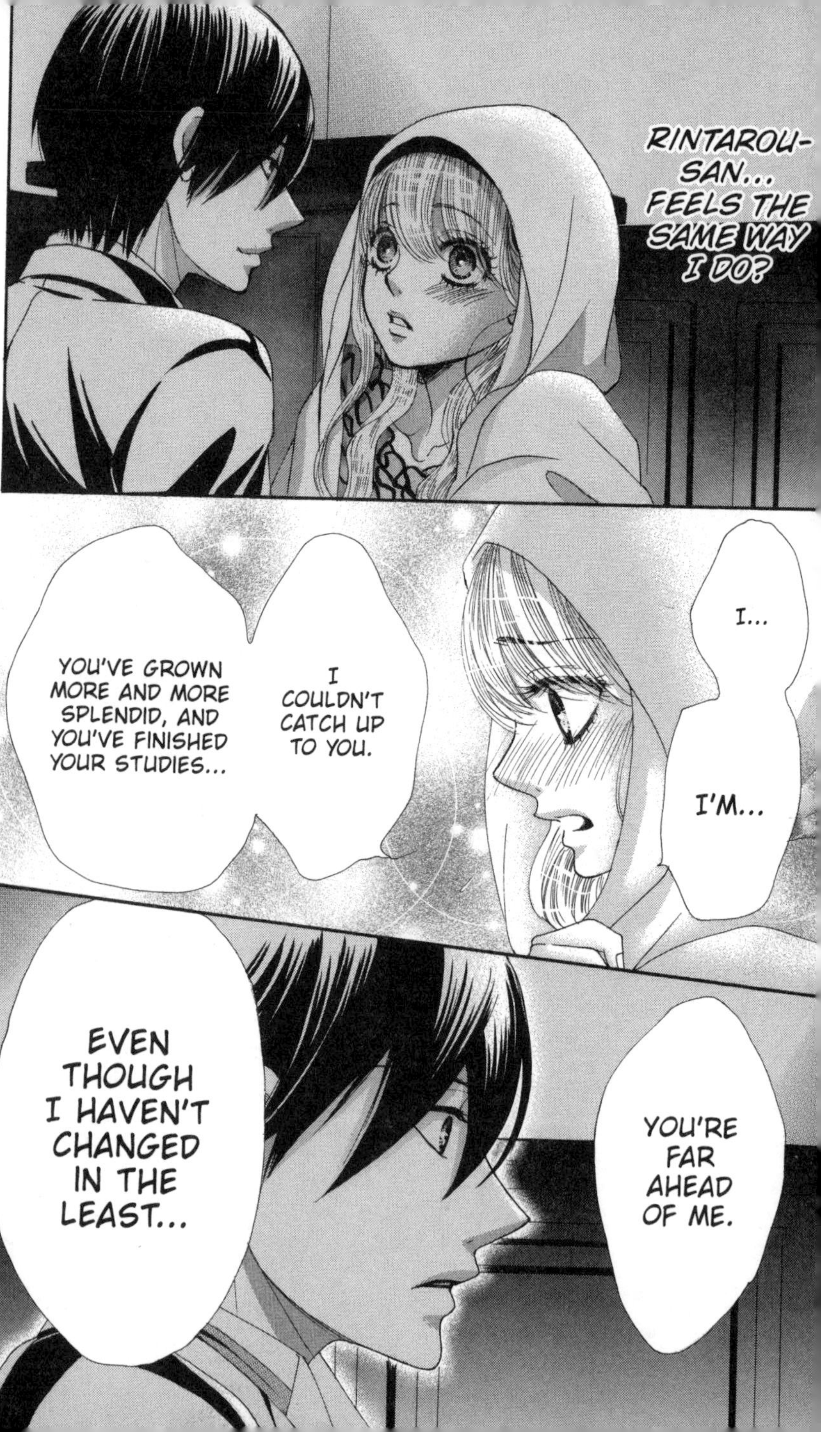
RINTAROU-SAN... FEELS THE SAME WAY I DO?
I...
I'M...
I COULDN'T CATCH UP TO YOU.
YOU'VE GROWN MORE AND MORE SPLENDID, AND YOU'VE FINISHED YOUR STUDIES...
YOU'RE FAR AHEAD OF ME.
EVEN THOUGH I HAVEN'T CHANGED IN THE LEAST...

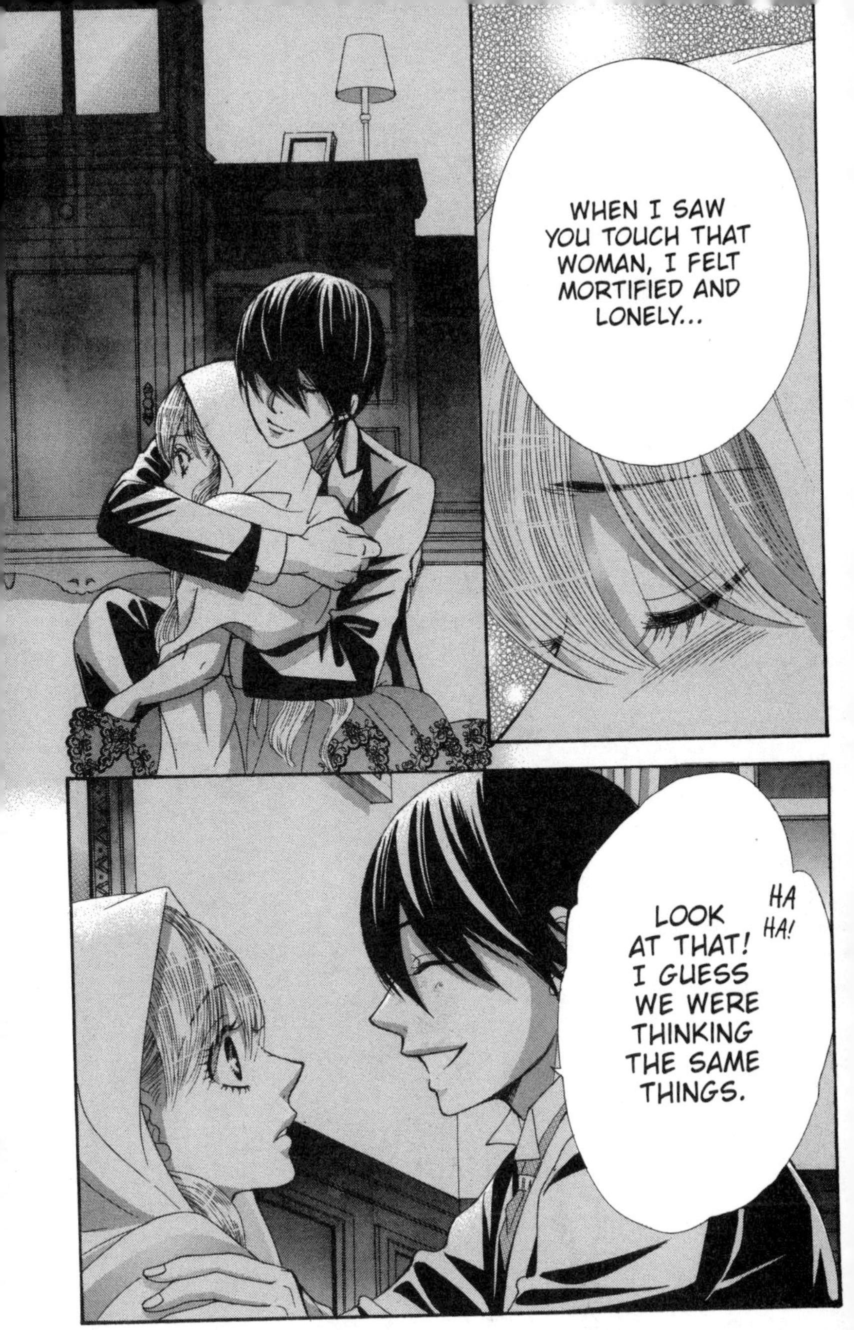
WHEN I SAW YOU TOUCH THAT WOMAN, I FELT MORTIFIED AND LONELY...
HA HA!
LOOK AT THAT! I GUESS WE WERE THINKING THE SAME THINGS.

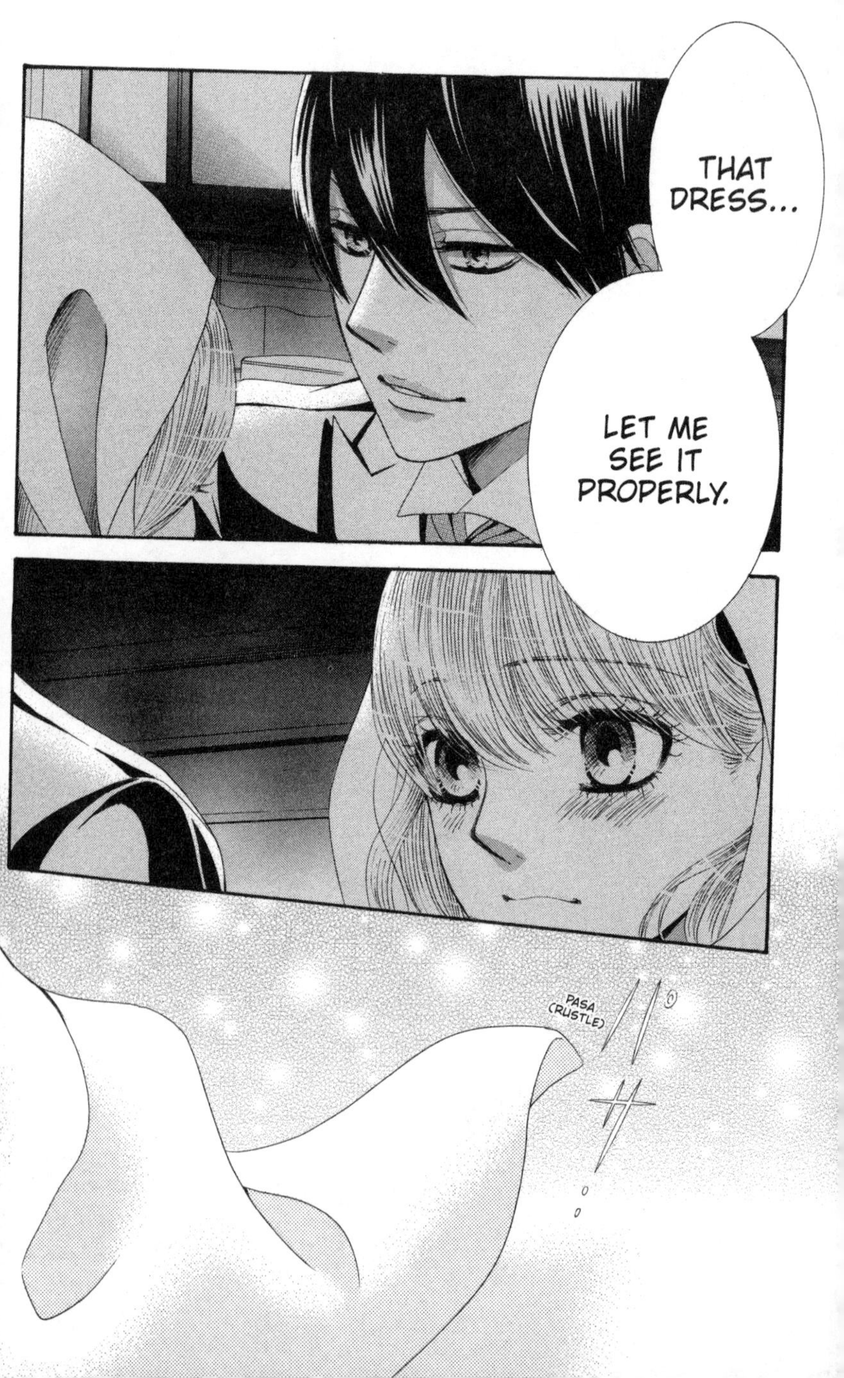
THAT DRESS...
LET ME SEE IT PROPERLY.
PASA (RUSTLE)

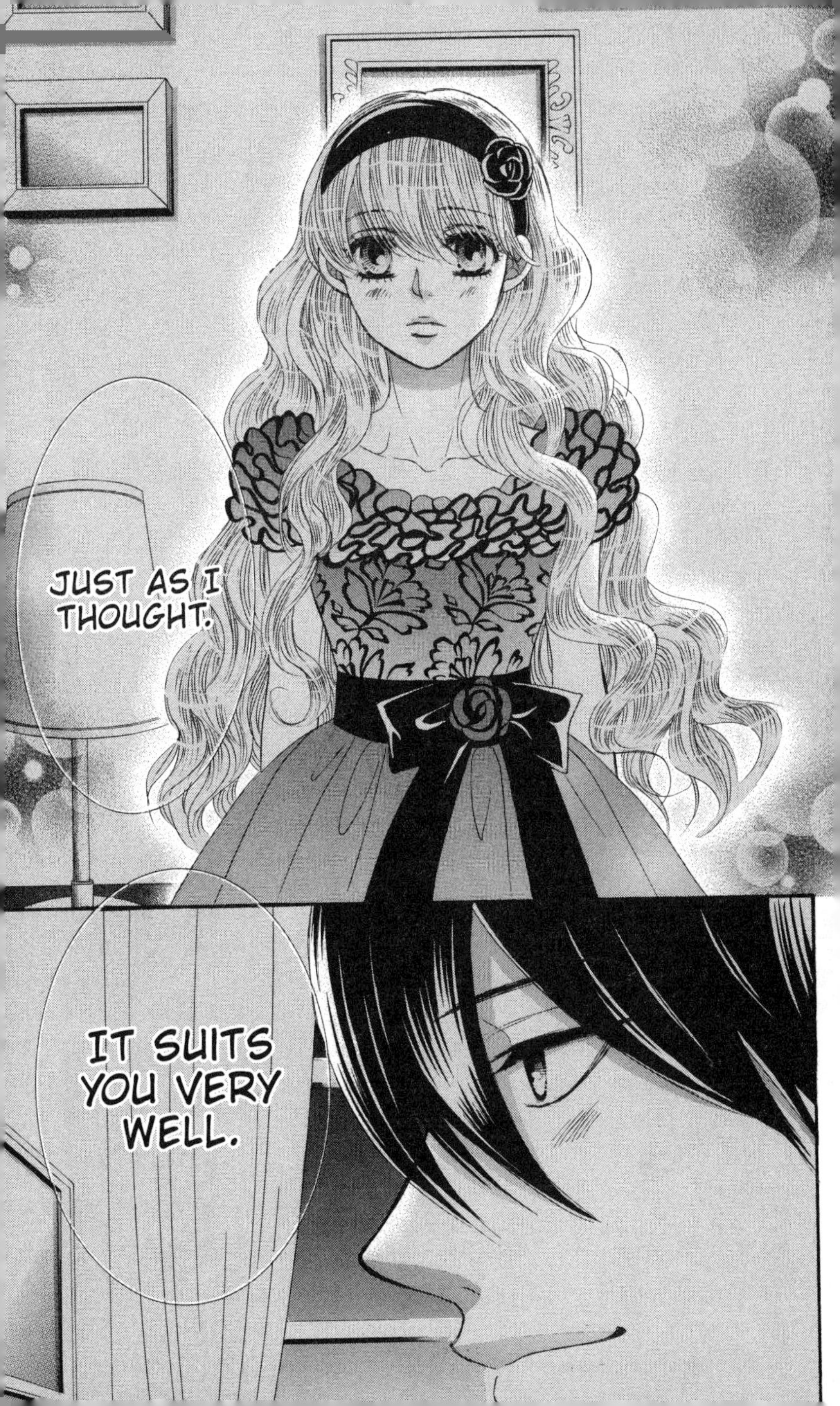
JUST AS I THOUGHT.
IT SUITS YOU VERY WELL.

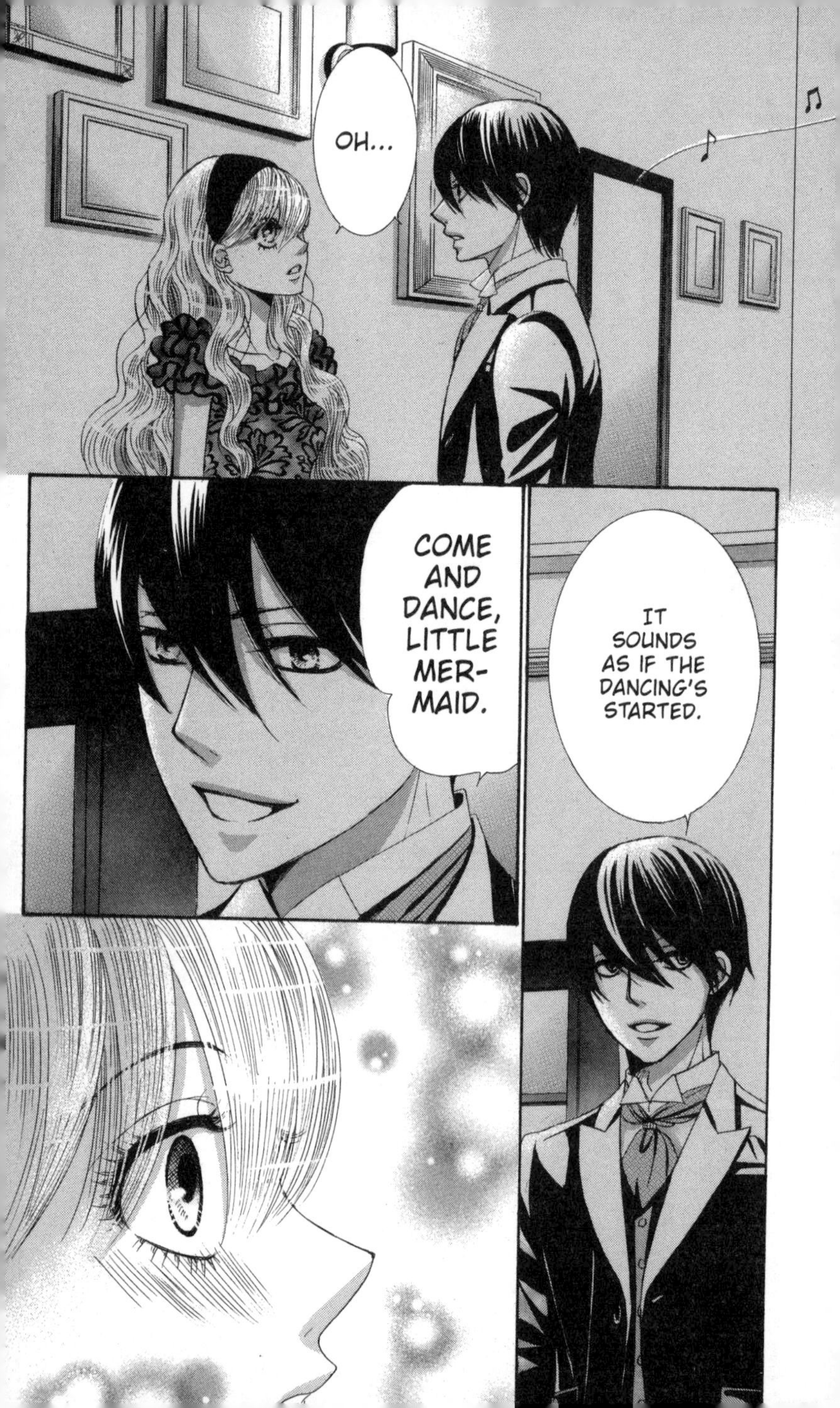
OH...
IT SOUNDS AS IF THE DANCING'S STARTED.
COME AND DANCE, LITTLE MER-MAID.

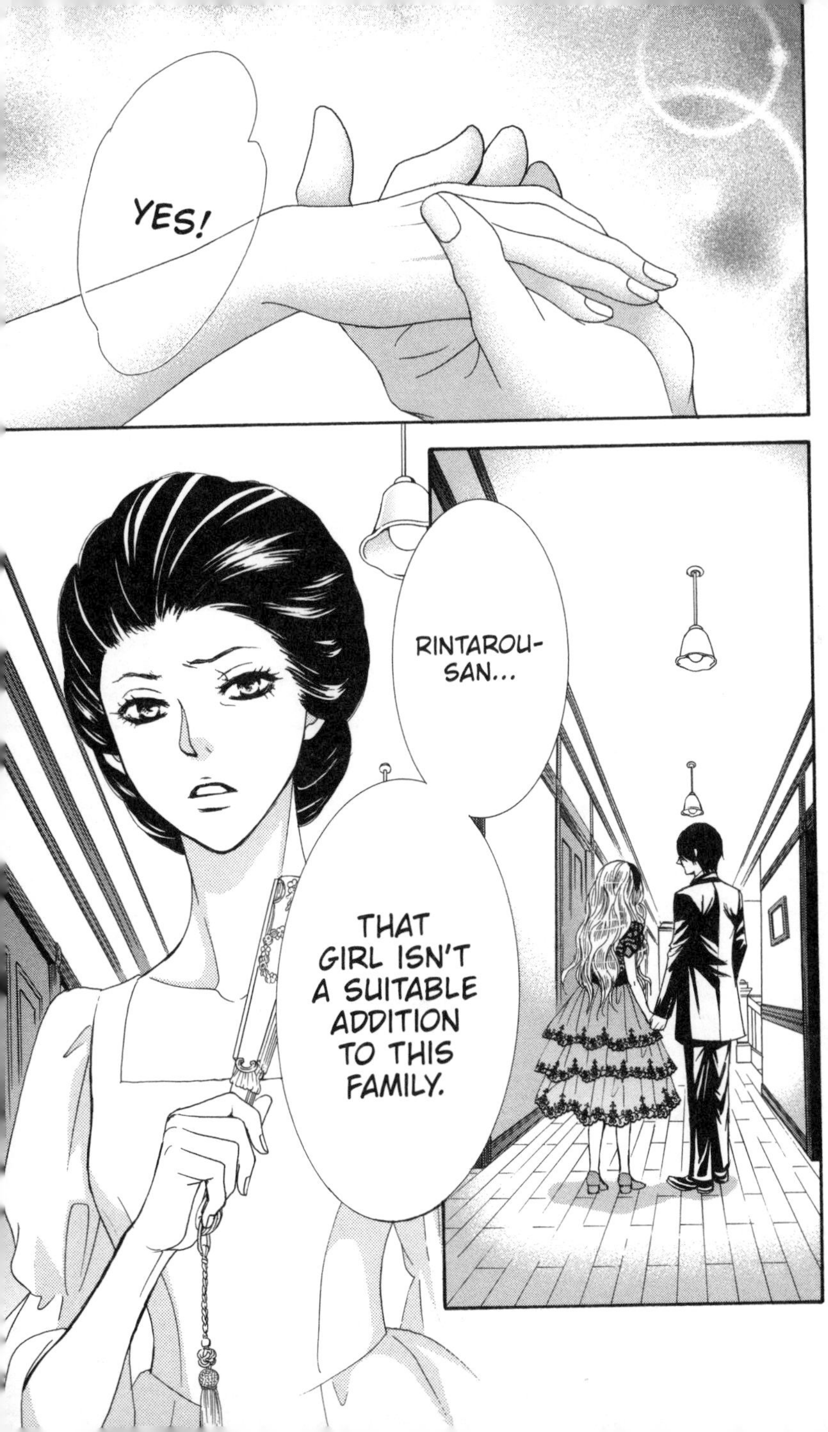
YES!
RINTAROU-SAN...
THAT GIRL ISN'T A SUITABLE ADDITION TO THIS FAMILY.

Episode 15

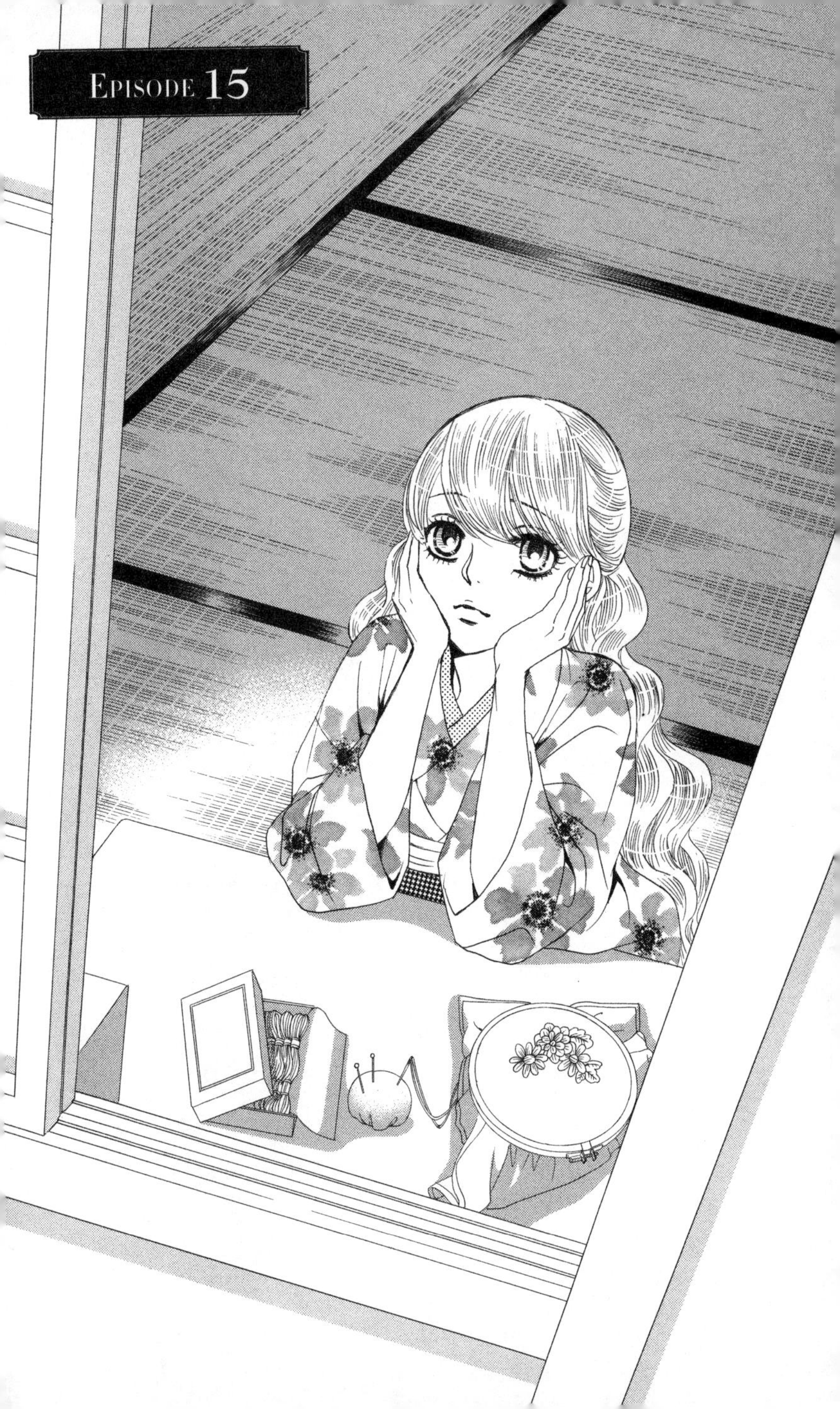

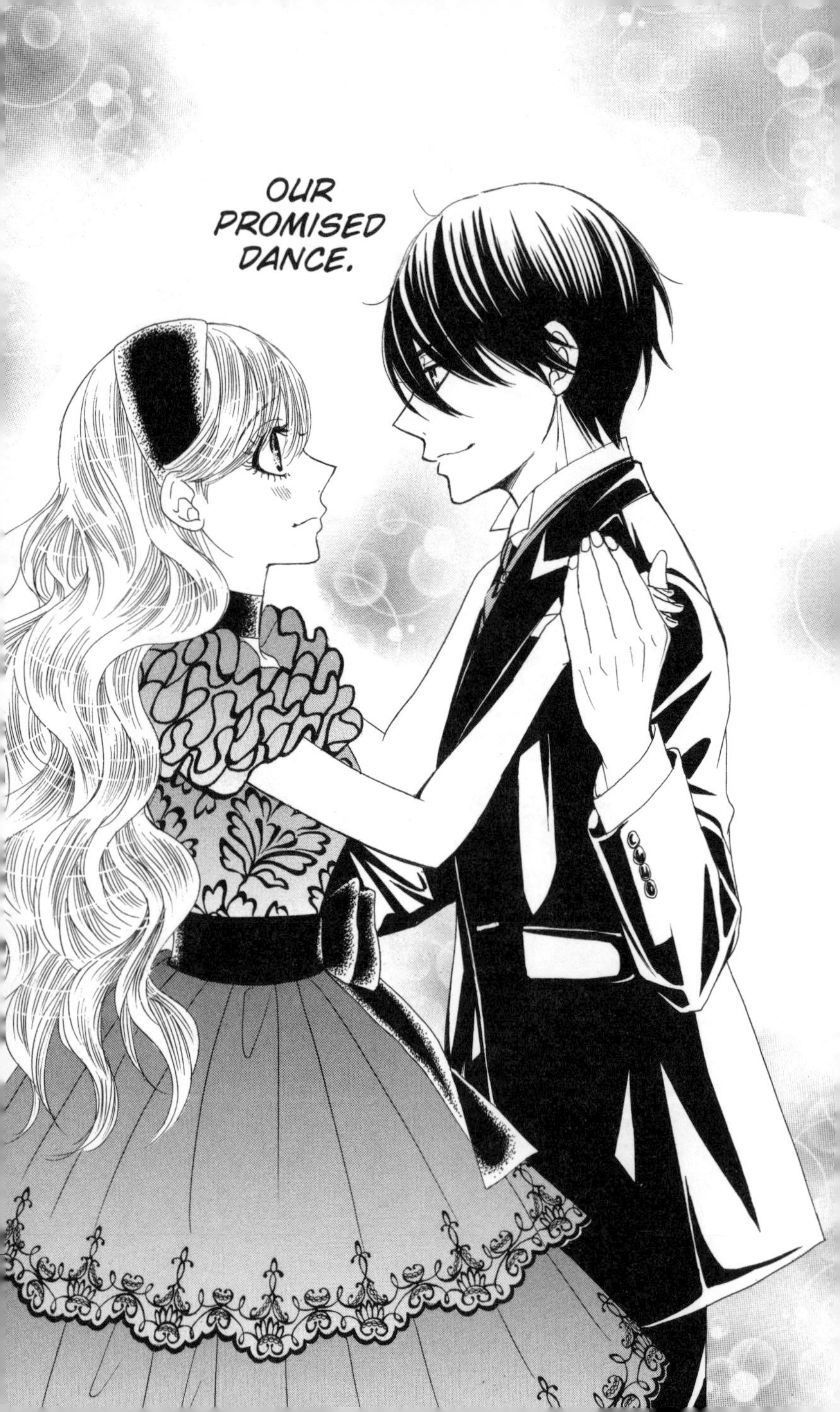
OUR PROMISED DANCE.

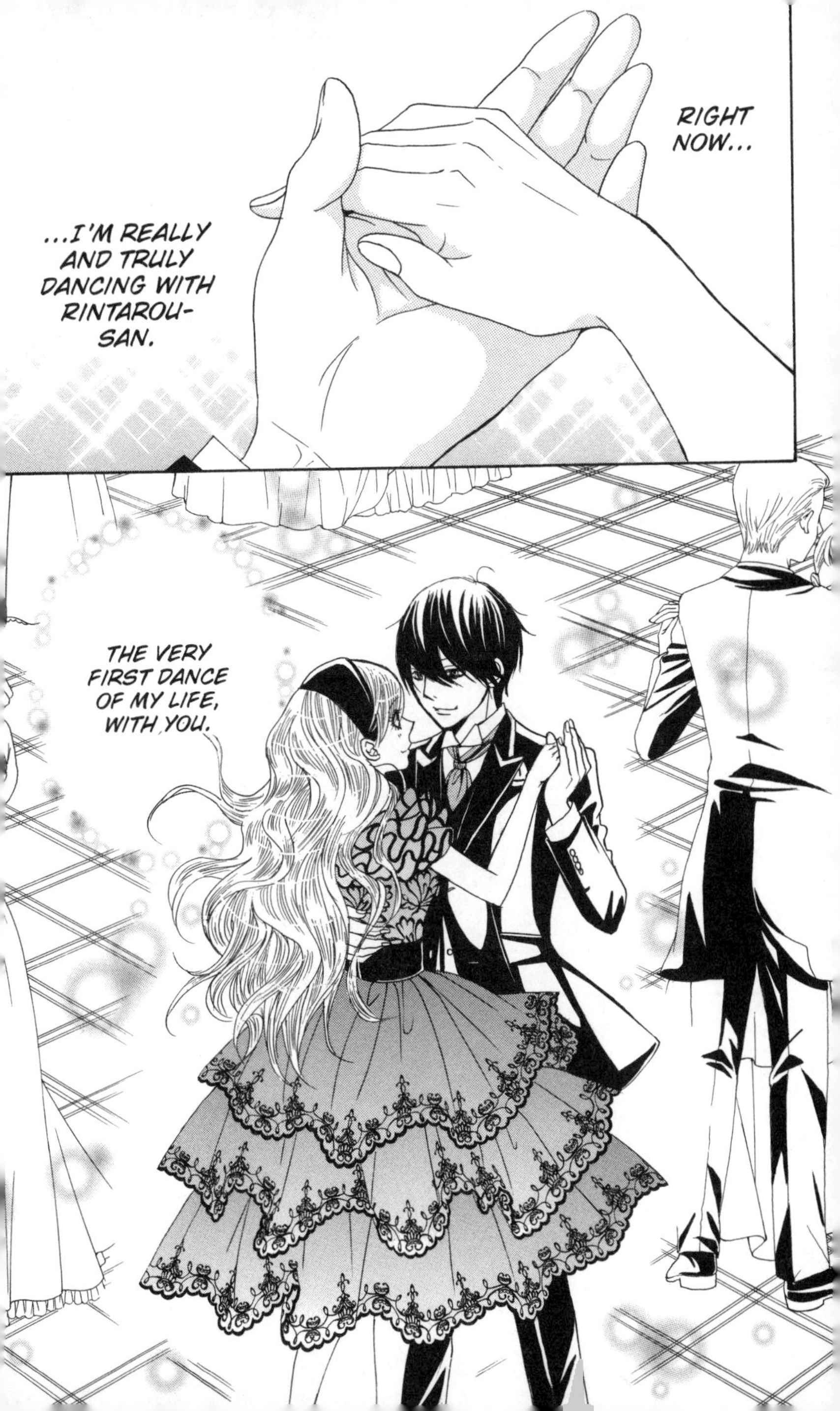
RIGHT NOW...
...I'M REALLY AND TRULY DANCING WITH RINTAROU-SAN.
THE VERY FIRST DANCE OF MY LIFE, WITH YOU.

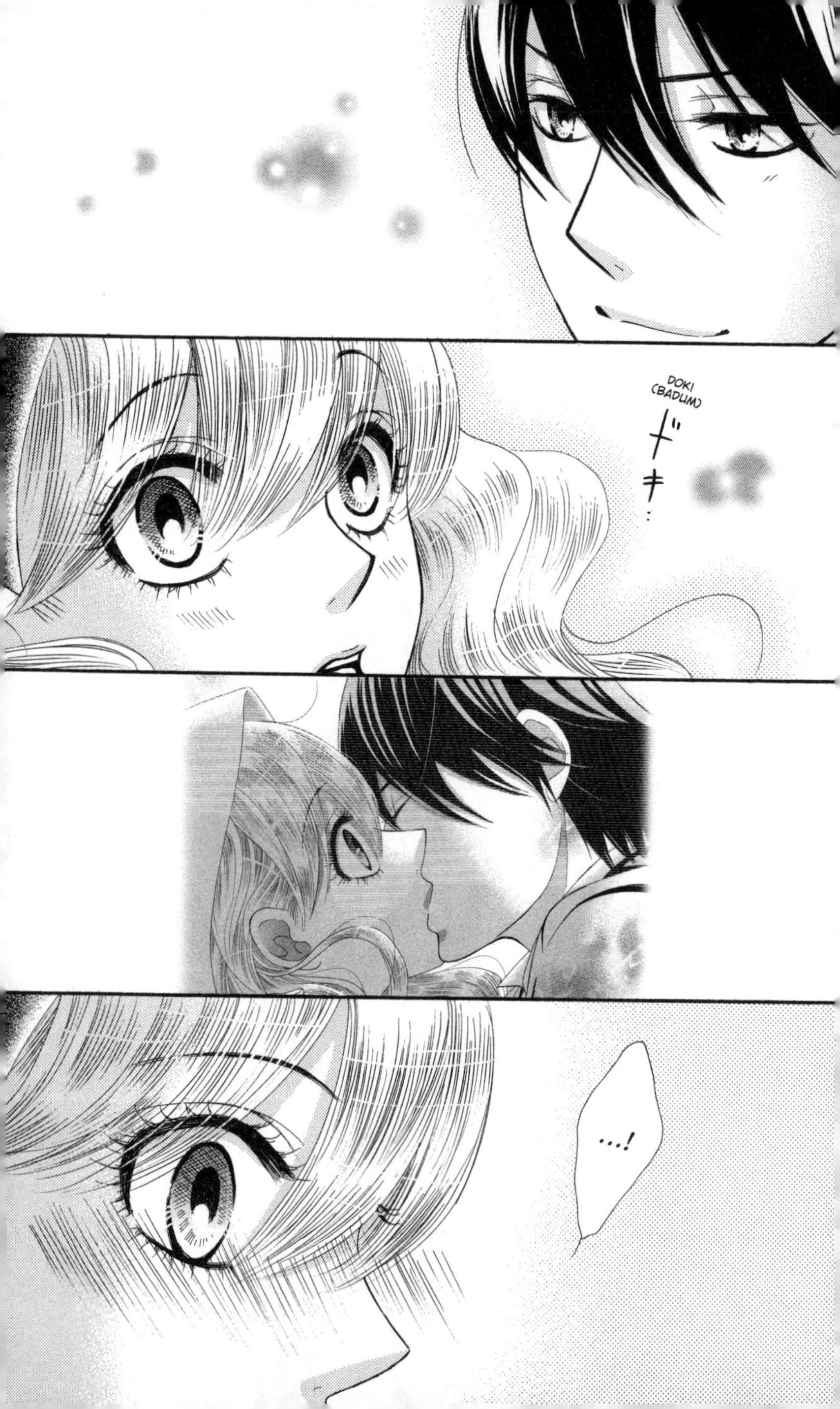
DOKI (BADUM)
ドキ
...!

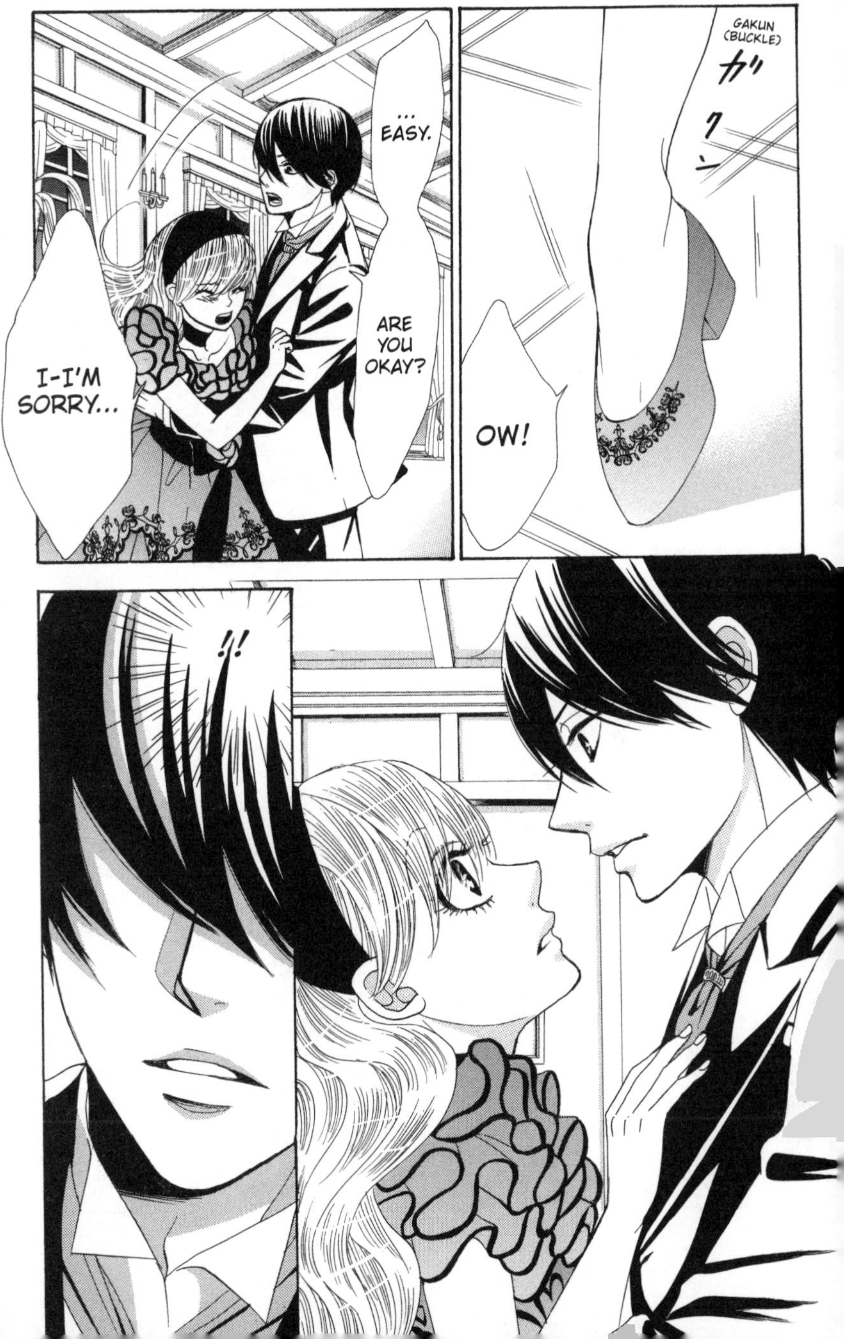
GAKUN (BUCKLE)
ガクン
OW!
... EASY.
ARE YOU OKAY?
I-I'M SORRY...
!!

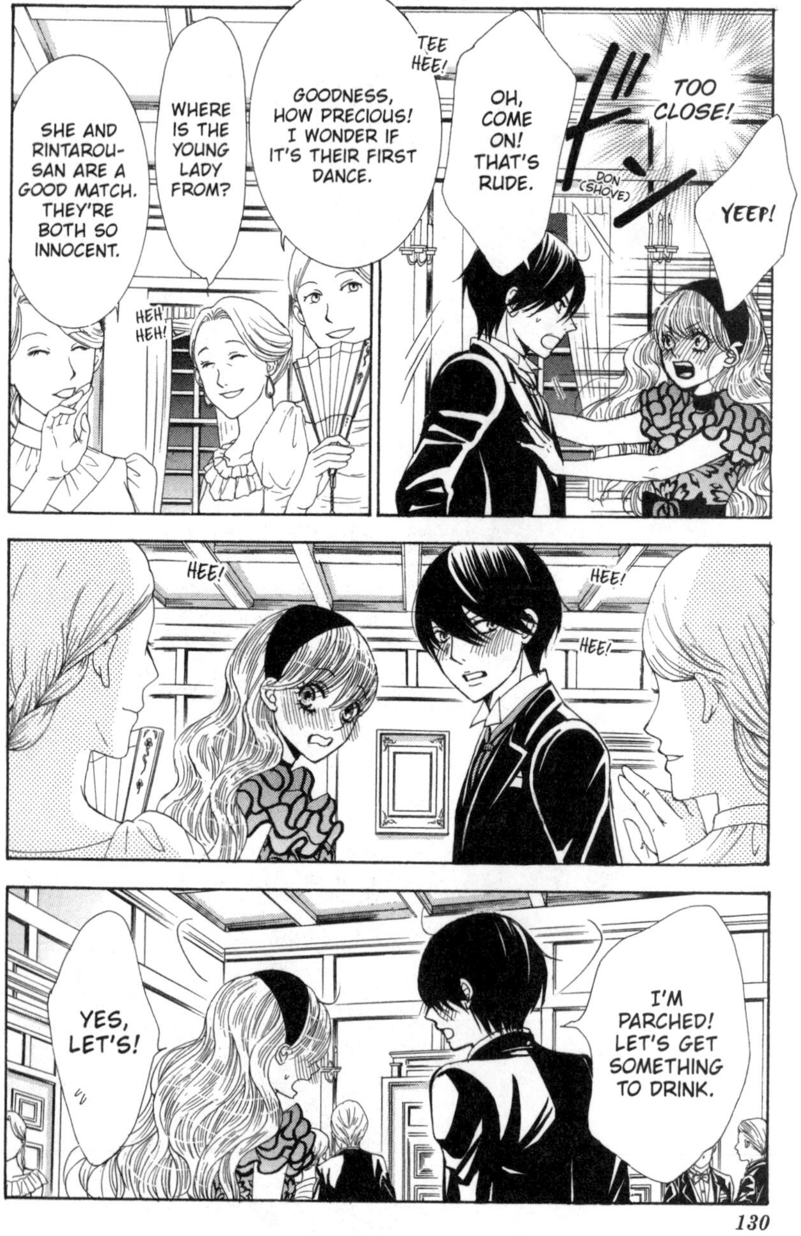
TOO CLOSE!
DON (SHOVE)
YEEP!
OH, COME ON! THAT'S RUDE.
TEE HEE!
GOODNESS, HOW PRECIOUS! I WONDER IF IT'S THEIR FIRST DANCE.
WHERE IS THE YOUNG LADY FROM?
SHE AND RINTAROU-SAN ARE A GOOD MATCH. THEY'RE BOTH SO INNOCENT.
HEH HEH!
HEE!
HEE!
HEE!
I'M PARCHED! LET'S GET SOMETHING TO DRINK.
YES, LET'S!

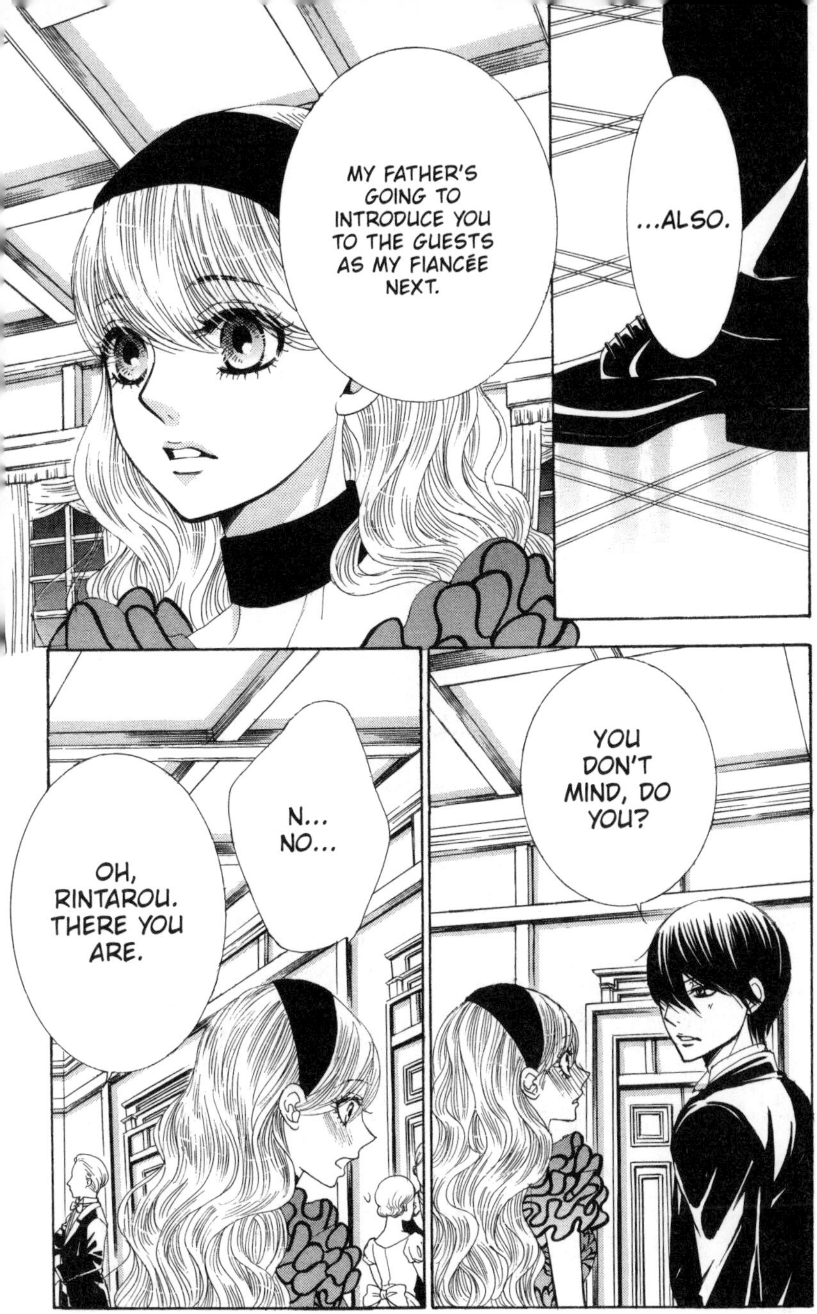
...ALSO.
MY FATHER'S GOING TO INTRODUCE YOU TO THE GUESTS AS MY FIANCÉE NEXT.
YOU DON'T MIND, DO YOU?
N... NO...
OH, RINTAROU. THERE YOU ARE.

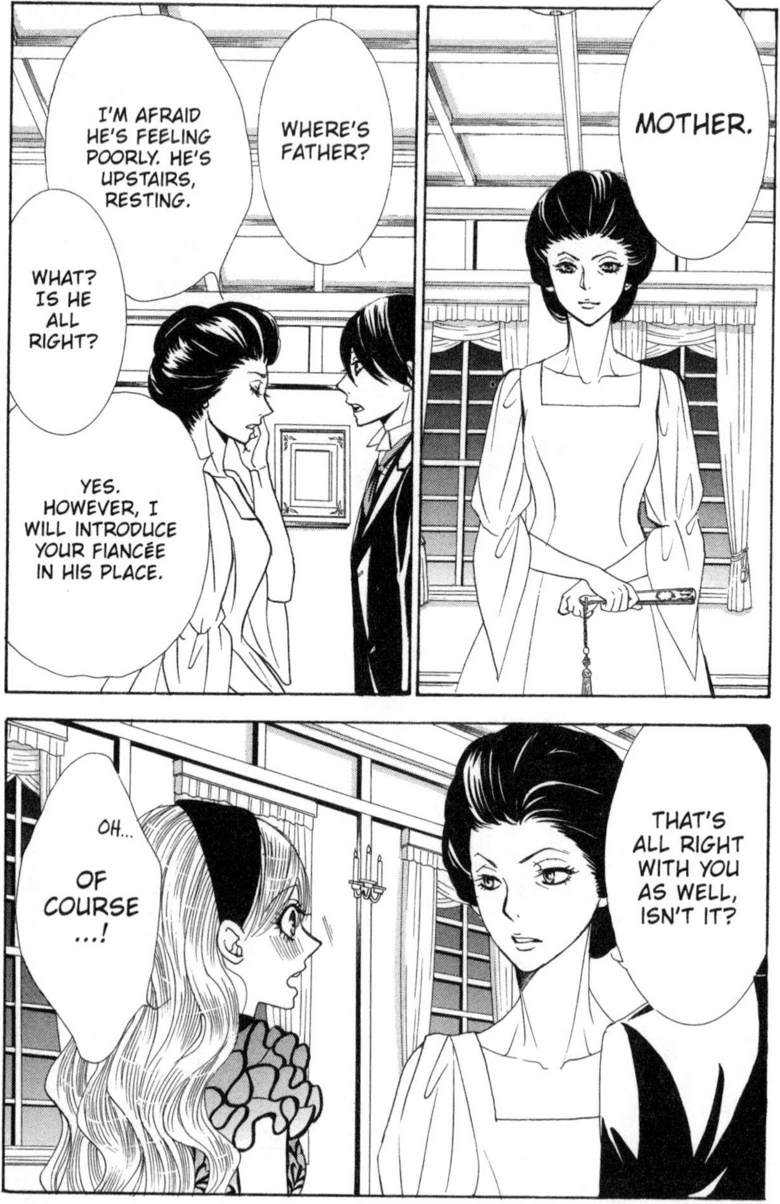
MOTHER.
WHERE'S FATHER?
I'M AFRAID HE'S FEELING POORLY. HE'S UPSTAIRS, RESTING.
WHAT? IS HE ALL RIGHT?
YES. HOWEVER, I WILL INTRODUCE YOUR FIANCÉE IN HIS PLACE.
THAT'S ALL RIGHT WITH YOU AS WELL, ISN'T IT?
OH...
OF COURSE ...!

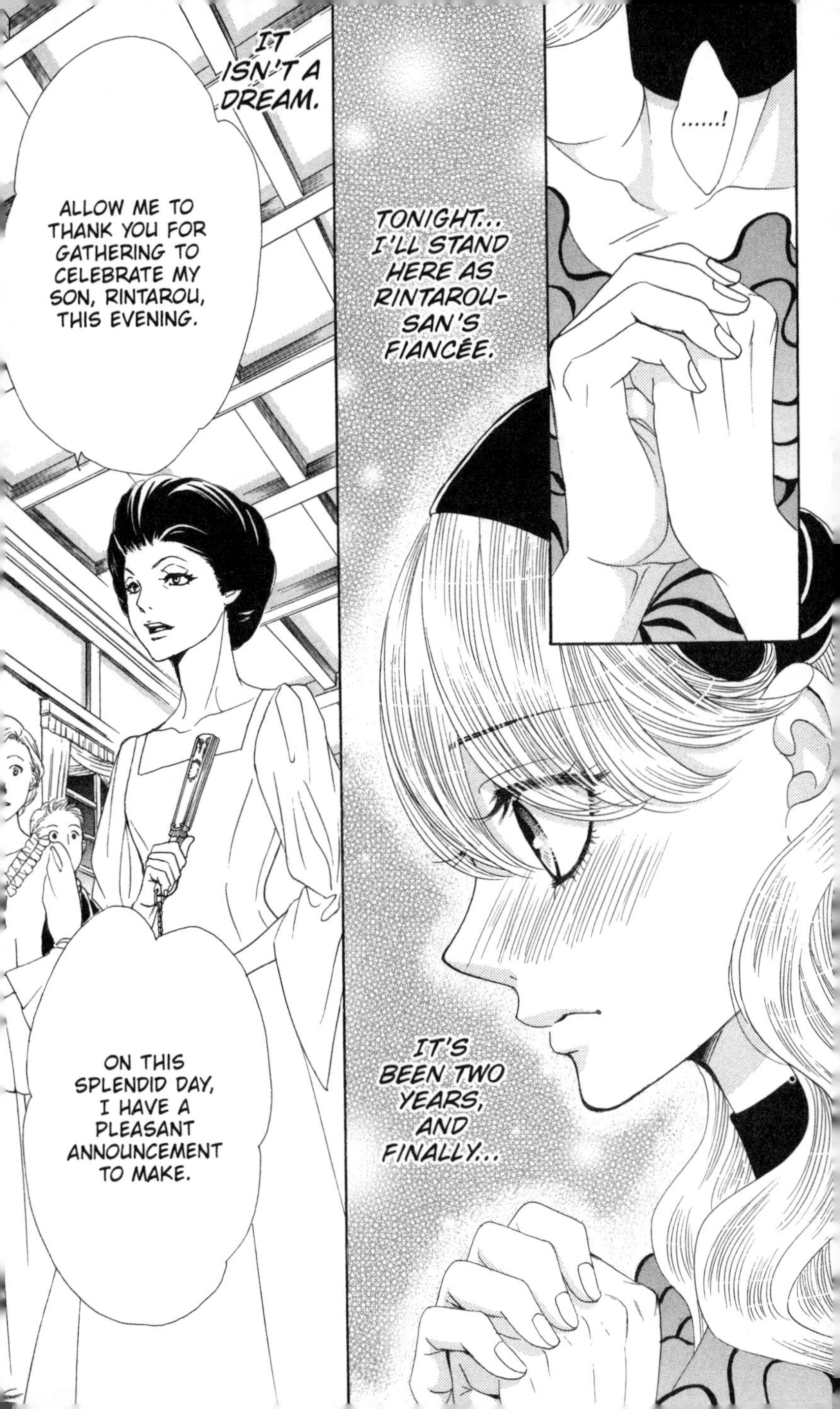
......!
TONIGHT... I'LL STAND HERE AS RINTAROU-SAN'S FIANCÉE.
IT'S BEEN TWO YEARS, AND FINALLY...
IT ISN'T A DREAM.
ALLOW ME TO THANK YOU FOR GATHERING TO CELEBRATE MY SON, RINTAROU, THIS EVENING.
ON THIS SPLENDID DAY, I HAVE A PLEASANT ANNOUNCEMENT TO MAKE.

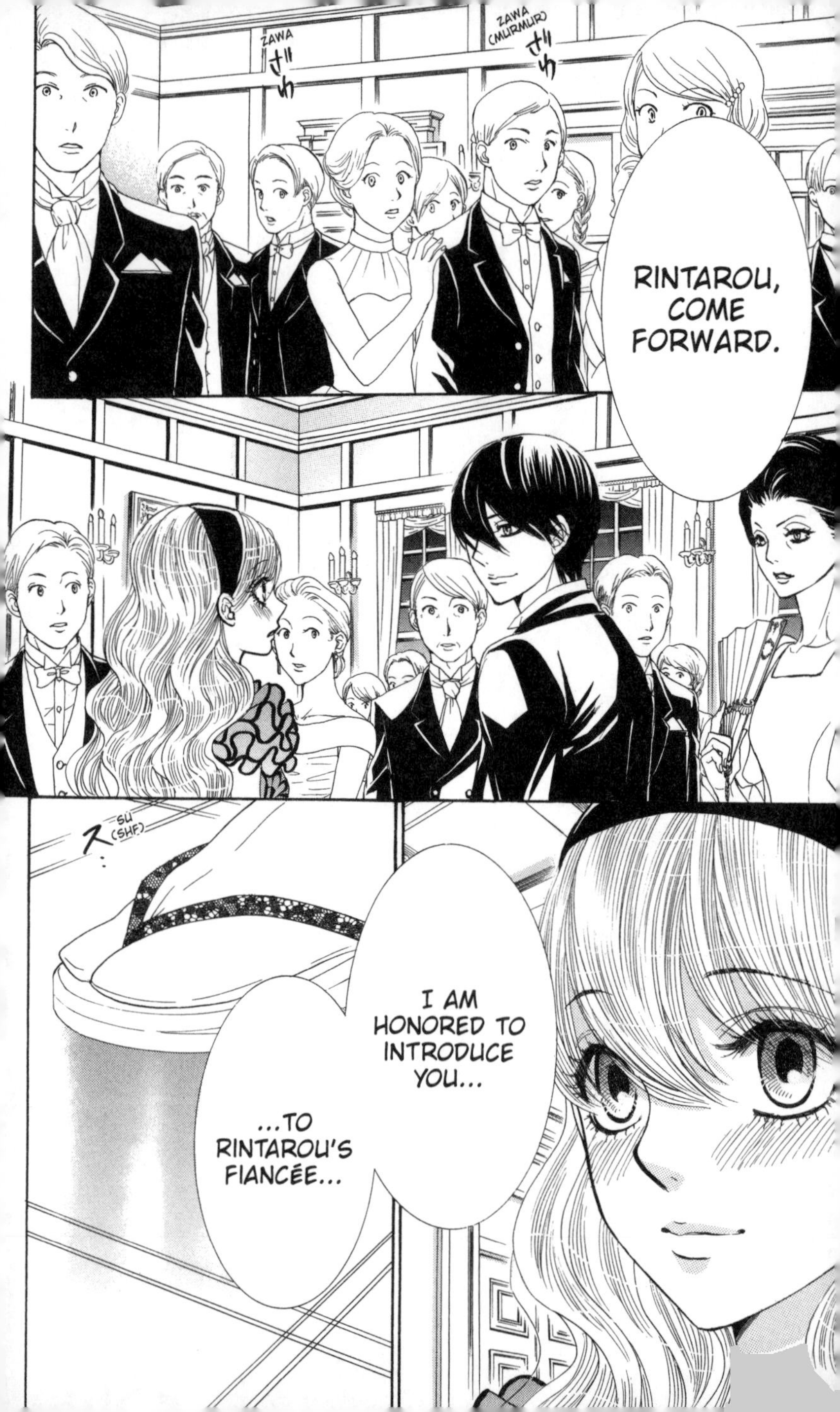
ZAWA (MURMUR)
ZAWA
RINTAROU, COME FORWARD.
I AM HONORED TO INTRODUCE YOU...
...TO RINTAROU'S FIANCÉE...
SU (SHF)

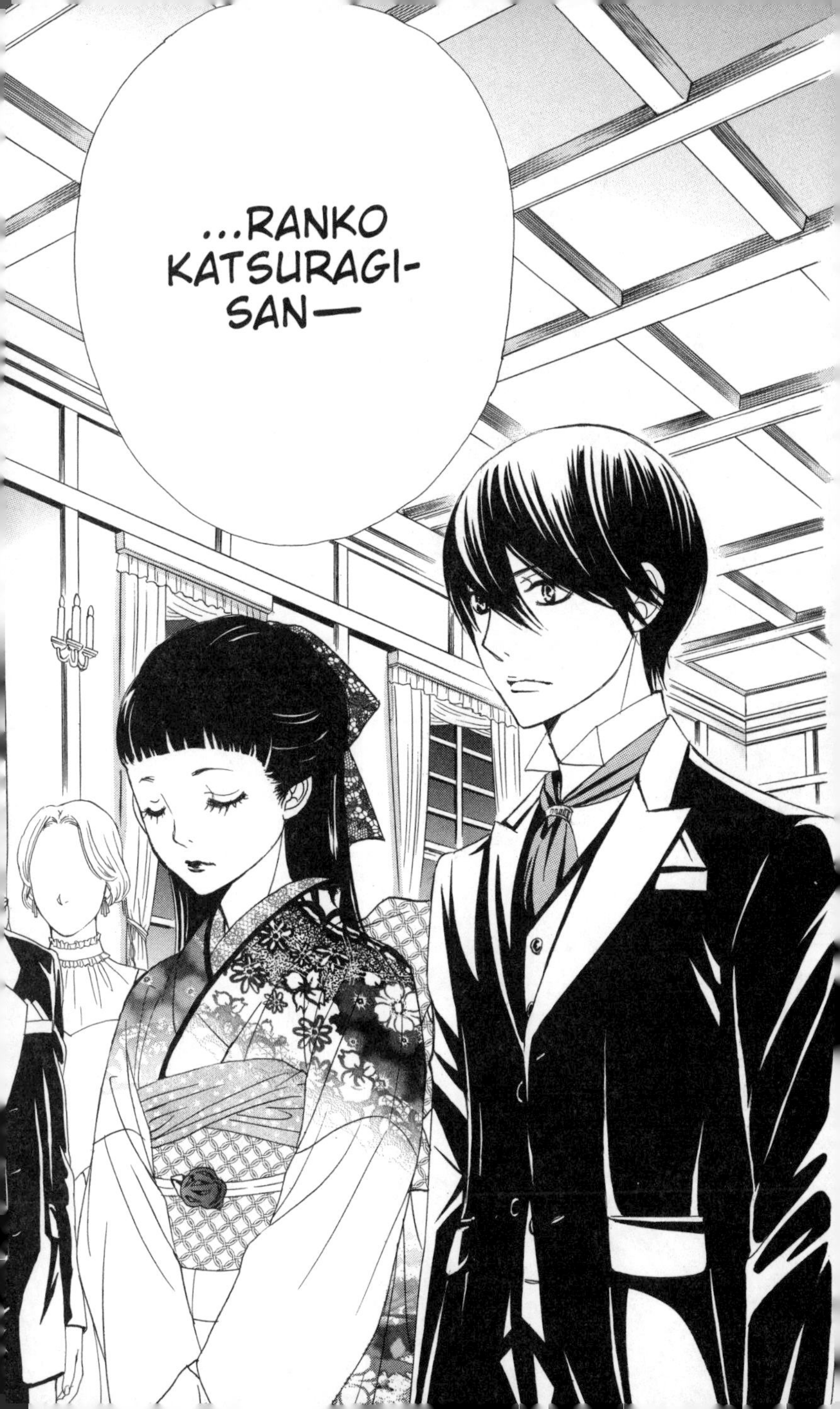
...RANKO KATSURAGI-SAN—

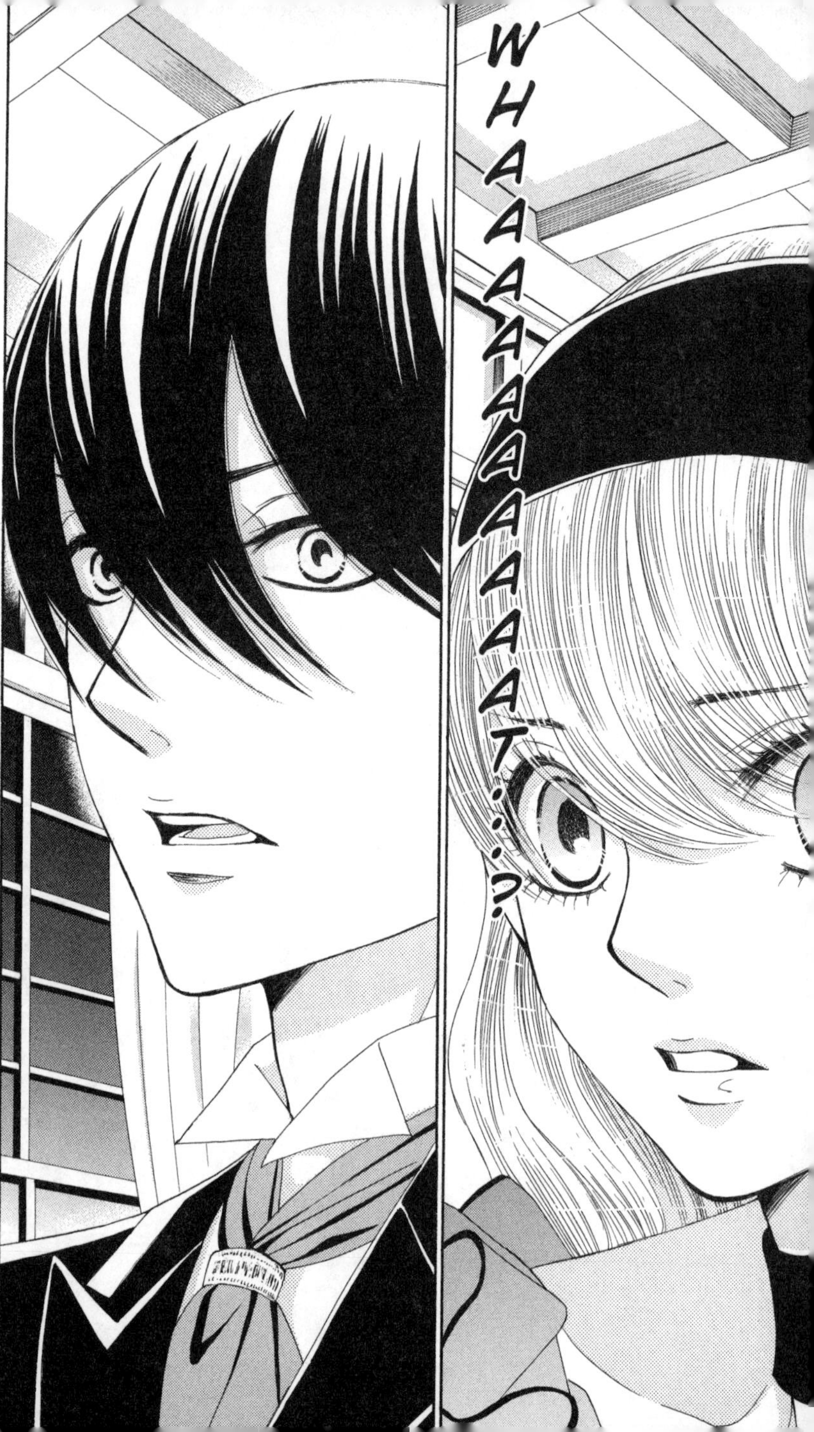
WHAAAAAAAAAAAAAT...?

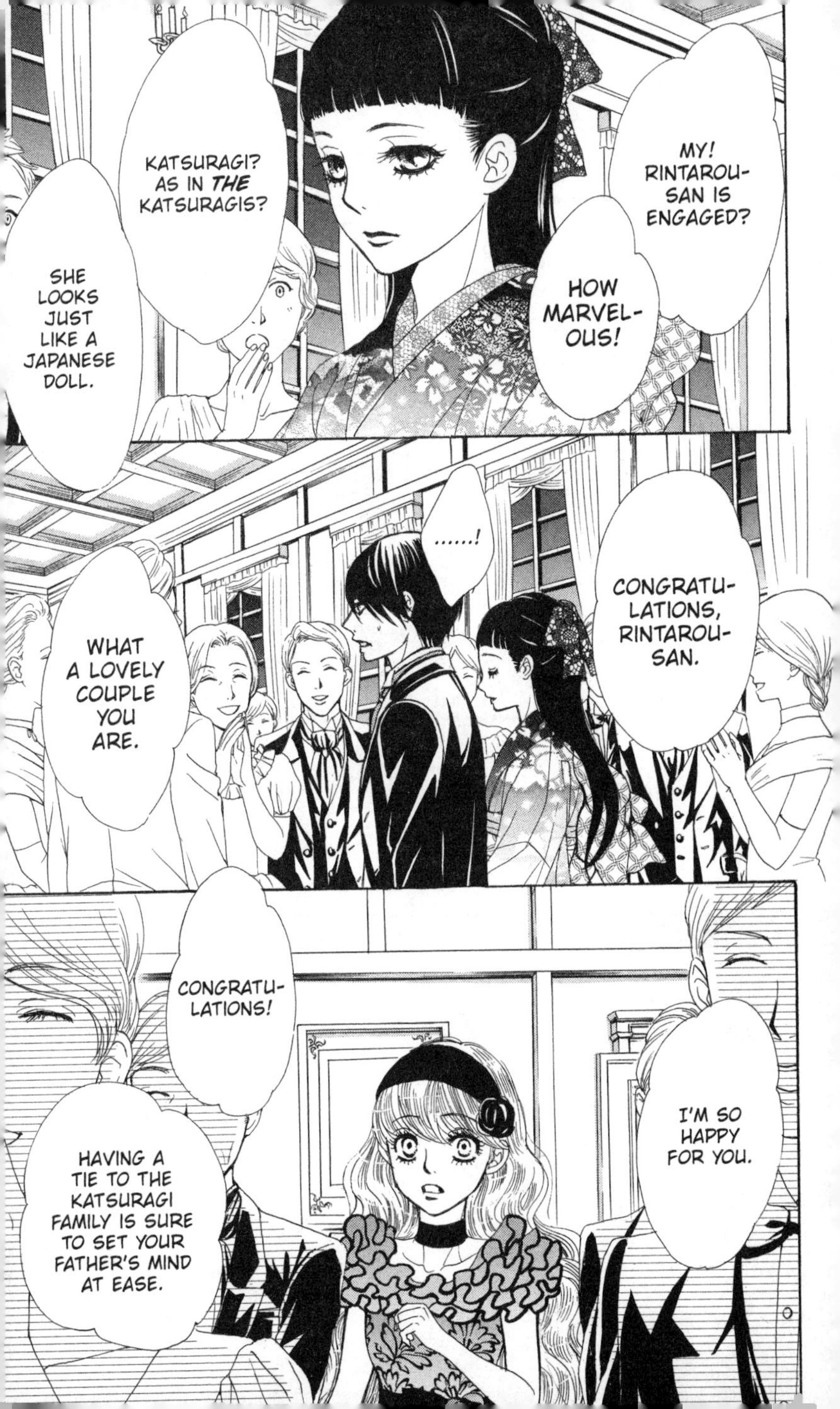
MY! RINTAROU-SAN IS ENGAGED?
HOW MARVEL-OUS!
KATSURAGI? AS IN *THE* KATSURAGIS?
SHE LOOKS JUST LIKE A JAPANESE DOLL.
CONGRATU-LATIONS, RINTAROU-SAN.
......!
WHAT A LOVELY COUPLE YOU ARE.
I'M SO HAPPY FOR YOU.
CONGRATU-LATIONS!
HAVING A TIE TO THE KATSURAGI FAMILY IS SURE TO SET YOUR FATHER'S MIND AT EASE.

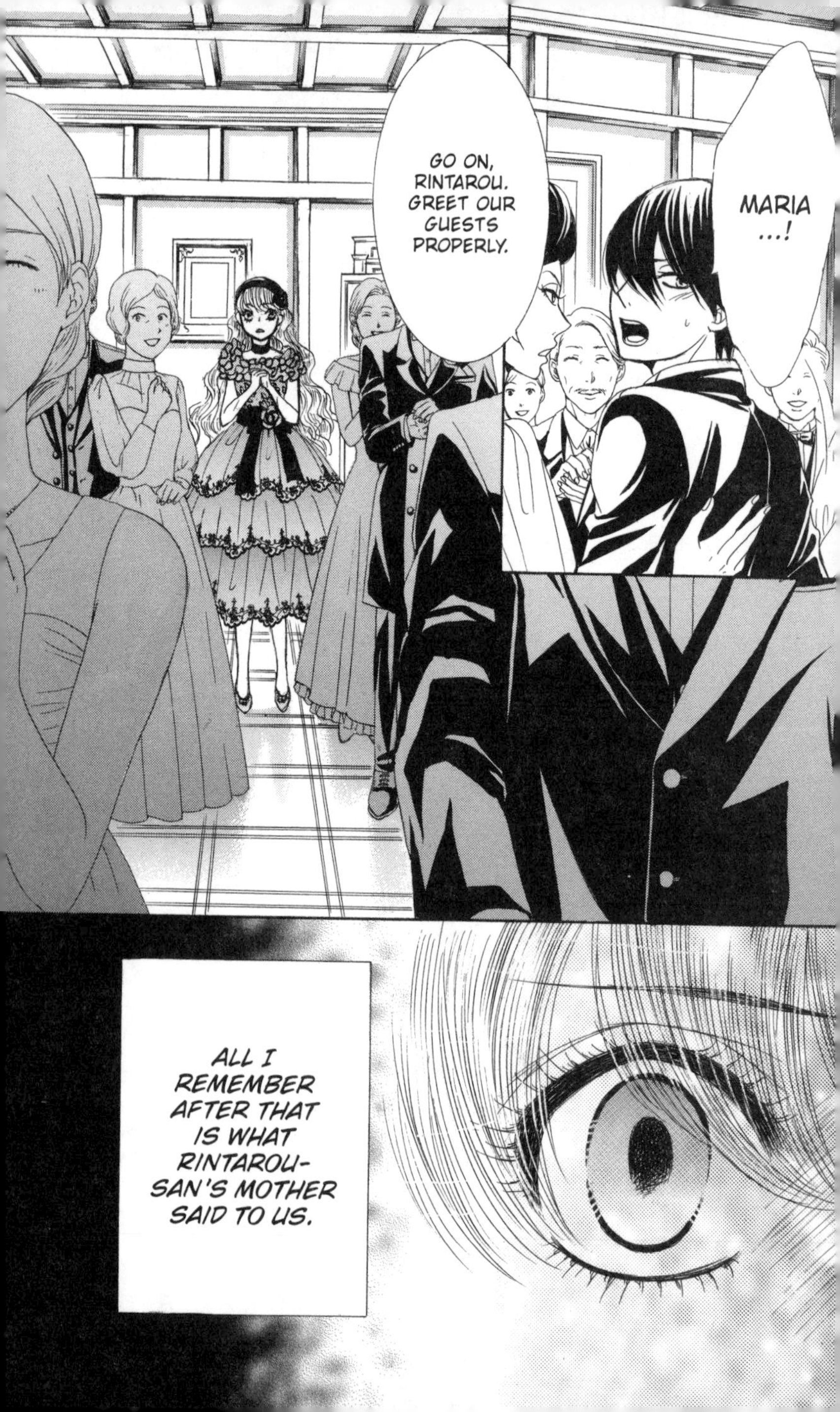
MARIA ...!
GO ON, RINTAROU. GREET OUR GUESTS PROPERLY.
ALL I REMEMBER AFTER THAT IS WHAT RINTAROU-SAN'S MOTHER SAID TO US.

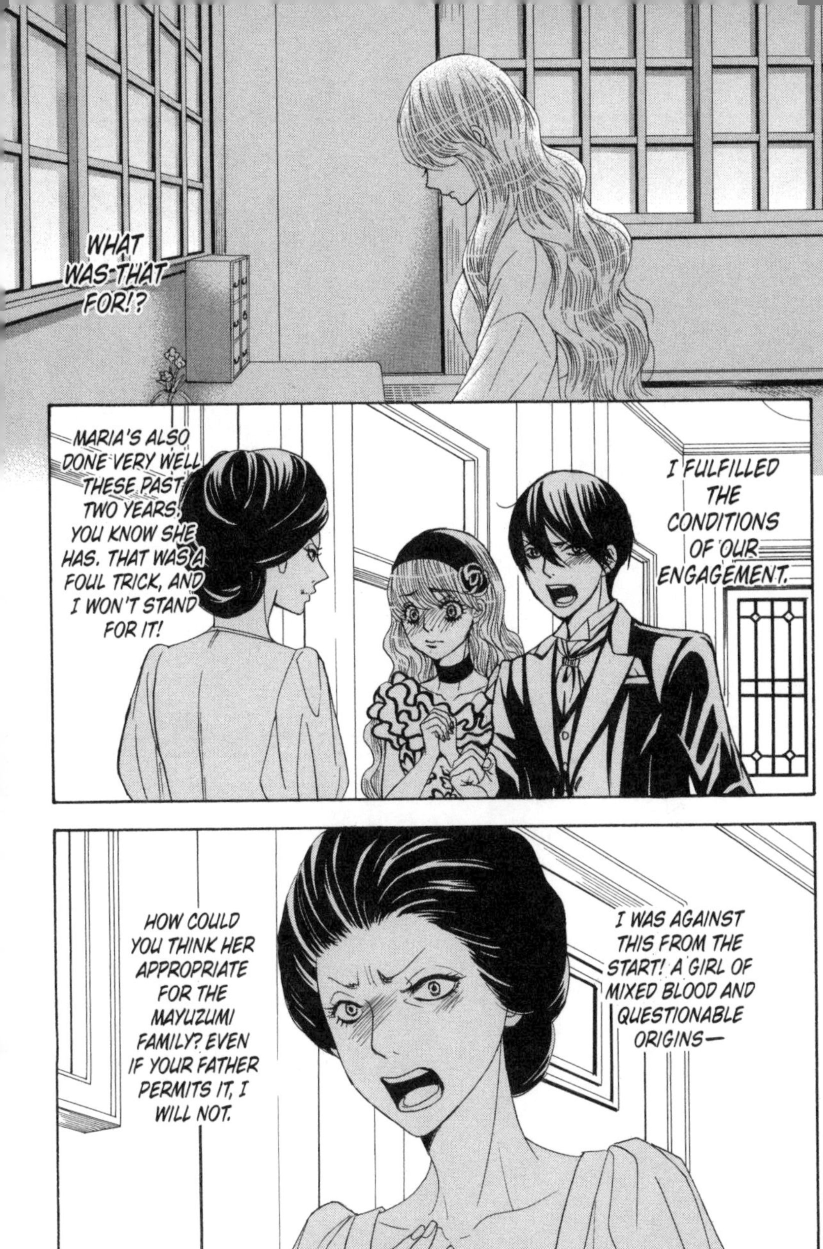
WHAT WAS THAT FOR!?
I FULFILLED THE CONDITIONS OF OUR ENGAGEMENT.
MARIA'S ALSO DONE VERY WELL THESE PAST TWO YEARS. YOU KNOW SHE HAS. THAT WAS A FOUL TRICK, AND I WON'T STAND FOR IT!
I WAS AGAINST THIS FROM THE START! A GIRL OF MIXED BLOOD AND QUESTIONABLE ORIGINS—
HOW COULD YOU THINK HER APPROPRIATE FOR THE MAYUZUMI FAMILY? EVEN IF YOUR FATHER PERMITS IT, I WILL NOT.

......!

I COULD NEVER ALLOW IT!

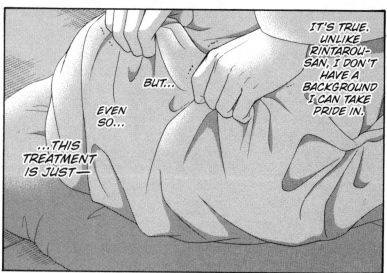

IT'S TRUE. UNLIKE RINTAROU-SAN, I DON'T HAVE A BACKGROUND I CAN TAKE PRIDE IN.

BUT...

EVEN SO...

...THIS TREATMENT IS JUST—

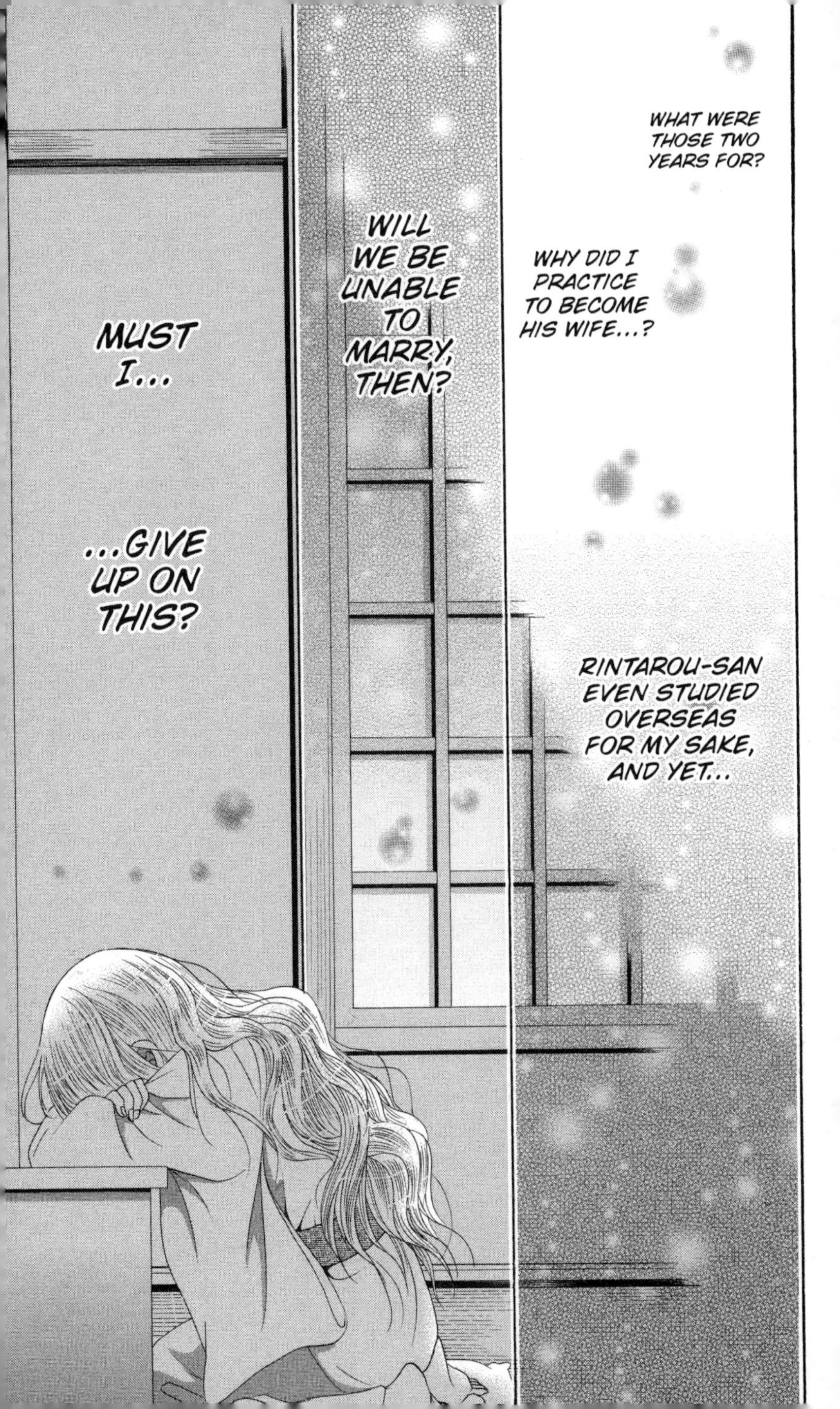
WHAT WERE THOSE TWO YEARS FOR?
WHY DID I PRACTICE TO BECOME HIS WIFE...?
RINTAROU-SAN EVEN STUDIED OVERSEAS FOR MY SAKE, AND YET...
WILL WE BE UNABLE TO MARRY, THEN?
MUST I...
...GIVE UP ON THIS?

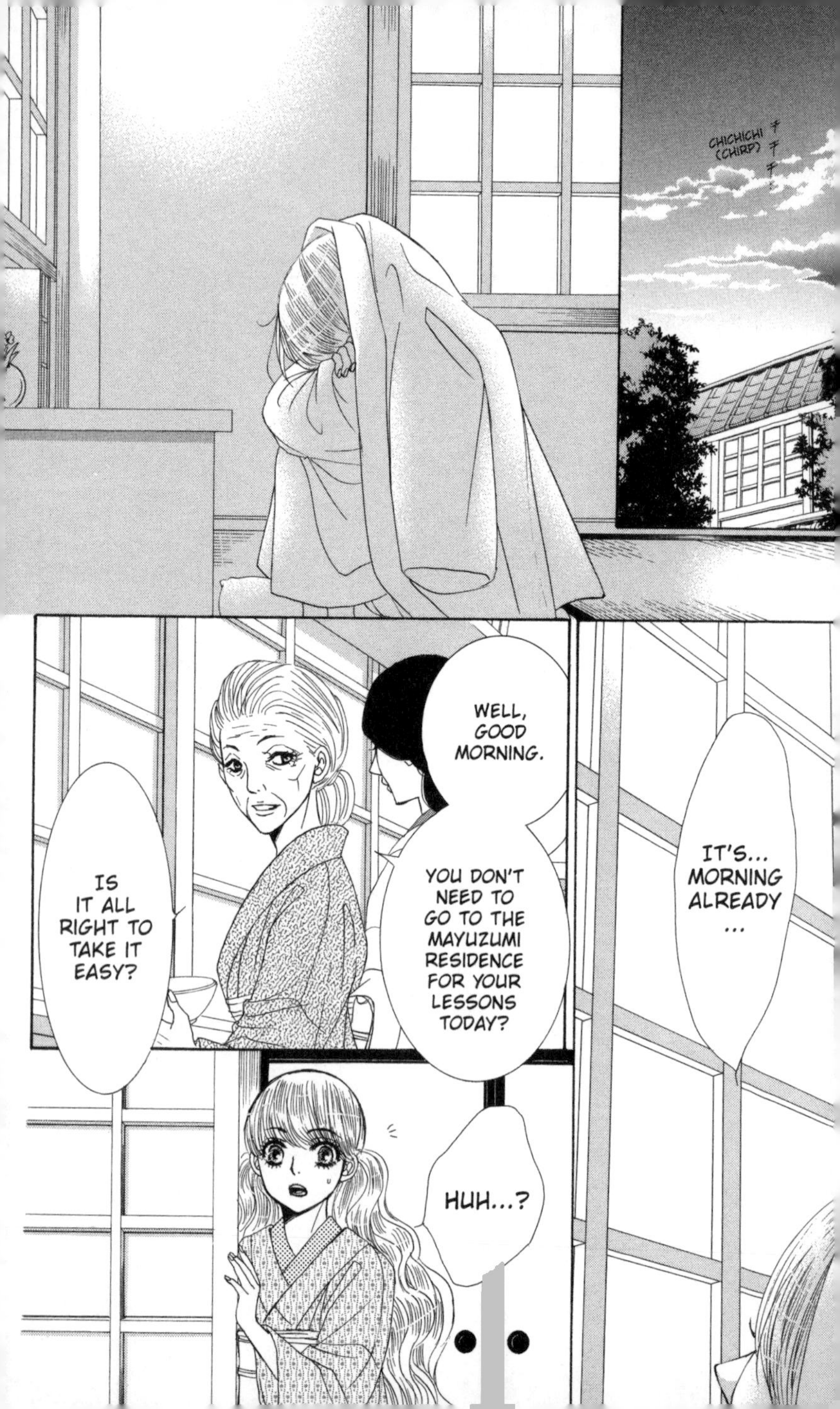
CHICHICHI (CHIRP)
チチチ
IT'S... MORNING ALREADY...
WELL, GOOD MORNING.
YOU DON'T NEED TO GO TO THE MAYUZUMI RESIDENCE FOR YOUR LESSONS TODAY?
IS IT ALL RIGHT TO TAKE IT EASY?
HUH...?

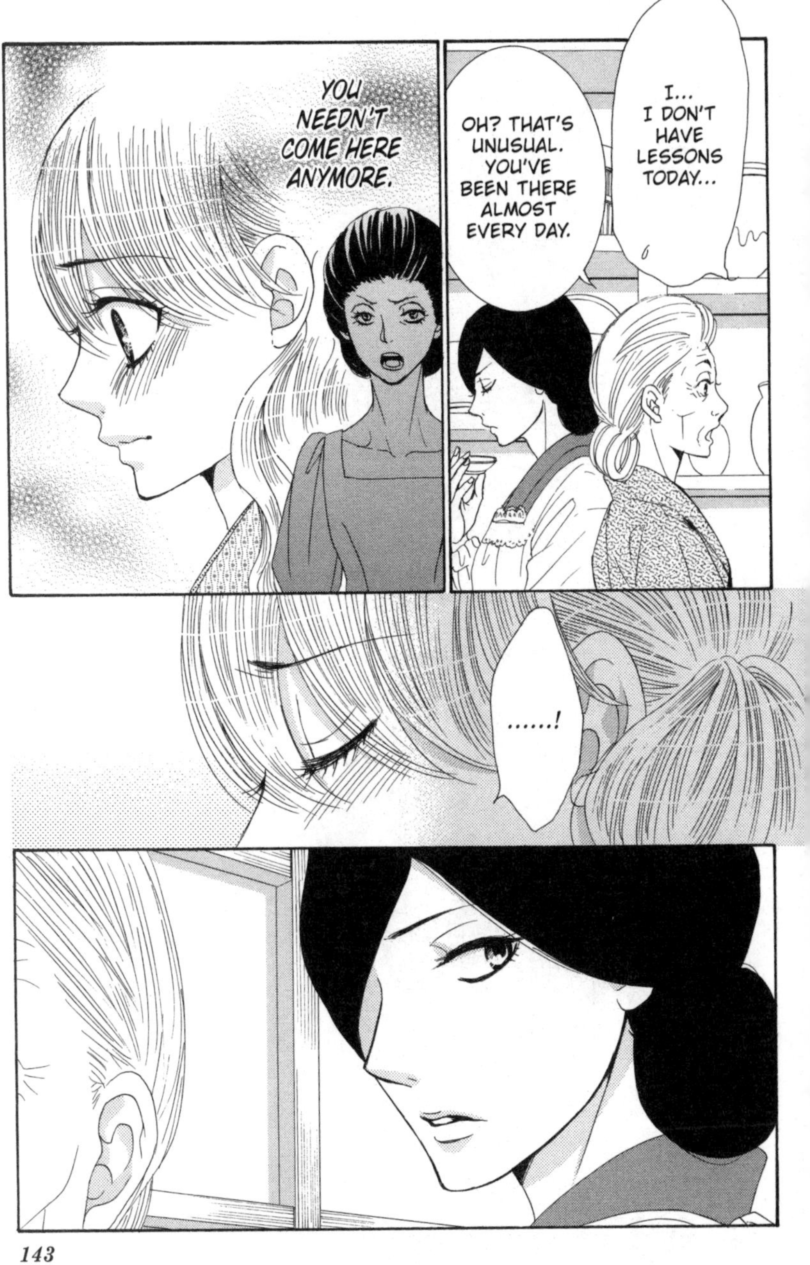
I...
I DON'T HAVE LESSONS TODAY...
OH? THAT'S UNUSUAL. YOU'VE BEEN THERE ALMOST EVERY DAY.
YOU NEEDN'T COME HERE ANYMORE.
......!

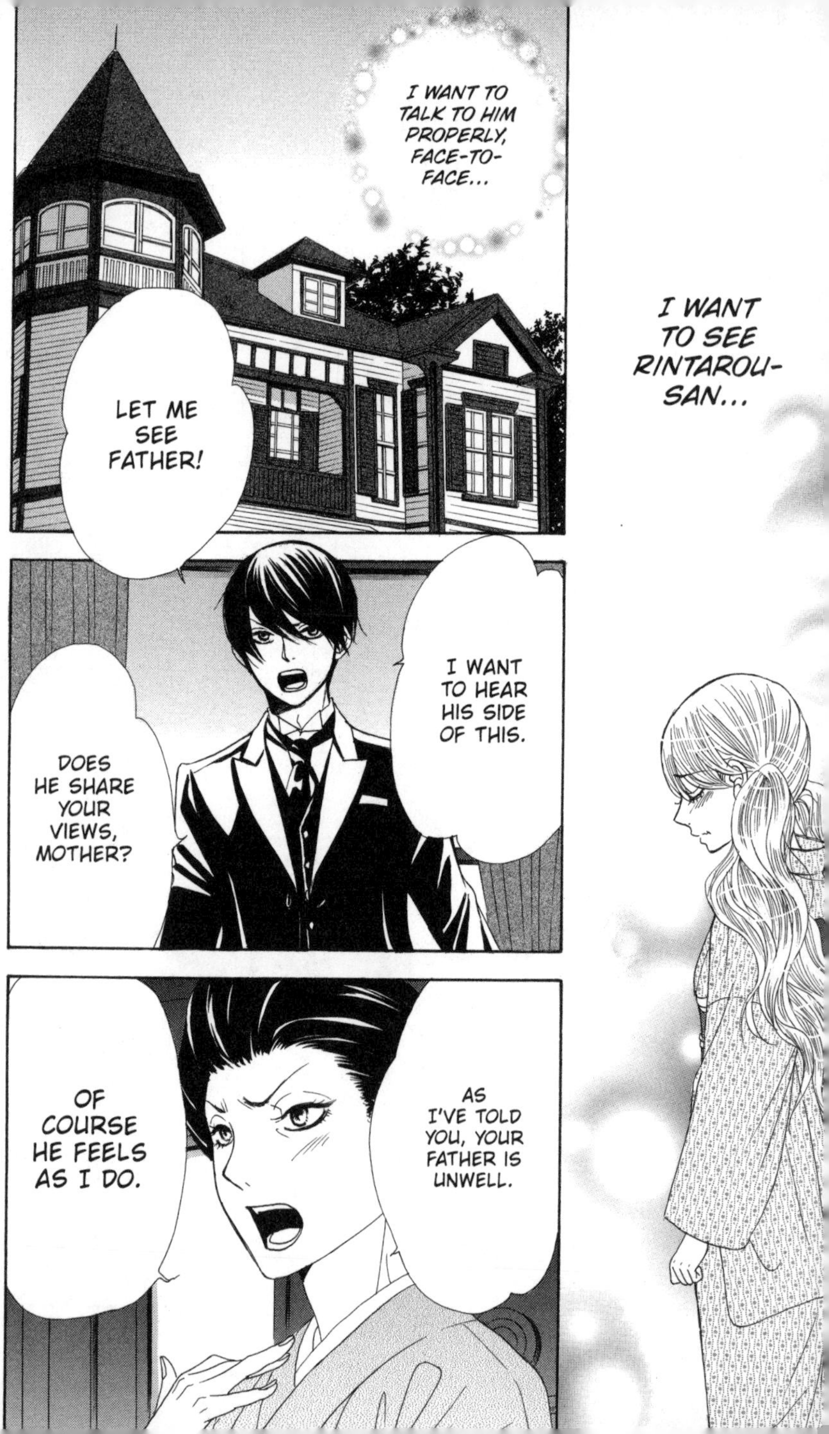
I WANT TO SEE RINTAROU-SAN...
I WANT TO TALK TO HIM PROPERLY, FACE-TO-FACE...
LET ME SEE FATHER!
I WANT TO HEAR HIS SIDE OF THIS.
DOES HE SHARE YOUR VIEWS, MOTHER?
AS I'VE TOLD YOU, YOUR FATHER IS UNWELL.
OF COURSE HE FEELS AS I DO.

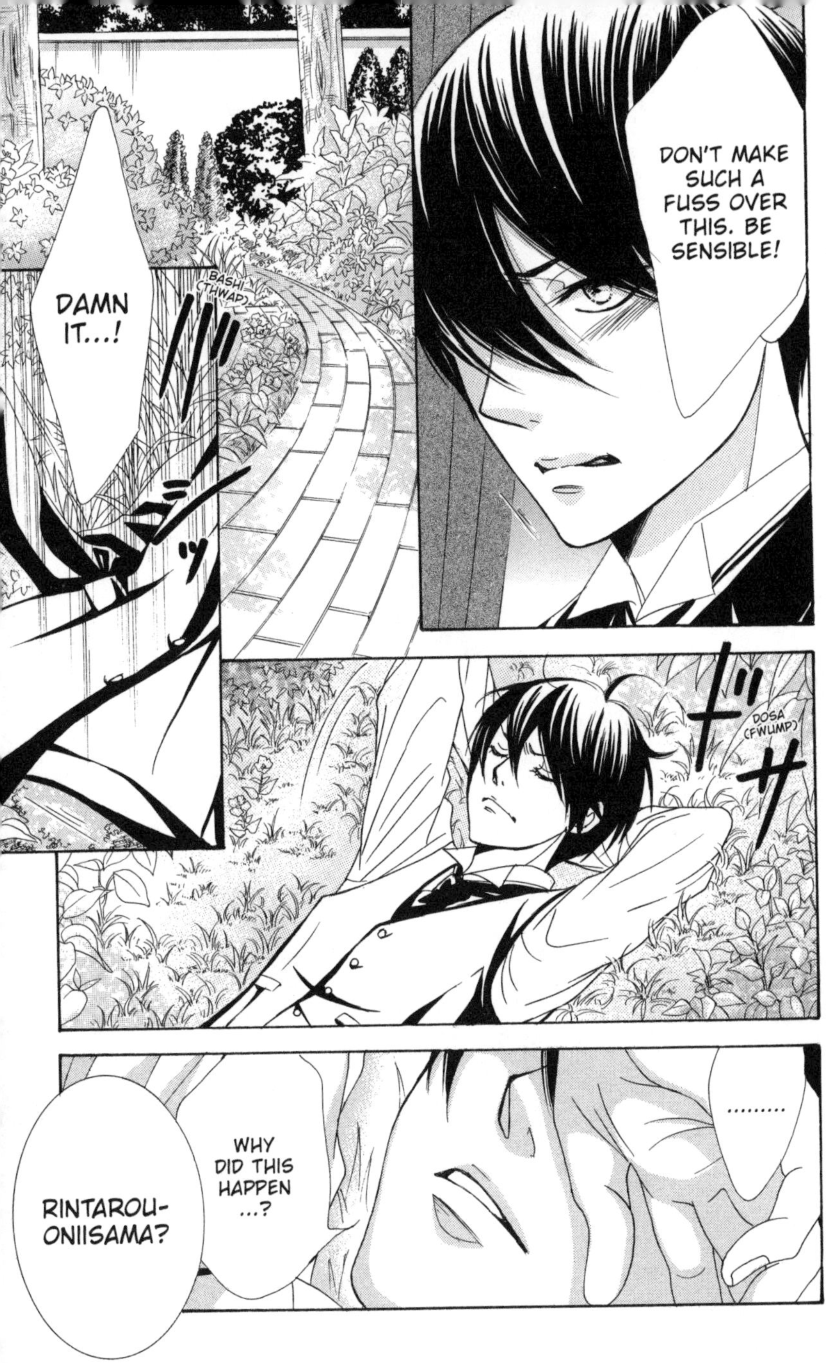
DON'T MAKE SUCH A FUSS OVER THIS. BE SENSIBLE!
DAMN IT...!
BASHI (THWAP)
DOSA (FWUMP)
....
WHY DID THIS HAPPEN ...?
RINTAROU-ONIISAMA?

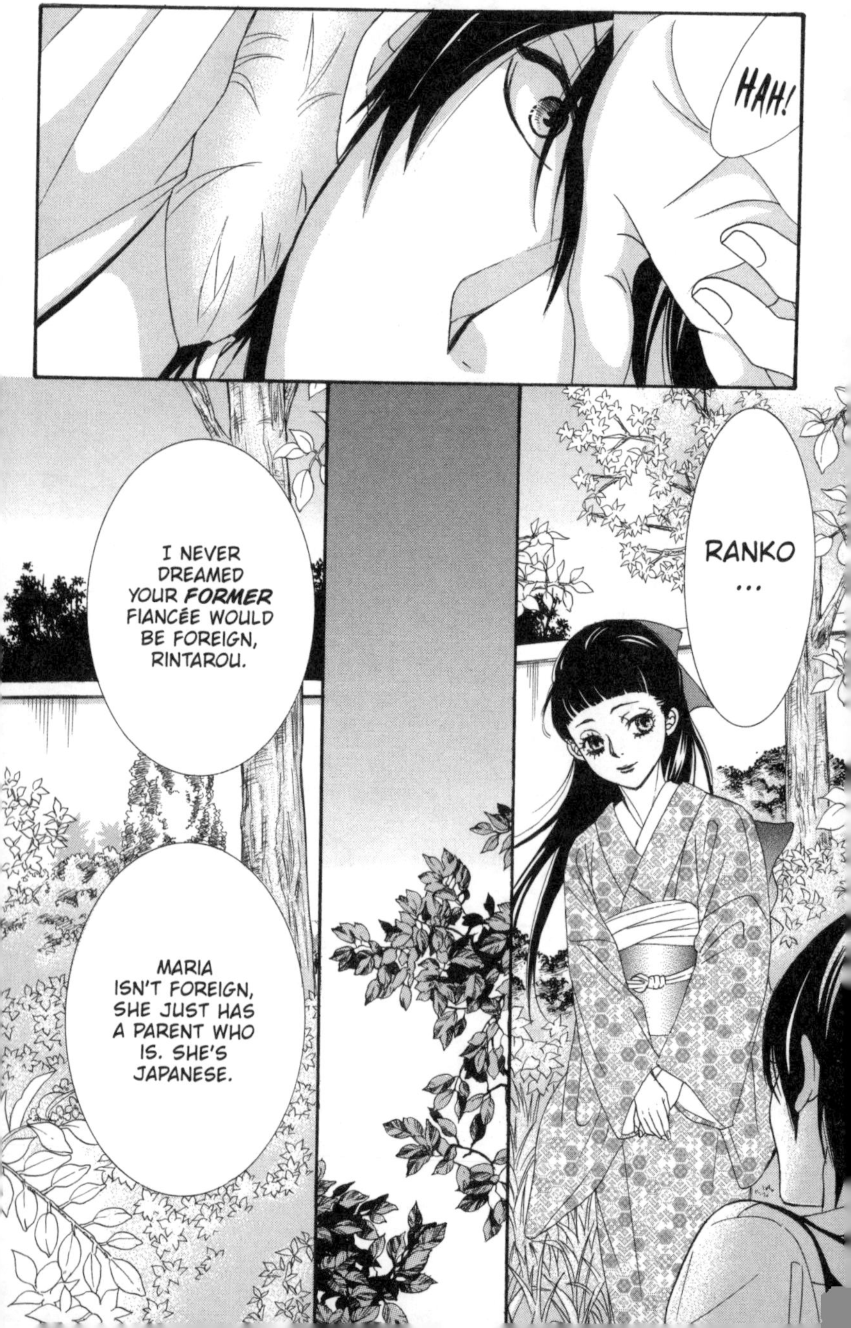
HAH!
RANKO ...
I NEVER DREAMED YOUR ***FORMER*** FIANCÉE WOULD BE FOREIGN, RINTAROU.
MARIA ISN'T FOREIGN, SHE JUST HAS A PARENT WHO IS. SHE'S JAPANESE.

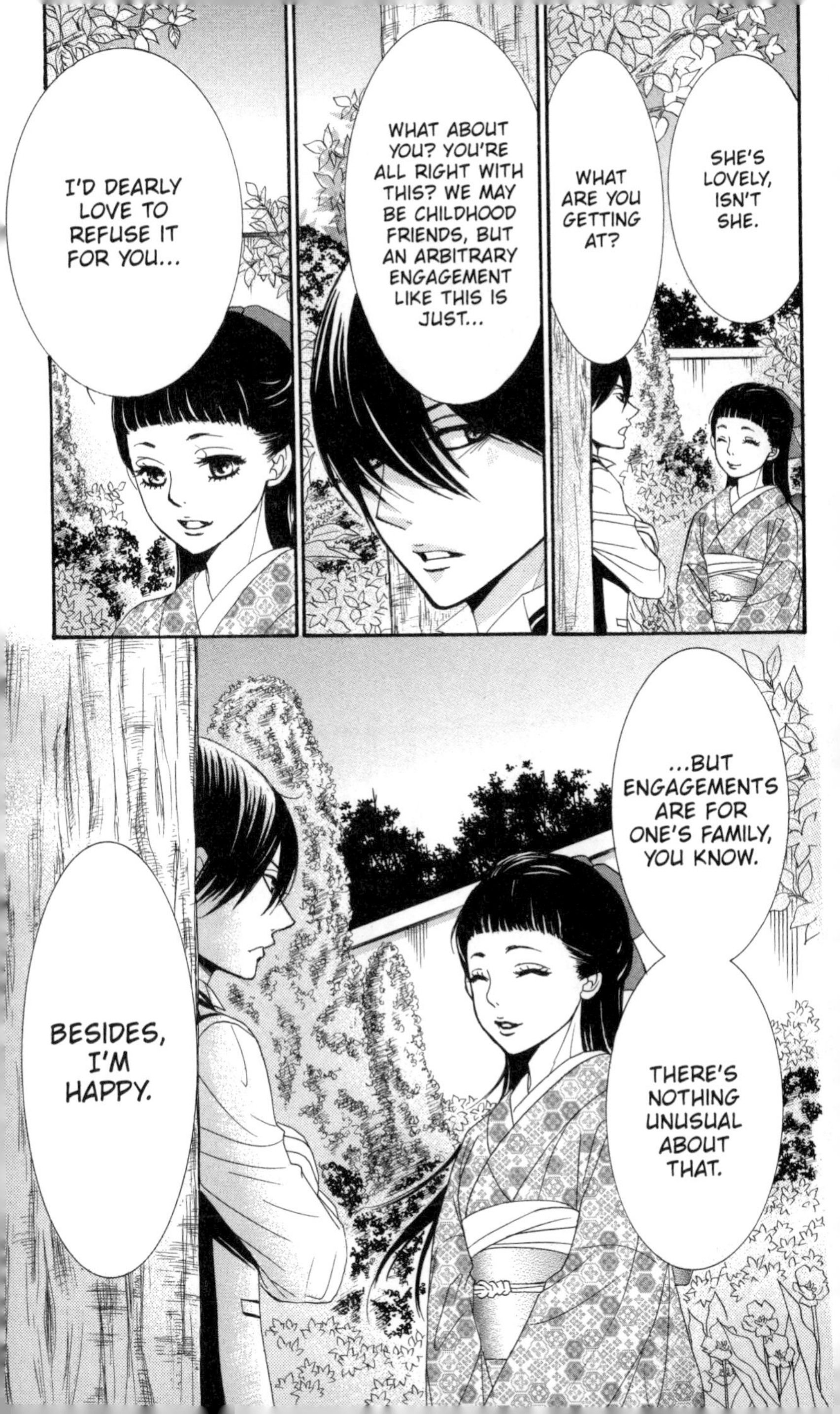
SHE'S LOVELY, ISN'T SHE.
WHAT ARE YOU GETTING AT?
WHAT ABOUT YOU? YOU'RE ALL RIGHT WITH THIS? WE MAY BE CHILDHOOD FRIENDS, BUT AN ARBITRARY ENGAGEMENT LIKE THIS IS JUST...
I'D DEARLY LOVE TO REFUSE IT FOR YOU...
...BUT ENGAGEMENTS ARE FOR ONE'S FAMILY, YOU KNOW.
THERE'S NOTHING UNUSUAL ABOUT THAT.
BESIDES, I'M HAPPY.

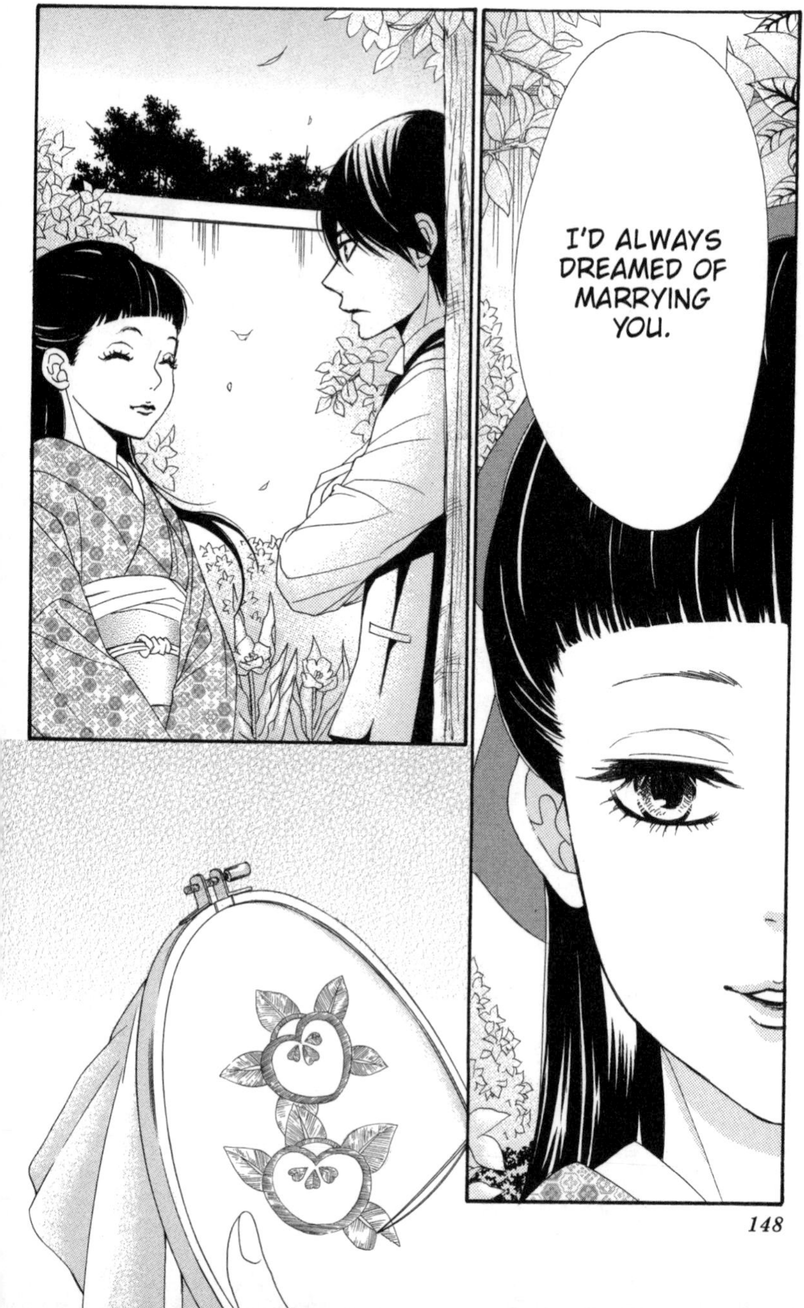
I'D ALWAYS DREAMED OF MARRYING YOU.

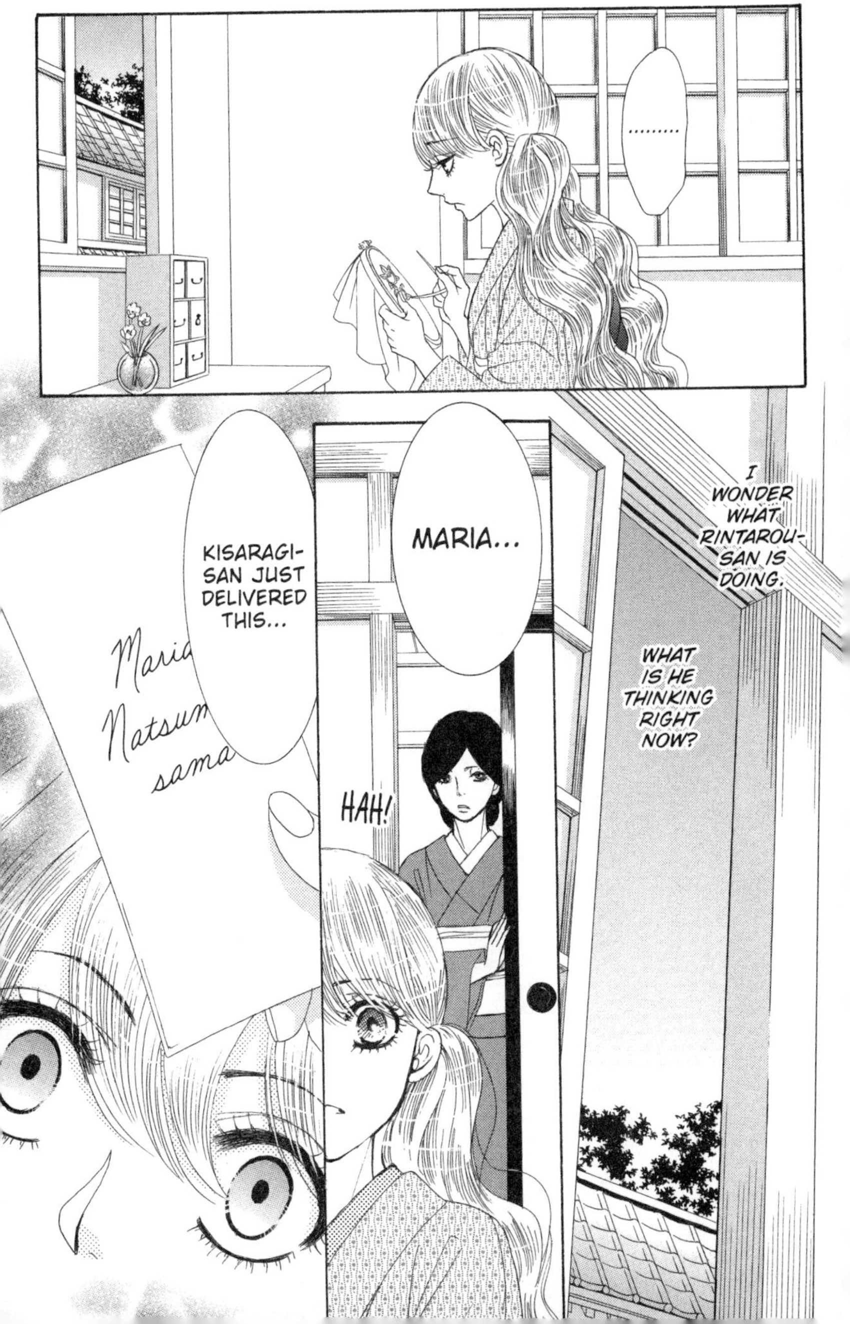
....
I WONDER WHAT RINTAROU-SAN IS DOING.
WHAT IS HE THINKING RIGHT NOW?
MARIA...
KISARAGI-SAN JUST DELIVERED THIS...
HAH!

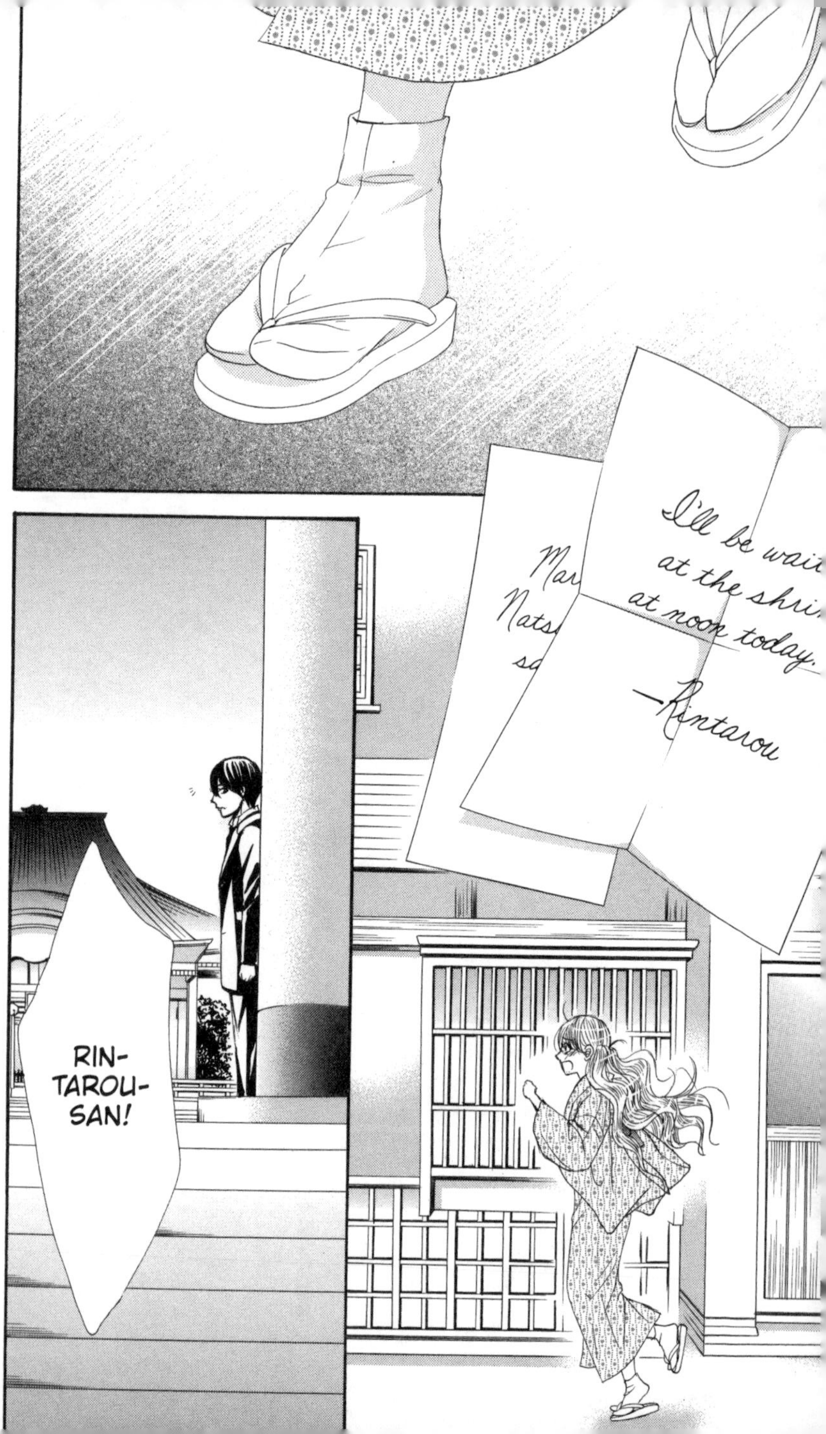

I'll be wait
at the shri
at noon today.
—Rintarou
RIN-TAROU-SAN!

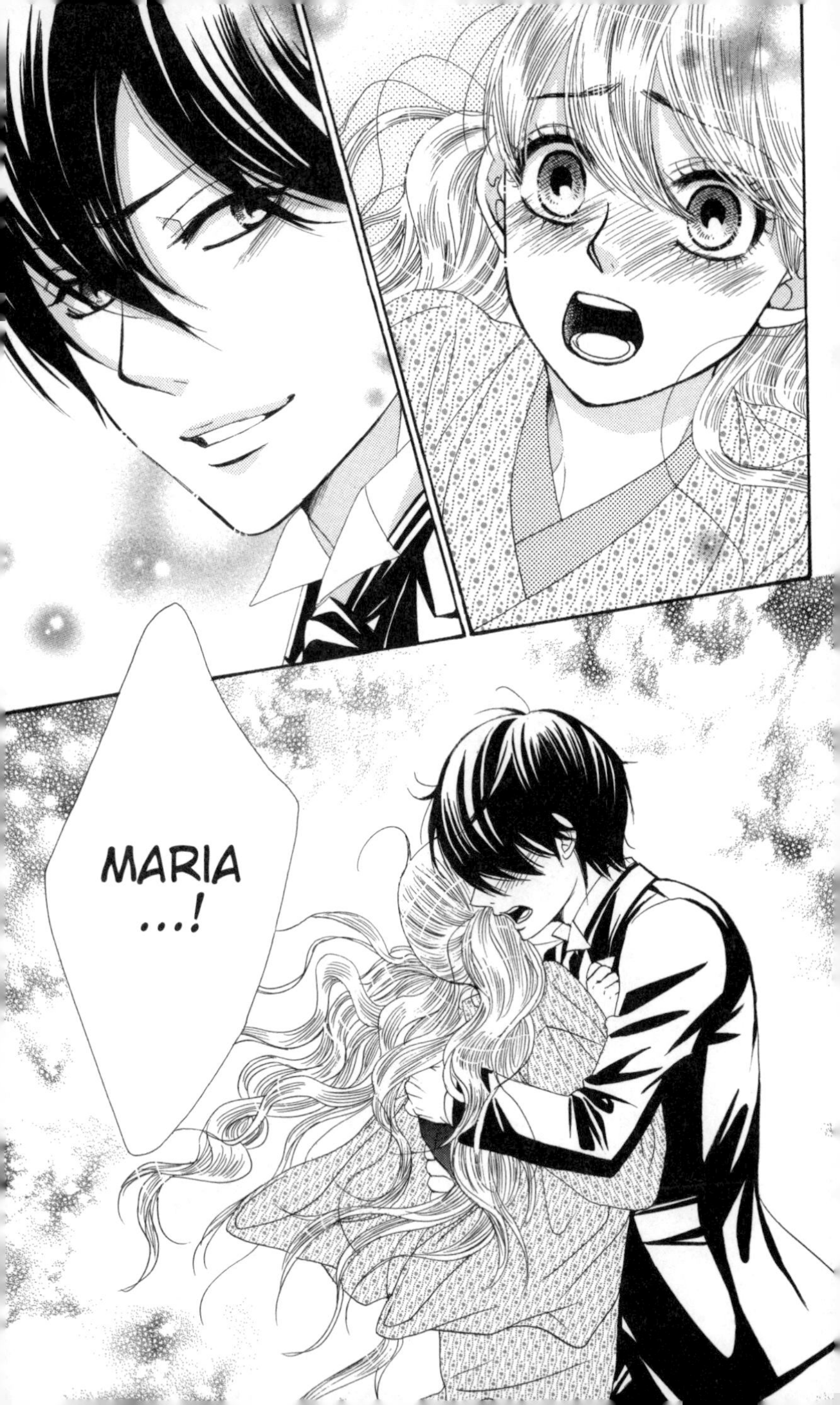
MARIA ...!

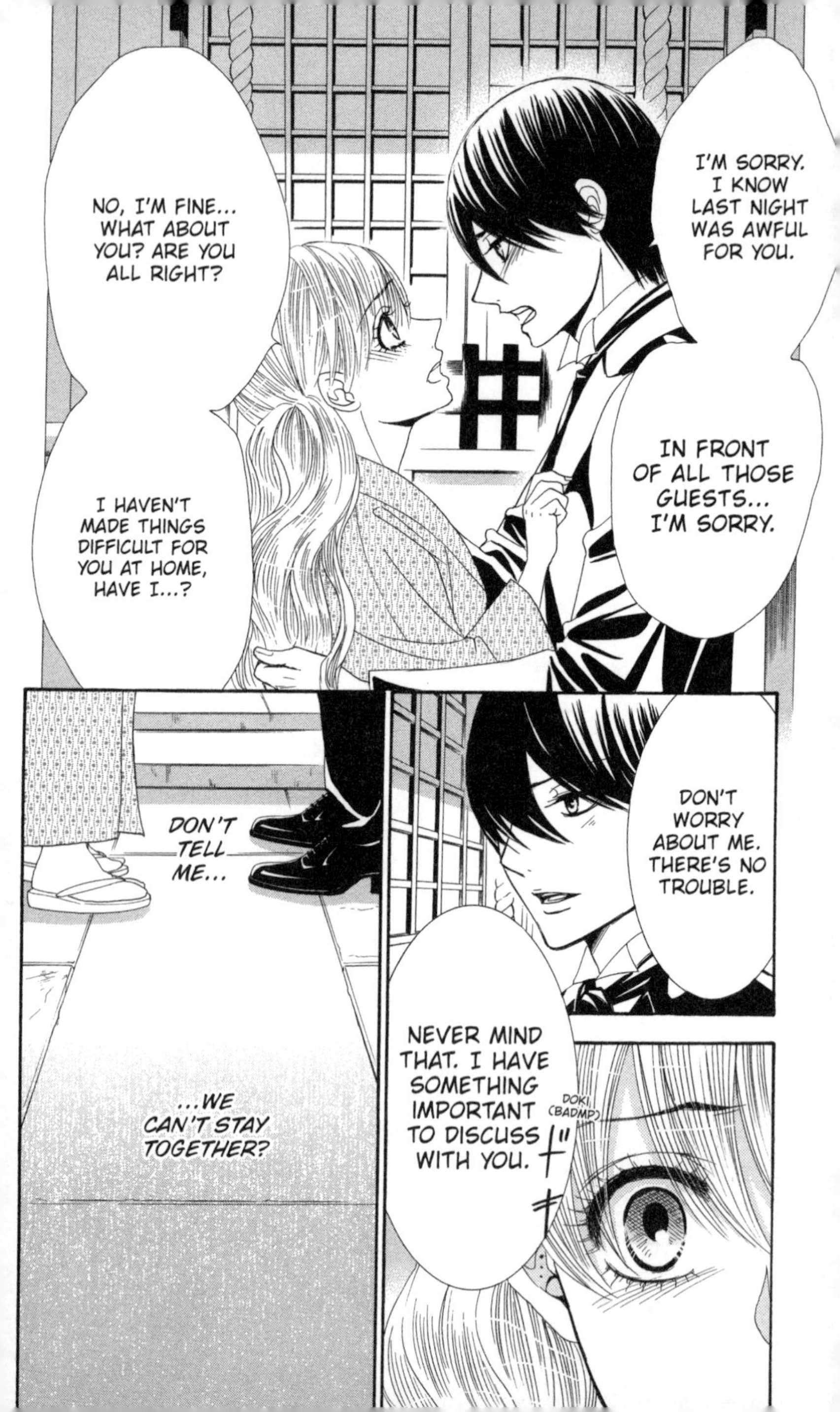
I'M SORRY. I KNOW LAST NIGHT WAS AWFUL FOR YOU.
IN FRONT OF ALL THOSE GUESTS... I'M SORRY.
NO, I'M FINE... WHAT ABOUT YOU? ARE YOU ALL RIGHT?
I HAVEN'T MADE THINGS DIFFICULT FOR YOU AT HOME, HAVE I...?
DON'T WORRY ABOUT ME. THERE'S NO TROUBLE.
NEVER MIND THAT. I HAVE SOMETHING IMPORTANT TO DISCUSS WITH YOU.
DOKI (BADMP)
DON'T TELL ME...
...WE CAN'T STAY TOGETHER?

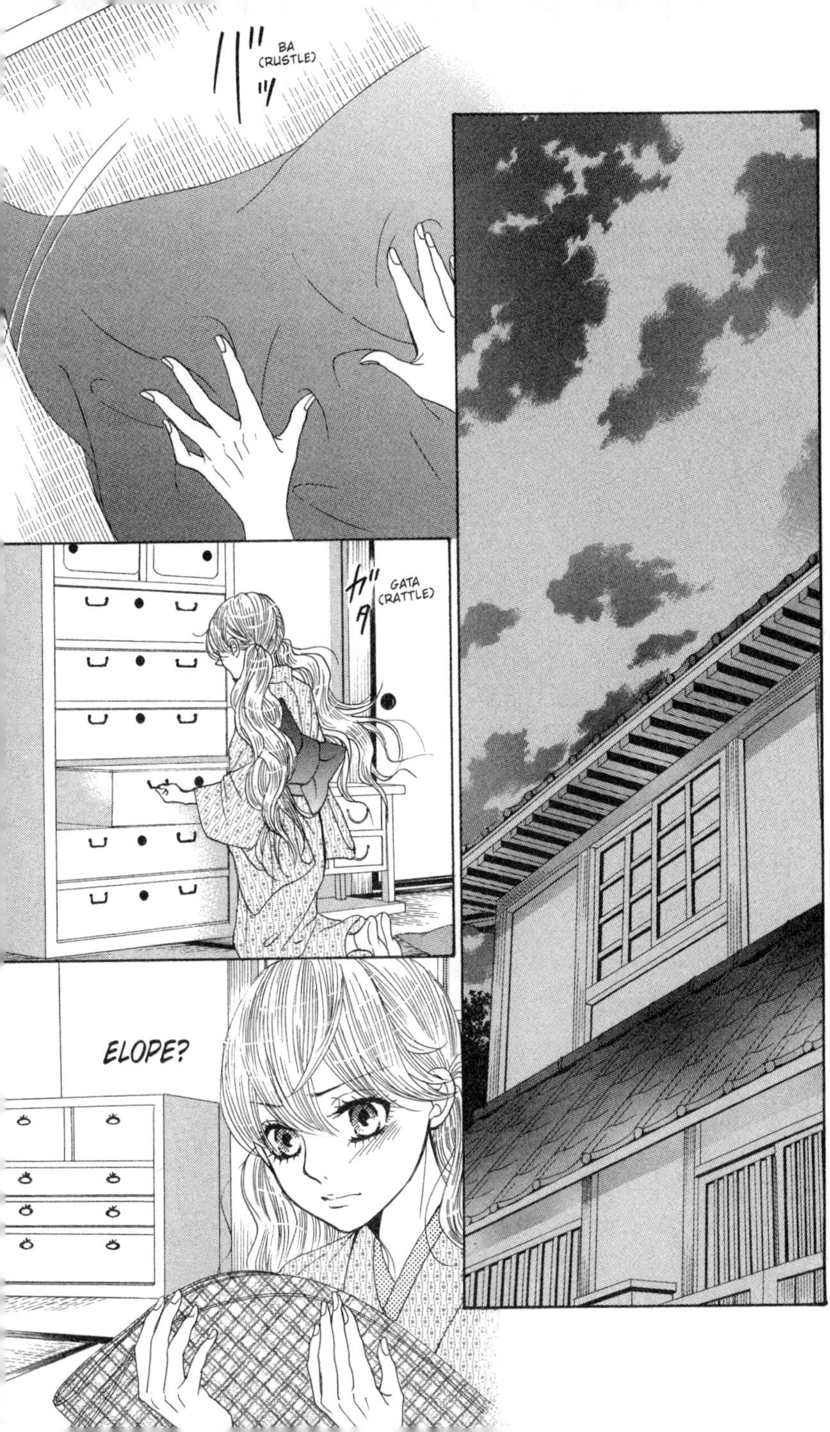
BA (RUSTLE)
GATA (RATTLE)
ELOPE?

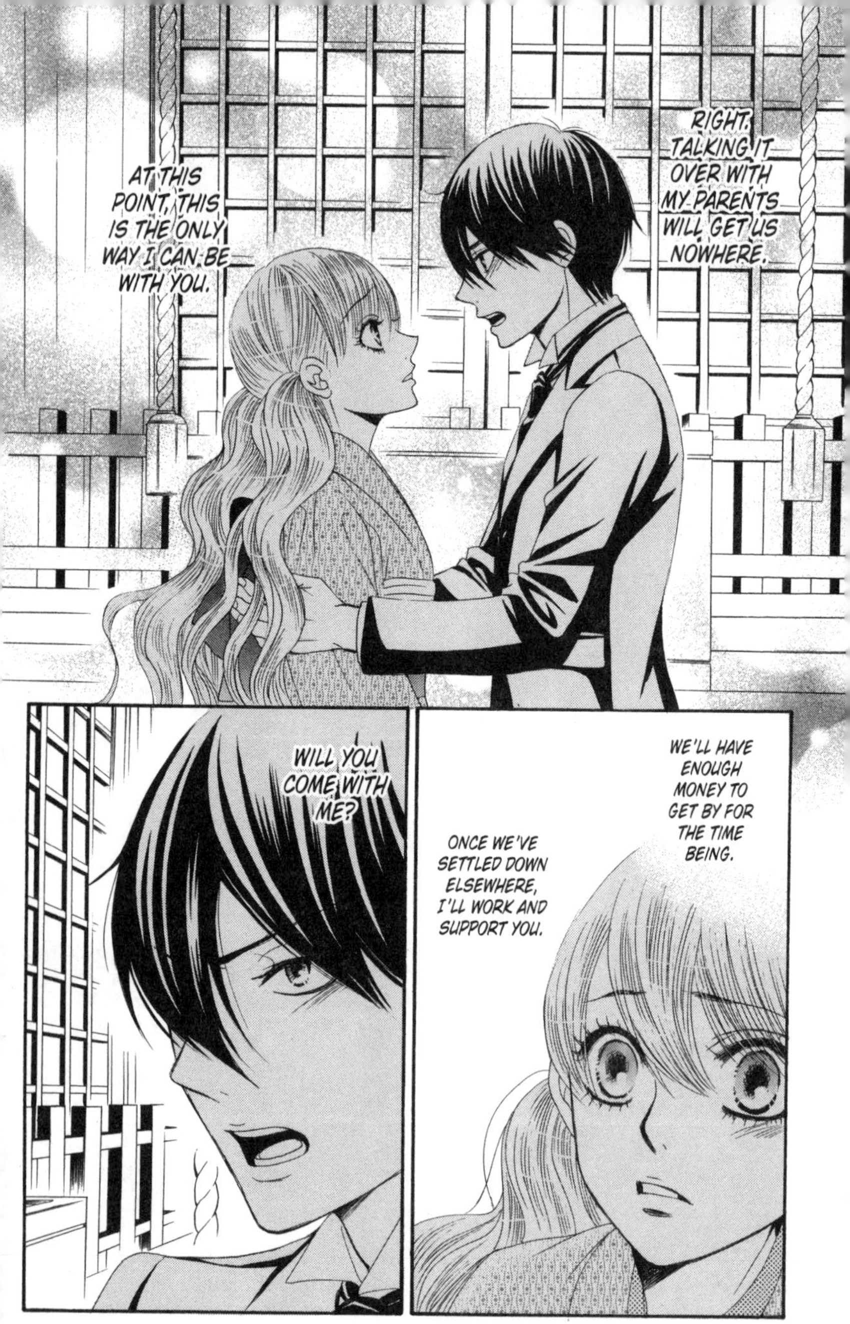
RIGHT. TALKING IT OVER WITH MY PARENTS WILL GET US NOWHERE.
AT THIS POINT, THIS IS THE ONLY WAY I CAN BE WITH YOU.
WE'LL HAVE ENOUGH MONEY TO GET BY FOR THE TIME BEING.
ONCE WE'VE SETTLED DOWN ELSEWHERE, I'LL WORK AND SUPPORT YOU.
WILL YOU COME WITH ME?

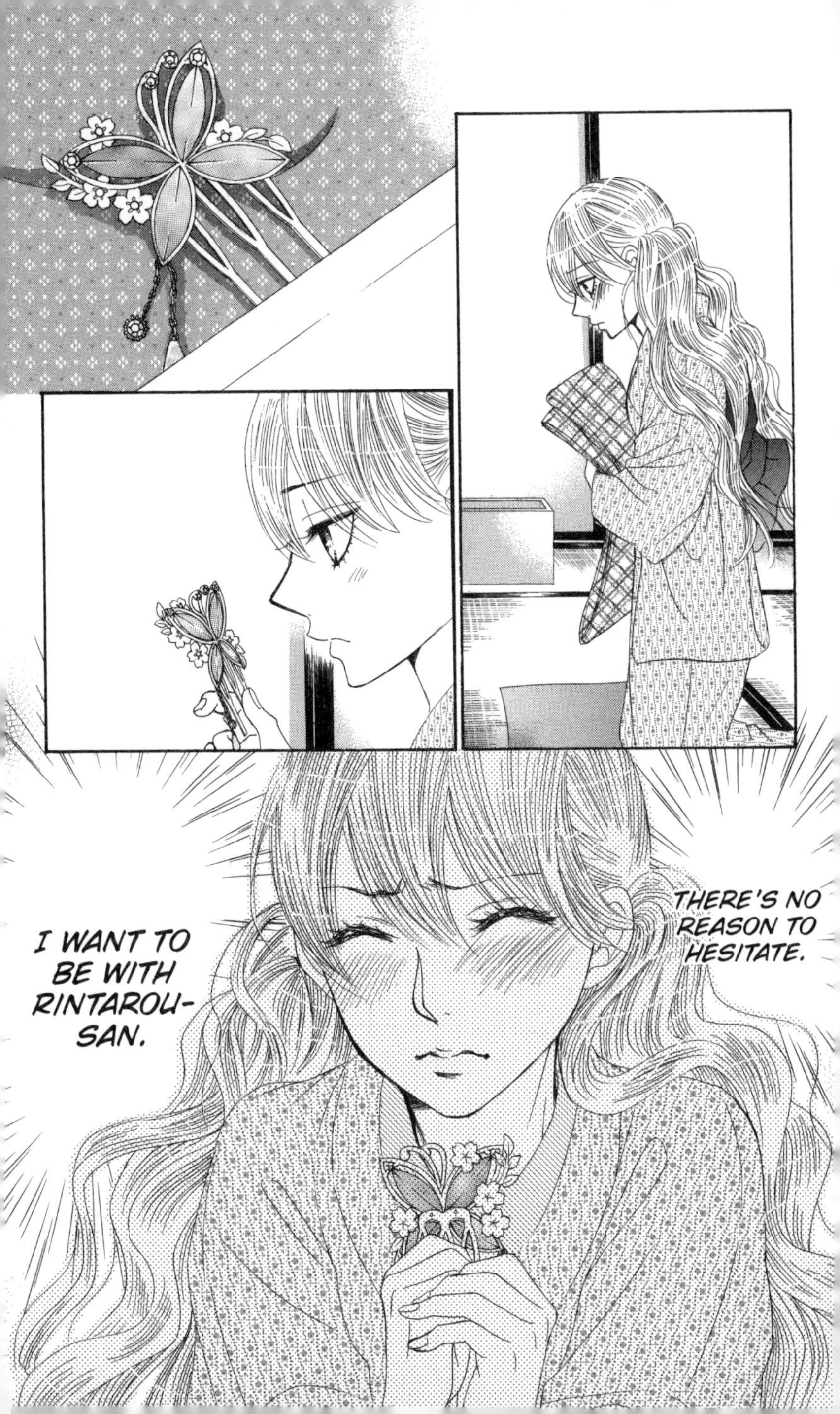
THERE'S NO REASON TO HESITATE.
I WANT TO BE WITH RINTAROU-SAN.

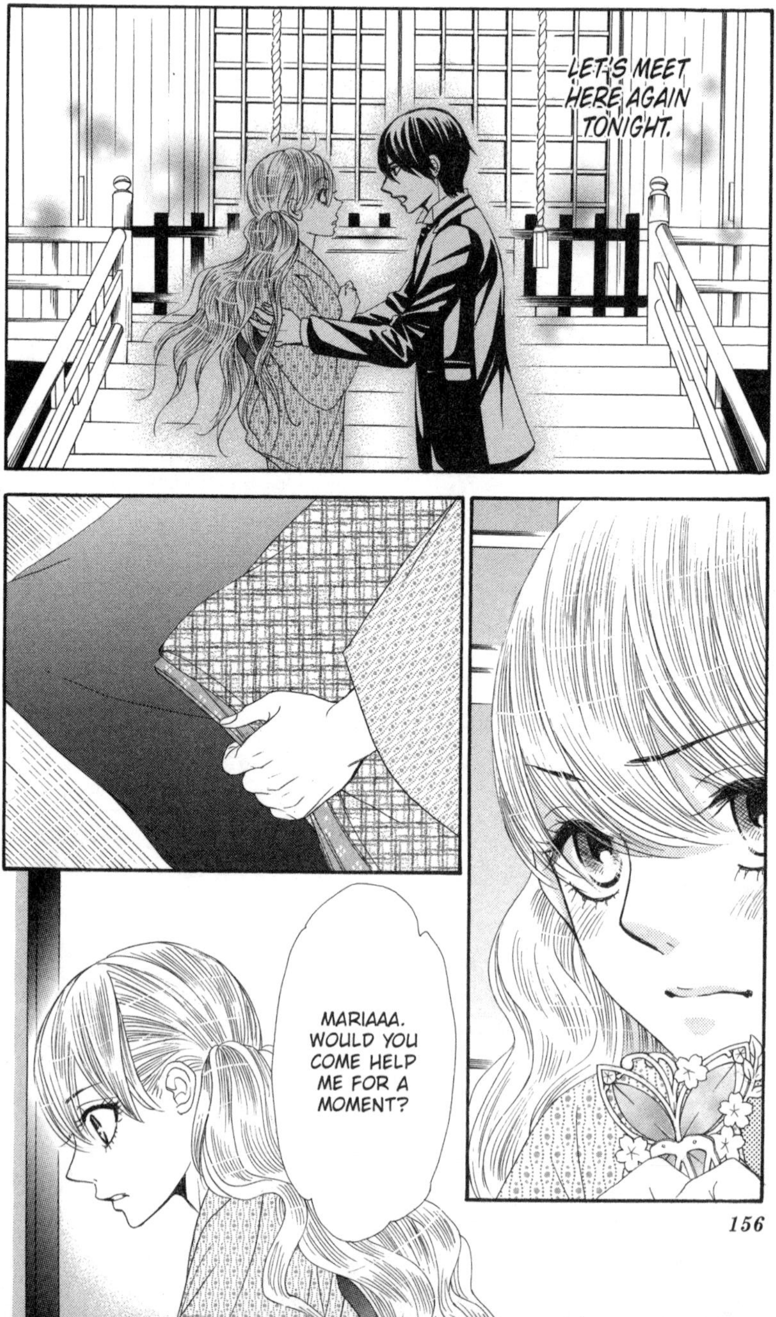
LET'S MEET HERE AGAIN TONIGHT.
MARIAAA. WOULD YOU COME HELP ME FOR A MOMENT?

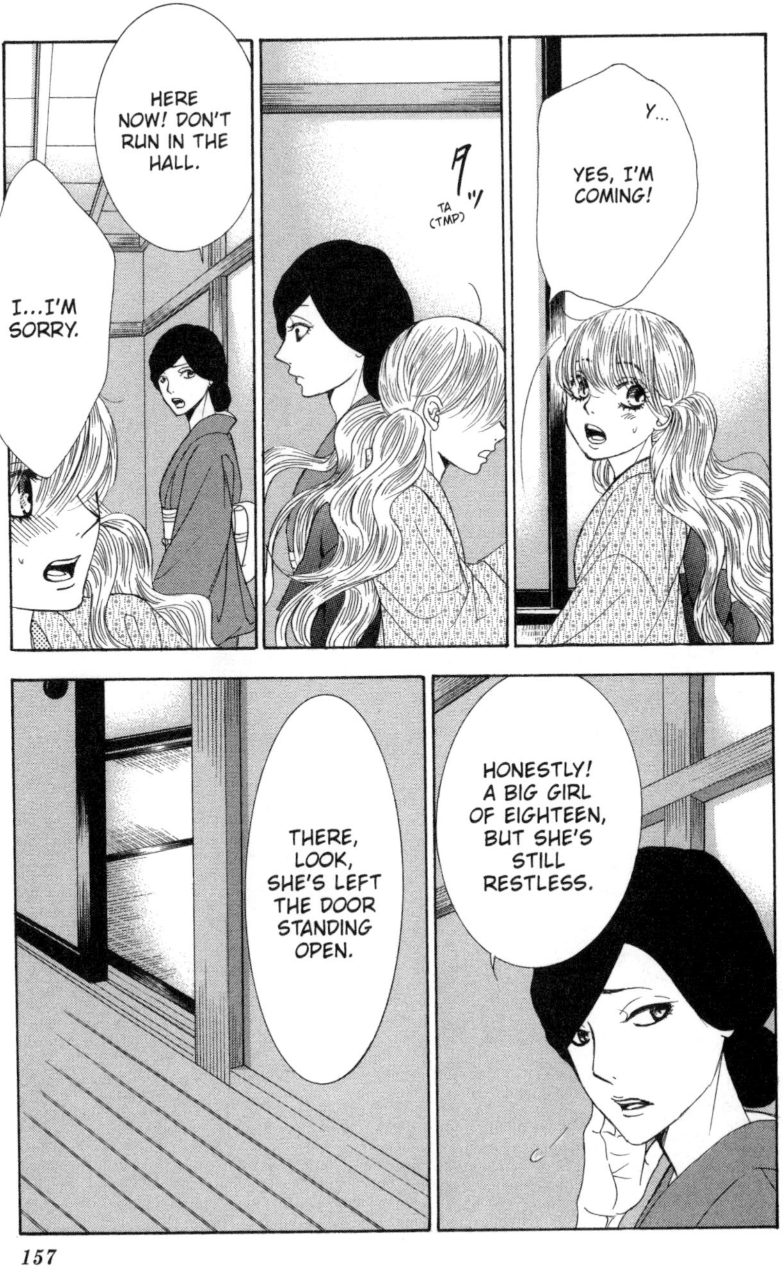
Y...
YES, I'M COMING!
TA (TMP)
HERE NOW! DON'T RUN IN THE HALL.
I...I'M SORRY.
HONESTLY! A BIG GIRL OF EIGHTEEN, BUT SHE'S STILL RESTLESS.
THERE, LOOK, SHE'S LEFT THE DOOR STANDING OPEN.

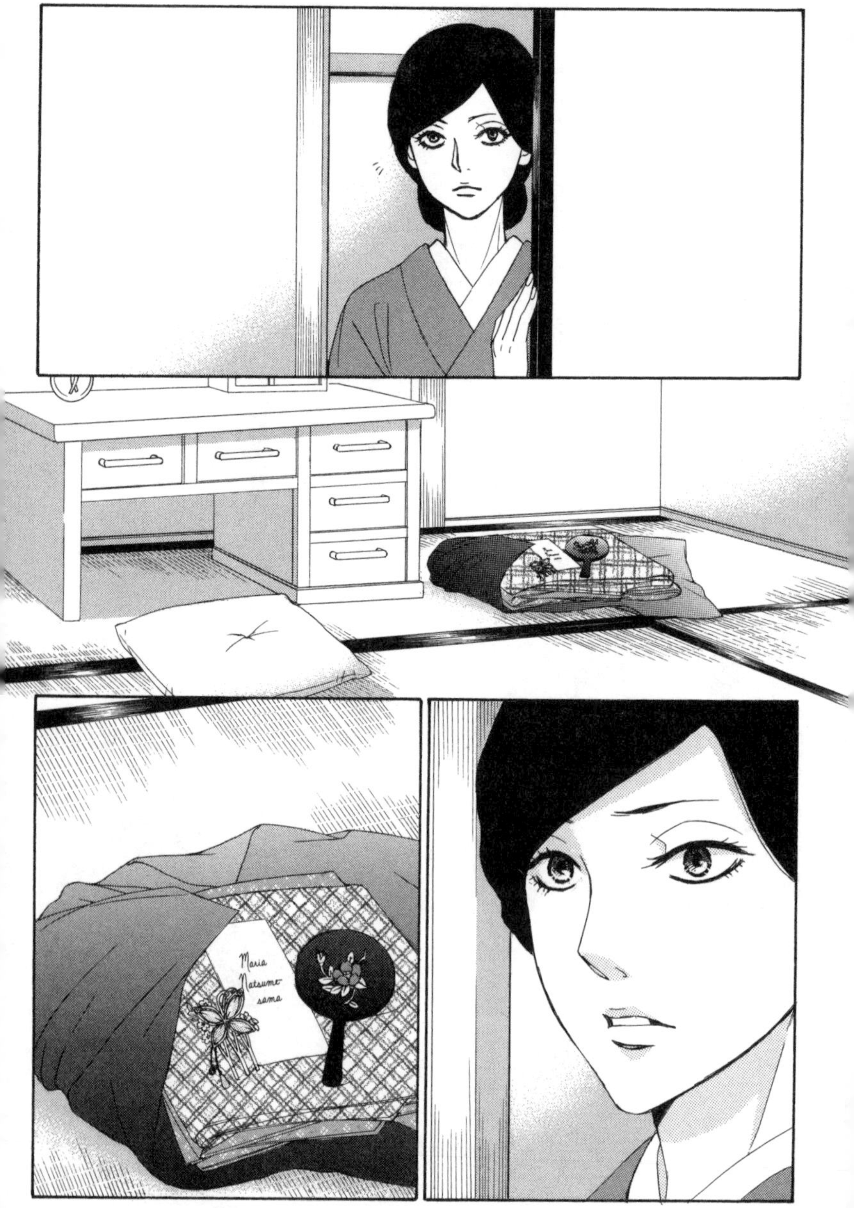
Maria
Natsume-
sama

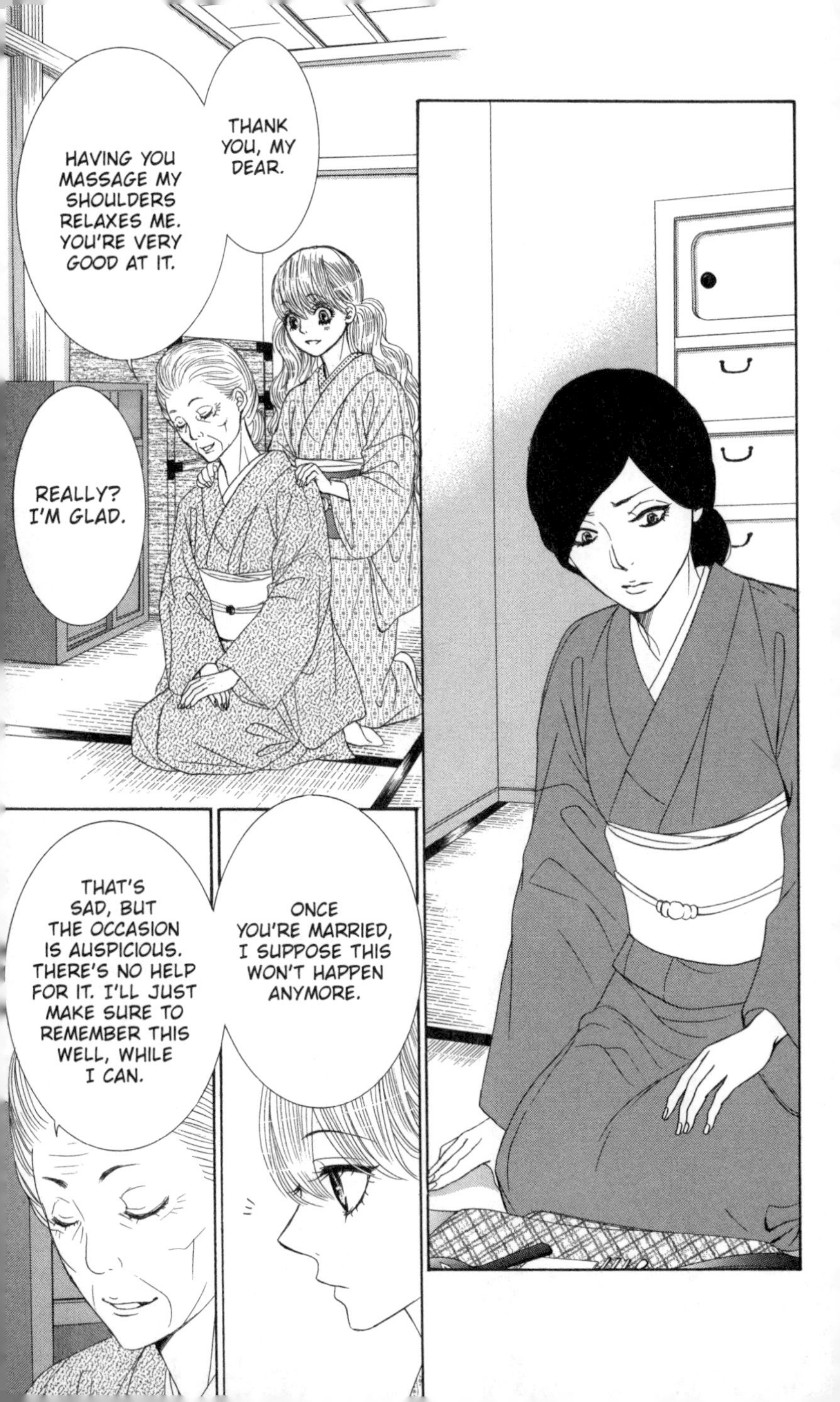
THANK YOU, MY DEAR.
HAVING YOU MASSAGE MY SHOULDERS RELAXES ME. YOU'RE VERY GOOD AT IT.
REALLY? I'M GLAD.
ONCE YOU'RE MARRIED, I SUPPOSE THIS WON'T HAPPEN ANYMORE.
THAT'S SAD, BUT THE OCCASION IS AUSPICIOUS. THERE'S NO HELP FOR IT. I'LL JUST MAKE SURE TO REMEMBER THIS WELL, WHILE I CAN.

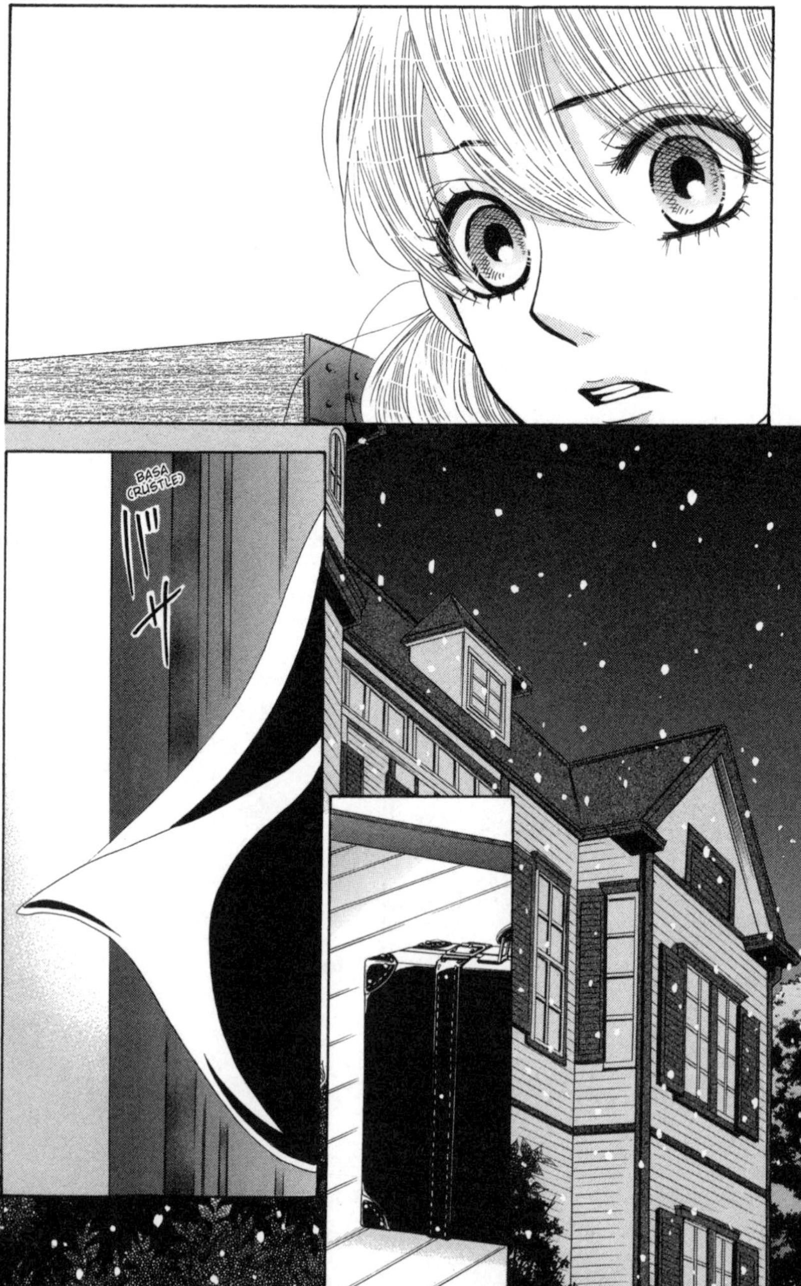
BASA (RUSTLE)

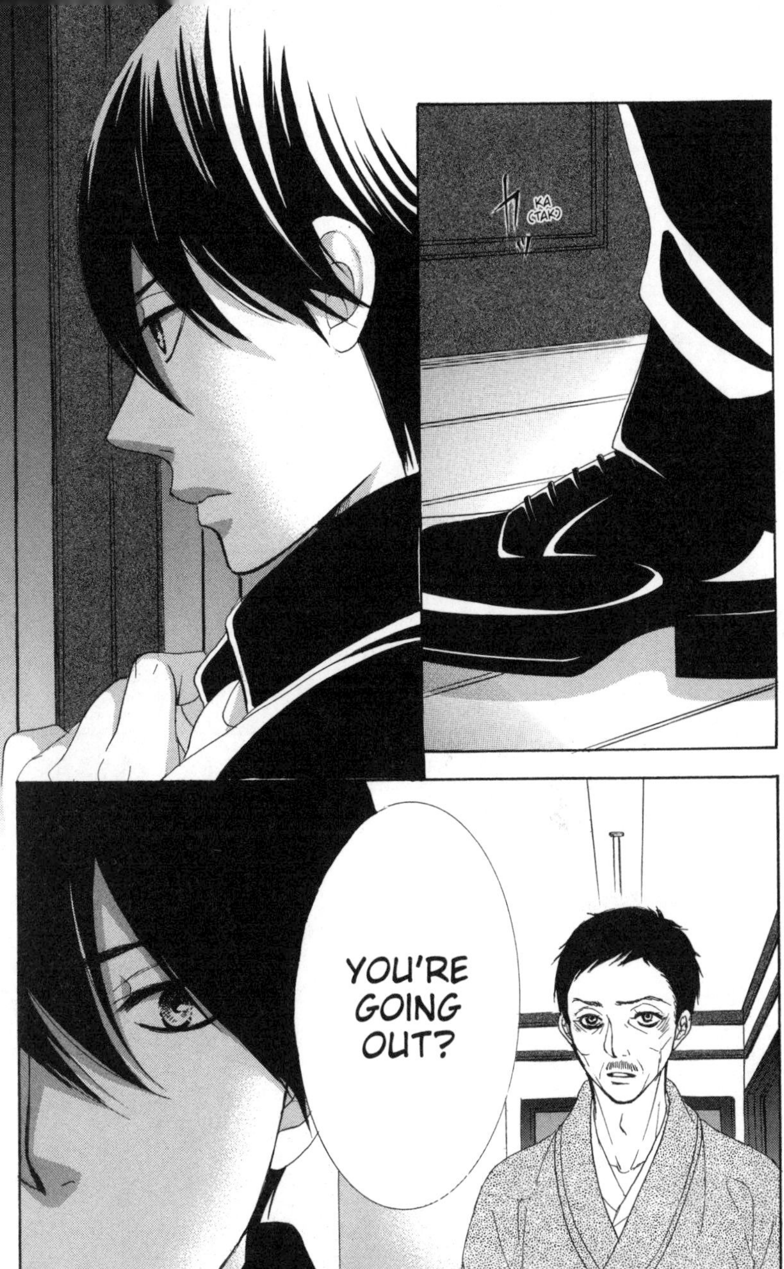
KA (TAK)
YOU'RE GOING OUT?

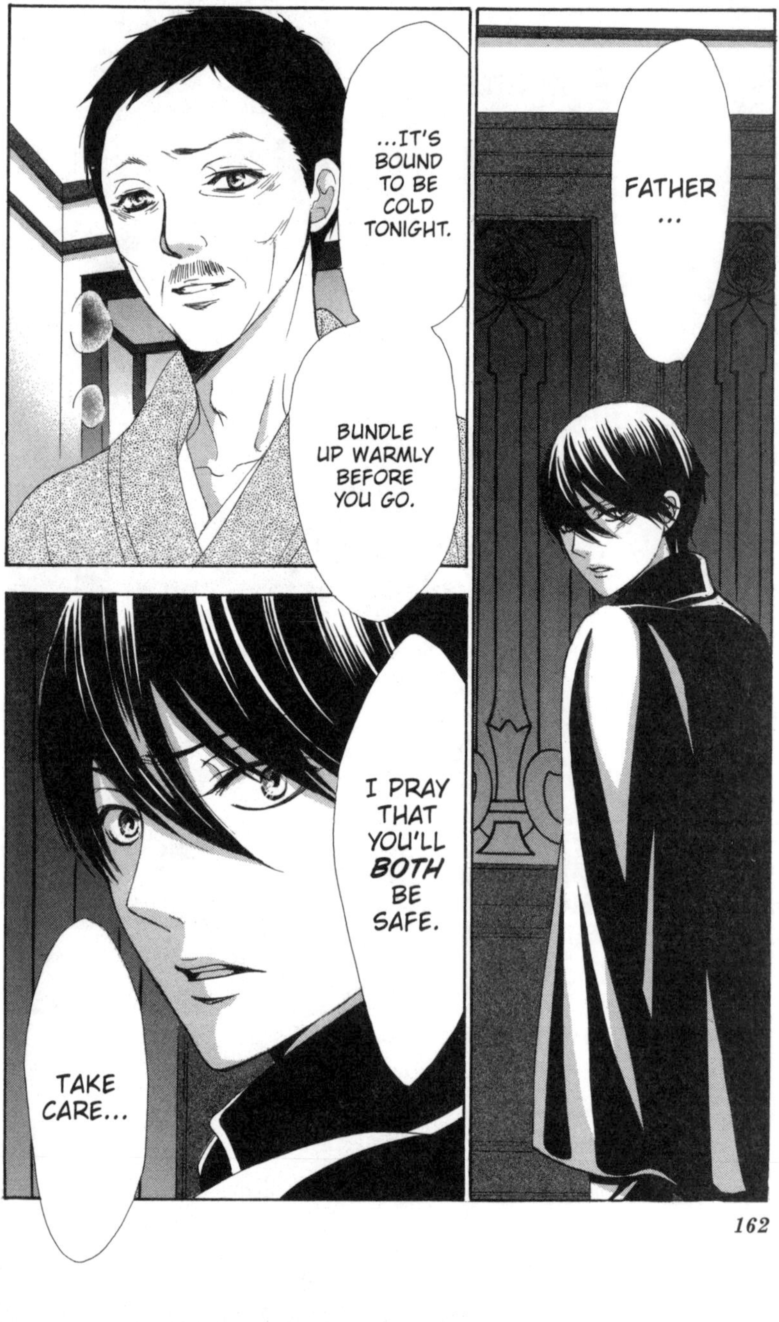
FATHER ...
...IT'S BOUND TO BE COLD TONIGHT.
BUNDLE UP WARMLY BEFORE YOU GO.
I PRAY THAT YOU'LL *BOTH* BE SAFE.
TAKE CARE...

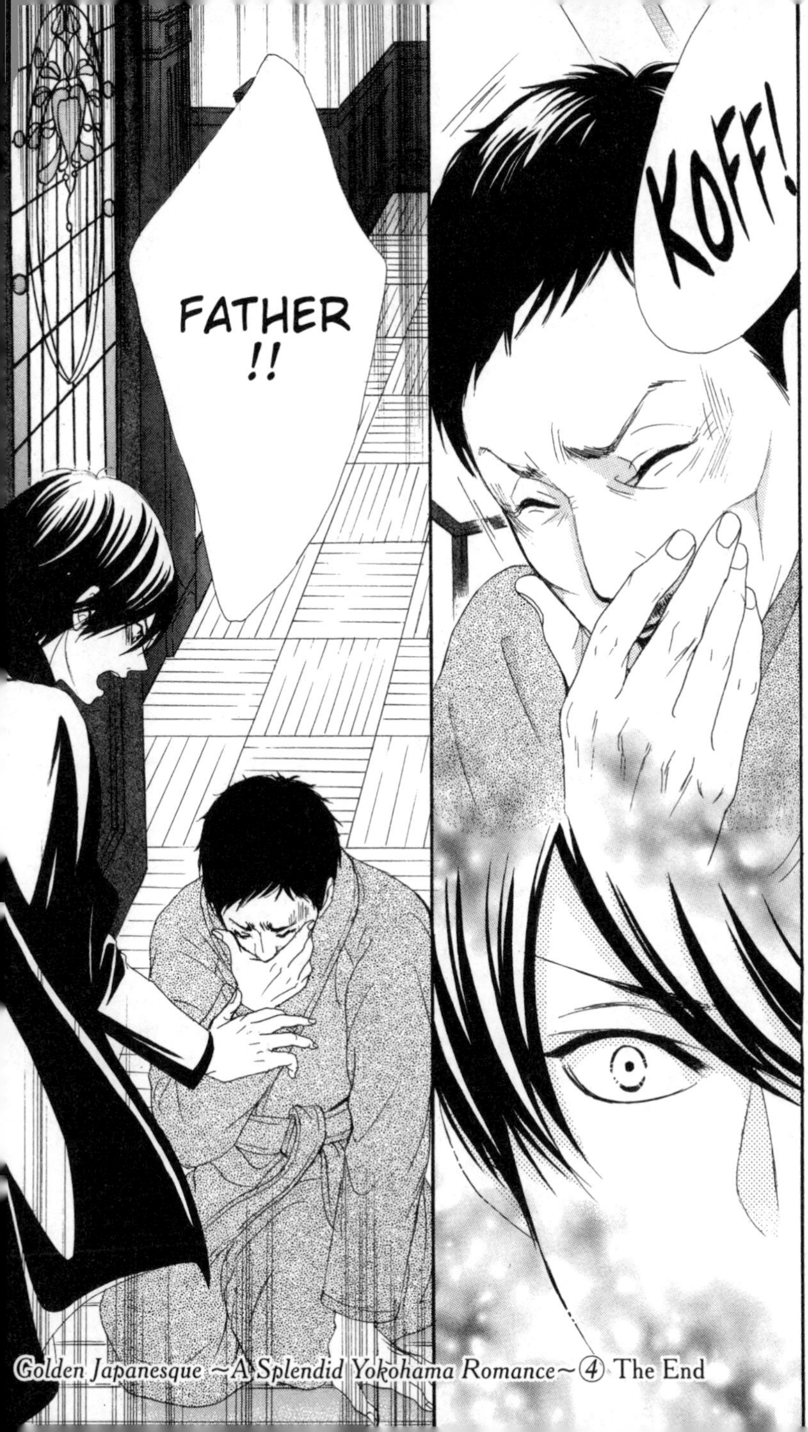
KOFF!
FATHER !!

Golden Japanesque ~A Splendid Yokohama Romance~ ④ The End

Special Thanks

■Assistants■

Alice Tsukada
Nozomi Hirama
Ikuko Shiroya
Yuri Sato
T. Sato

■Editor■
Sanae Morihara

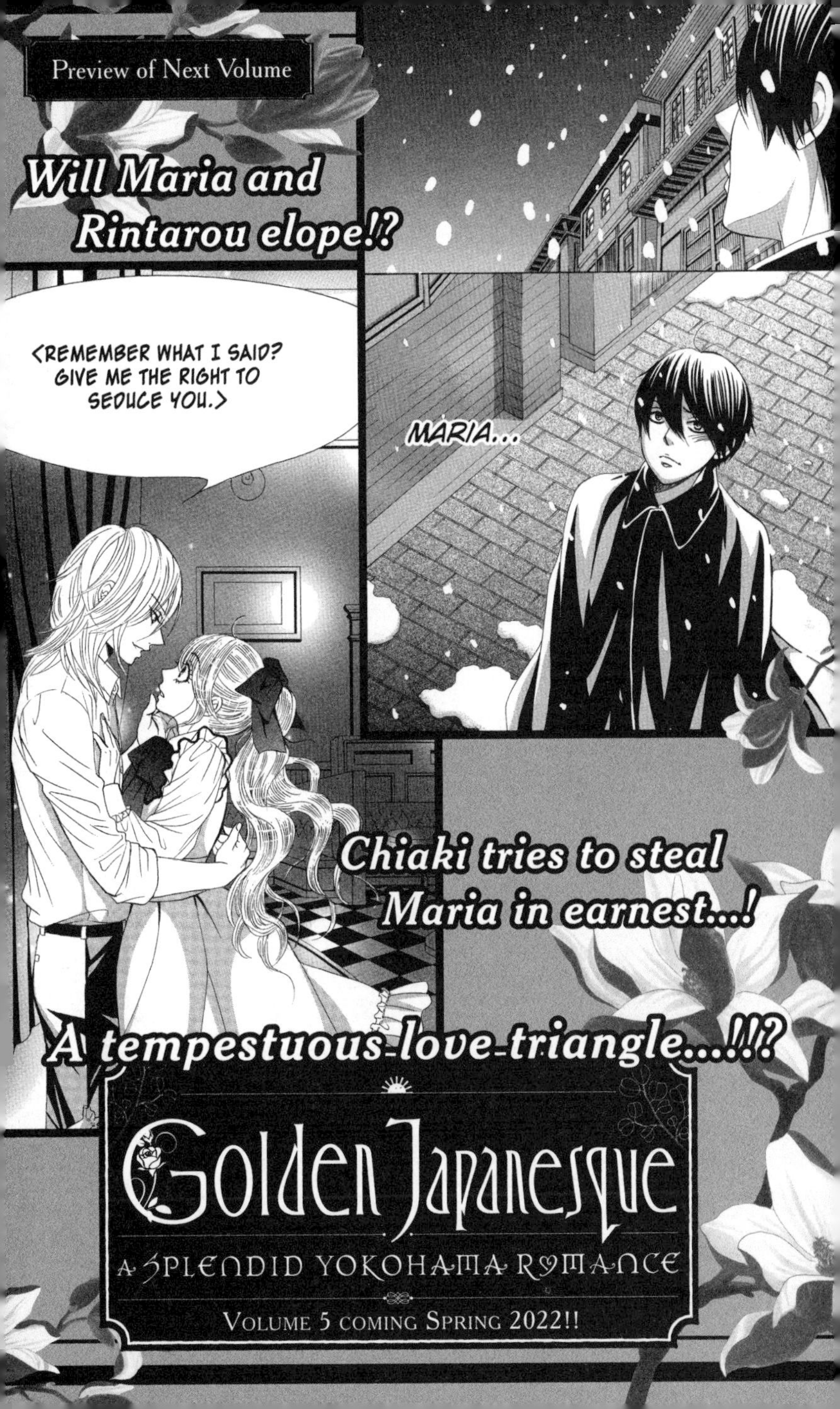
Preview of Next Volume
Will Maria and Rintarou elope!?
MARIA...
<REMEMBER WHAT I SAID? GIVE ME THE RIGHT TO SEDUCE YOU.>
Chiaki tries to steal Maria in earnest...!
A tempestuous love triangle...!!?
Golden Japanesque
A Splendid Yokohama Romance
Volume 5 coming Spring 2022!!

Translation Notes

GENERAL

no honorific: Indicates familiarity or closeness; if used without permission or reason, addressing someone in this manner would constitute an insult.

-san: The Japanese equivalent of Mr./Mrs./Miss. If a situation calls for politeness, this is the fail-safe honorific.

-sama: Conveys great respect; may also indicate that the social status of the speaker is lower than that of the addressee.

-shi: An impersonal honorific used in formal speech or writing, e.g., legal documents.

-dono: Roughly equivalent to "master" or "milord."

-kun: Used most often when referring to boys, this indicates affection or familiarity. Occasionally used by older men among their peers, but it may also be used by anyone referring to a person of lower standing.

-chan: An affectionate honorific indicating familiarity used mostly in reference to girls; also used in reference to cute persons or animals of either gender.

-(o)nii/(o)nee: Meaning "big brother"/ "big sister," it can also refer to those older but relatively close in age to the speaker. It can be combined with other honorifics, such as *-san*, *-chan*, or *-sama*.

-senpai: An honorific for describing someone with more immediate seniority, such as an upperclassman or senior club member.

Golden Japanesque is set in the Meiji era, which lasted from1868 to 1912 and is known as a time of great Western influence in Japan. The era is named after the Meiji emperor, and it coincides with his reign. Referring to a given year in terms of an emperor's reign is typical in Japan—for example, Meiji Year 1 refers to 1868. The Meiji era is followed by Taisho (1912 to 1926), Showa (1926 to 1989), Heisei (1989 to 2019), and Reiwa (2019 to present).

Yokohama Port was opened to foreign trade in 1859.

The Japanese language uses three different sets of characters in writing: *hiragana* and *katakana* (which are akin to alphabets) and *kanji* (Chinese characters). Achieving full literacy in Japanese requires mastering all three, with *kanji* being by far the most complex and difficult. However, it was even more challenging in the Meiji era, as that's when attempts to simplify and formalize the written language had only began to take place. Prior to then, written and spoken Japanese could also be incredibly different from each other.

PAGE 013

Rice cakes, or *daifuku*, are buns made of sweet red bean paste wrapped in sweetened *mochi* (cakes made from rice flour). Chiaki has taken to calling Maria "Beany Rice Cake" in reference to a version of the snack that's studded with salted beans (*mame daifuku*), as well as how her turning red then white resembles the red beans and white mochi of sweet-bean rice cakes.

PAGE 026

Chiaki is Rintarou's cousin, but he calls him **Aki-nii** as if he were an older brother he was fairly close to.

PAGE 145

Similar to his relationship with Chiaki, Rintarou and Ranko are not from the same family; however, the fact that she's calling him **Rintarou-oniisama** ("brother") most likely means that they were rather close when they were growing up.

PAGE 153

This is a ***furoshiki***, or traditional wrapping cloth. Objects are placed in the middle of the cloth, after which the corners are tied together in the middle, forming a handle. They're very versatile, and can be used to wrap and transport almost anything, from lunchboxes or gifts to clothes and toiletries. Although there's a shop selling Western-style suitcases in Maria's neighborhood (See Volume 1), most of the local people probably still use *furoshiki* when they travel domestically.

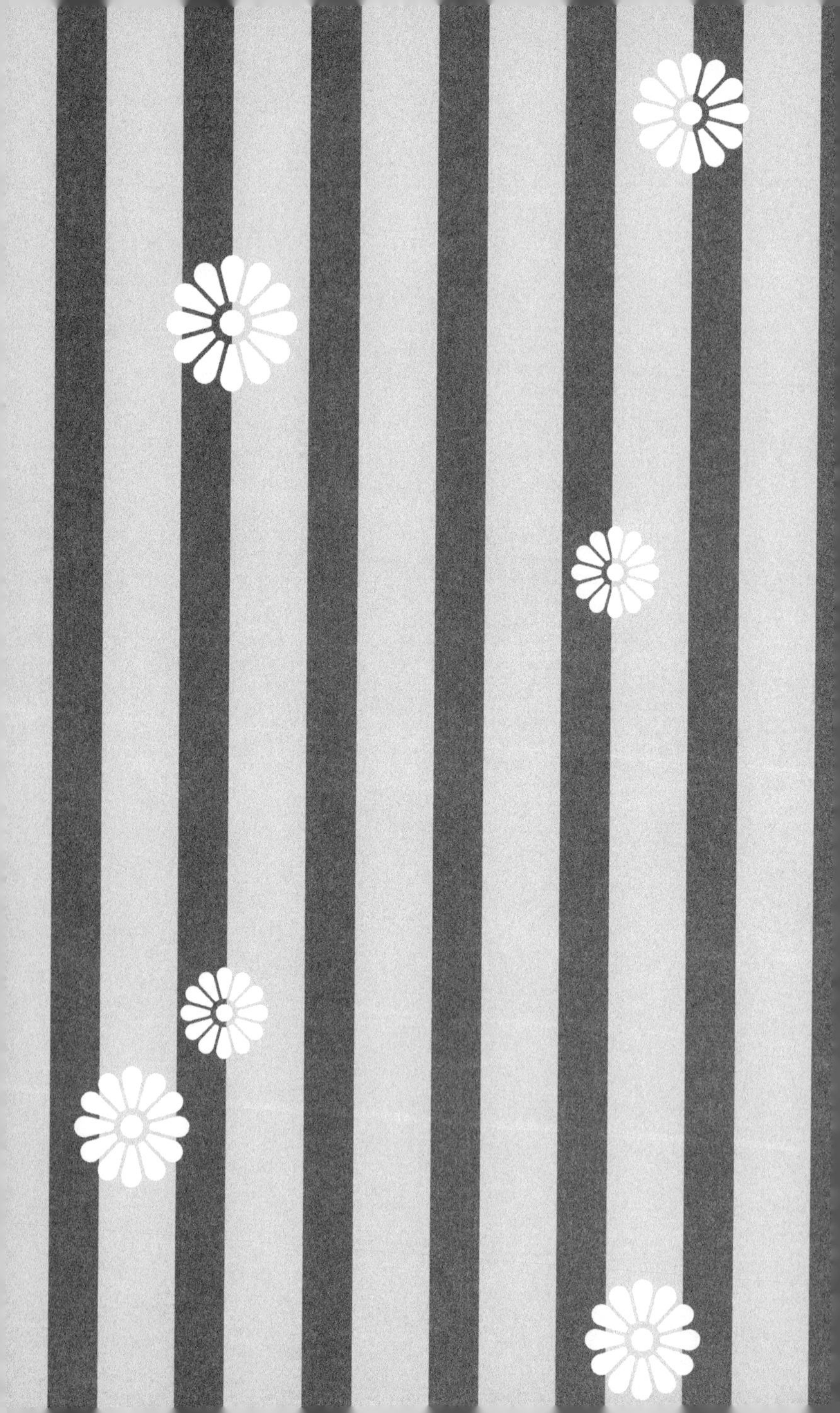

A Loner's Worst Nightmare: Human Interaction!

MY YOUTH R♥MANTIC COMEDY iS WRØNG, AS I EXPECTED

Wataru Watari
Illustration Ponkan⑧

1

Volumes 1–12 on sale now!

MY YOUTH R♥MANTIC COMEDY iS WRØNG, AS I EXPECTED

Hachiman Hikigaya is a cynic. He believes "youth" is a crock—a sucker's game, an illusion woven from failure and hypocrisy. But when he turns in an essay for a school assignment espousing this view, he's sentenced to work in the Service Club, an organization dedicated to helping students with problems! Worse, the only other member of the club is the haughty Yukino Yukinoshita, a girl with beauty, brains, and the personality of a garbage fire. How will Hachiman the Cynic cope with a job that requires—*gasp!*—social skills?

Check out the manga too!

Yen Press

Light Novel © 2011 Wataru WATARI / SHOGAKUKAN, Illustrations by PONKAN⑧
Manga ©2013 Wataru WATARI, Naomichi IO, Ponkan⑧/SHOGAKUKAN

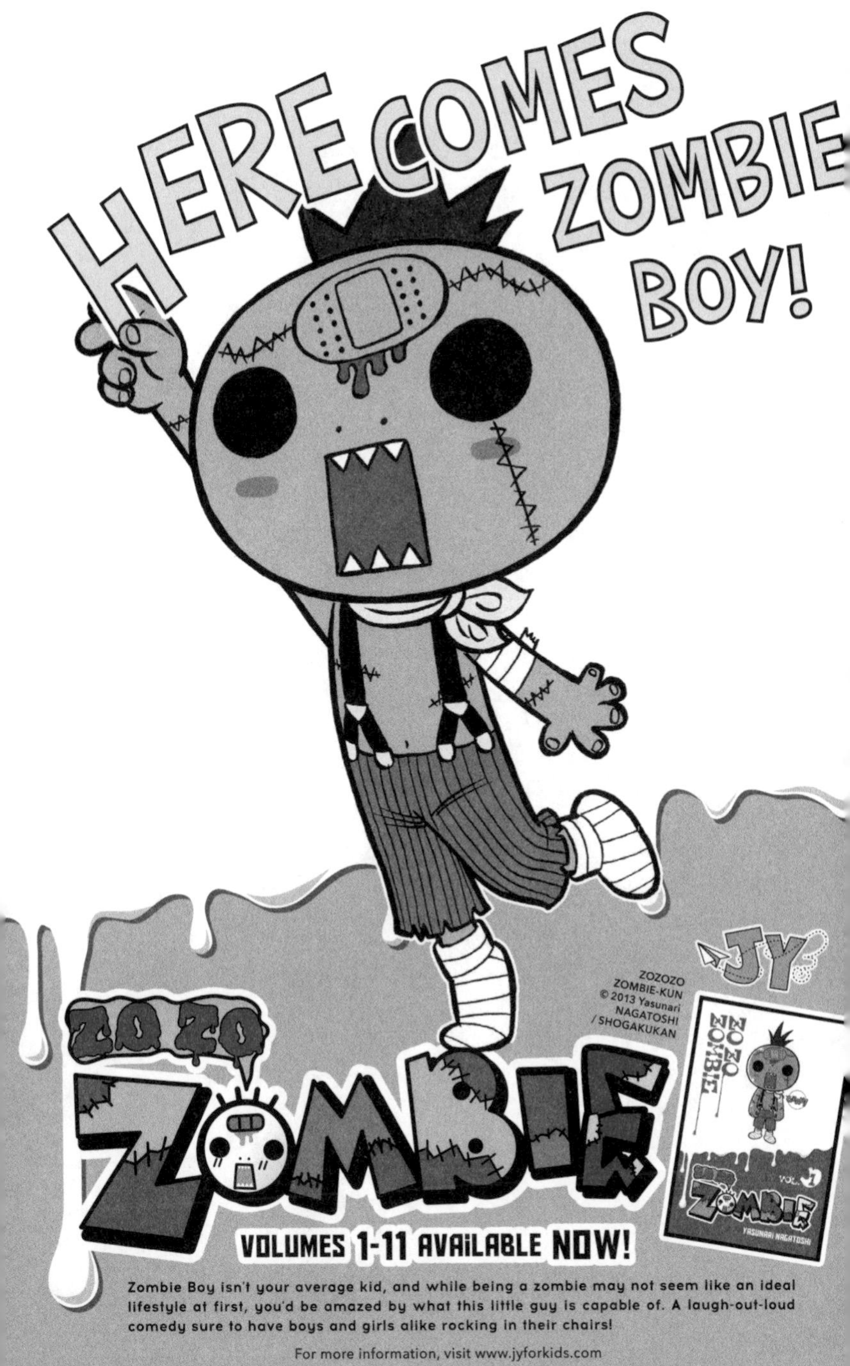
HERE COMES ZOMBIE BOY!
ZO ZO ZOMBIE
ZOZOZO ZOMBIE-KUN © 2013 Yasunari NAGATOSHI / SHOGAKUKAN
JY
VOLUMES 1-11 AVAILABLE NOW!
Zombie Boy isn't your average kid, and while being a zombie may not seem like an ideal lifestyle at first, you'd be amazed by what this little guy is capable of. A laugh-out-loud comedy sure to have boys and girls alike rocking in their chairs!
For more information, visit www.jyforkids.com

HORIMIYA ©HERO • DOZ ©Daisuke Hagiwara / SQUARE ENIX

Yen Press

HORIMIYA

A sweet "aww"-inspiring tale of school life begins when two similarly dissimilar teenagers discover that there are multiple sides to every story...and person!!!

VOLUMES 1-15

IN STORES NOW!

Toilet-bound Hanako-Kun

At Kamome Academy, rumors abound about the school's Seven Mysteries, one of which is Hanako-san. Said to occupy the third stall of the third floor girls' bathroom in the old school building, Hanako-san grants any wish when summoned. Nene Yashiro, an occult-loving high school girl who dreams of romance, ventures into this haunted bathroom...but the Hanako-san she meets there is nothing like she imagined! Kamome Academy's

Yen Press

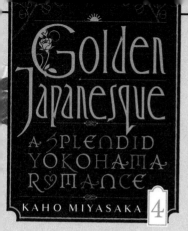

Golden Japanesque
A Splendid Yokohama Romance

KAHO MIYASAKA 4

Translation:
TAYLOR ENGEL

Lettering:
LYS BLAKESLEE

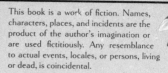

KINIRO JAPANESQUE
-YOKOHAMA KARENTAN- vol.4 by Kaho MIYASAKA
© 2019 Kaho MIYASAKA
All rights reserved.
Original Japanese edition published by SHOGAKUKAN.
English translation rights in the United States of America, Canada, the United Kingdom, Ireland, Australia and New Zealand arranged with SHOGAKUKAN through Tuttle-Mori Agency, Inc.

Yen Press
150 West 30th Street, 19th Floor
New York, NY 10001

Visit us at yenpress.com
  facebook.com/yenpress
  twitter.com/yenpress
  yenpress.tumblr.com
  instagram.com/yenpress

First Yen Press Edition: December 2021

Yen Press is an imprint of Yen Press, LLC.
The Yen Press name and logo are trademarks of Yen Press, LLC.

The publisher is not responsible for websites (or their content) that are not owned by the publisher.

Library of Congress Control Number:
2020948881

ISBNs: 978-1-9753-3555-7 (print)
       978-1-9753-3556-4 (ebook)

10 9 8 7 6 5 4 3 2 1

LSC-C

Printed in the United States of America